Between
the Devil and the Deep

BETWEEN THE DEVIL AND THE DEEP

A MEMOIR OF ACTING AND REACTING

PIETER-DIRK UYS

ZEBRA

Published by Zebra Press
an imprint of Struik Publishers
(a division of New Holland Publishing (South Africa) (Pty) Ltd)
PO Box 1144, Cape Town, 8000
New Holland Publishing is a member of Johnnic Communications Ltd

www.zebrapress.co.za

First published 2005

1 3 5 7 9 10 8 6 4 2

Publication © Zebra Press 2005
Text © Pieter-Dirk Uys 2005

Cover photograph © Fiona Barclay-Keating
Table Mountain photograph © Mark Skinner Image Library

PUBLISHING MANAGER: Marlene Fryer
EDITOR: Robert Plummer
PROOFREADER: Ronel Richter-Herbert
COVER AND TEXT DESIGNER: Natascha Adendorff
TYPESETTER: Monique van den Berg
PRODUCTION MANAGER: Valerie Kömmer

Set in 9.5 pt on 13.75 pt Berling Roman

Reproduction by Hirt & Carter (Cape) (Pty) Ltd
Printed and bound by Paarl Print, Oosterland Street, Paarl, South Africa

ISBN 1 77007 100 8

www.imagesofafrica.co.za

IMAGES OF AFRICA
PHOTO LIBRARY

Contents

PREFACE

My first memoir, *Elections & Erections*, focused on fear and fun. This second outing is about acting and reacting. There is still fear and fun, but now sex and democracy take a backseat to my life in the theatre – or rather, the theatre in my life.

Many people are not named in this book, but they have made this life so much more complete with their support, or so much more interesting with their resistance. They know who they are, and are probably grateful that there is not enough space to tell the whole truth. But a memoir is not a confession, or an accusation; it is a smell, a taste, a hot flush of memory. And, I hope, some truth. One thing is for sure: it's the story of a life blessed with opportunity, generosity, frustration and luck. And a hell of a lot of hardegat discipline.

Once again I am in the Zebra stable of Struik Publishers, and I wear my black and white stripes with pride. Editor Robert Plummer nurtured *Elections & Erections*, and has seamlessly pushed the edges of my envelope to embrace *Between the Devil and the Deep*, and for that I am very happy and relieved. And he can spell! (Although I think Evita's legs are better.)

Thanks to my wonderful photographer colleagues – Brian Astbury, Ruphin Coudyzer, Pat Bromilow-Downing and Anton Geldenhuys – for their images spanning thirty years.

Thanks to my favourite Metropole Hotel in Long Street, Cape Town, for allowing the usual three suspects to be snapped in the same bed for the cover by Fiona Barclay-Keating.

And, of course, thanks to the politicians here and there for never letting me down and without whom I would be speechless.

I want to dedicate this book to every teacher who inspires children to make their dreams come true.

PIETER-DIRK UYS
Darling
August 2005

1

ANGELS IN DARLING

He is just a little boy. Maybe seven, but he looks younger. This is Benny's first concert.

He sees his mother sitting in the third row with his granny. Behind them are Mevrou Brand and her eldest daughter Gail, who is pregnant with her second child. They are waiting for their Henry to play his piano piece. He is older than Benny, maybe eight. Overweight. Looks twelve.

The small venue is packed with people from the local Darling community.

A Wednesday afternoon in the sweltering summer. Hot, even though every door and window is open to hijack whatever breeze there is. A long goods train has just clattered past, crashing into the piano sounds with a shrill whistle and threatening rumble. At least it sounded in key.

The majority of the audience are coloured, the families of the children taking part. Still, there are enough white people to give a healthy rainbow balance. After all, this is Evita se Perron, formerly Darling railway station, now on the tourist map as a must-see for all visitors to the Western Cape.

They come in their hundreds, arriving in a Cape Town now glittering and throbbing with the reputation of being one of the international travel meccas of the planet. Table Mountain is a World Heritage Site. So is Robben Island, former home to the first rulers of a democratic South Africa. After a sombre visit to the Island in the morning, the tourists make the trip to Darling for coffee, koeksisters, bobotie or a show. From the sublime to the ridiculous. They park their cars on the gravel next to the railway line, and pay homage to the hostess, Mrs Evita Bezuidenhout, the most famous white woman in Africa! They come with a smile and a euro from Europe that is now a Union, with a dollar from the States now not so United, or a pound from Britain formerly Great. All those currencies look good in rands.

The visitor from Zimbabwe gets a free cooldrink. A million of his dollars can't buy anything but love. Others come from up the road in Africa – Kenya, Nigeria, Namibia. The African Renaissance whispering the urban legend that the dark continent is slowly waking up from its million-year slumber.

At Evita se Perron, the only signs of the troubled past are displayed on walls as part of the bizarre entertainment. In the garden known as Boerassic Park stand statues and likenesses of the historical fathers of apartheid, now hysterical reasons for mirth and contempt. And a great place for birds to sit and shit.

Funny thing, democracy.

It's imperfect and crooked and infuriating, but at least touched by human hands. Now everyone has the right to make fools of themselves, or heroes. The world still remembers the ultimate reality-television moment, when the Afrikaner leader of a white minority racist regime stood up in Parliament and cut his political throat with a slow-motion gesture that changed history.

FW de Klerk echoed Mikhail Gorbachev's perestroika with his own Pretoriastroika, and on 1 February 1990 made it legal for us to be illegal. The African National Congress and South African Communist Party were unbanned, and the political prisoners were soon released. Today South Africa is probably the only country in the world with a Communist Party with plans for the future. Not counting China. But we try not to count China. Didn't that message in the fortune cookie once say: 'In 2020 China will rule the world'?

It is not yet that year, and, for the moment, the rainbow rules the land. Nelson Mandela and Desmond Tutu are our inspirations. Our two old guardian angels, beating their tired wings across our heads and keeping away the goblins and dragons. Warning us of the viruses that came with this new century.

*   *   *

It was just an old grey feather. Lying in the path to Boerassic Park.

One of the cats must have caught a bird! There are always heaps of little feathers around the Perron, clustered on the small grass patch or scattered among the wily cacti and basil bushes that clot together to form a perfect impenetrable laager, protecting Evita's sacred land and keeping the invading plastic bags out.

The eight resident theatre cats get fed twice a day on expensive dry kernels. They wait, like a pride of tame, overfed lions, for Beryl to put out their individual plates, shiny new bowls, each with its proud name and proper place.

Windgat prowls her domain, the small venue where the children have their piano classes. They love hugging the battered old beast while waiting for teacher Mary-Ann to put them through their paces. Mary-Ann speaks their language, the tune of her West Coast accent imparting information without need for show or politeness.

'Okay, now listen to what horrible sounds you are making! This is not just a piano! This is a secret machine to make the angels dance! And if you make it sound like a farm animal with a sore belly, the angels will be frightened and fly away from Darling! Make the angels happy?'

They nod gravely.

'Okay, and keep your fingers lightly on the keys. You're not beating a cobra to death. You're making music! Try that again!'

Plonk! Plink! Plink? Plank! ... Blaaa!

The angels don't seem to mind, not even when there's a really bad blaaa! Only Windgat opens one eye and gives a small shudder. That the kids understand. They plink plonk plank again, without the horrible blaaa, and check the cat.

The Perron Prokofiev sleeps on.

*   *   *

Windgat lies next to the piano in her usual spot, eyes closed. Even when we all applaud.

The small boy called Benny gets down from the piano stool. When he plays, his feet don't reach the floor. He can't use the pedals yet. During lessons he lies on the floor and presses them with both hands while Mary-Ann plays the keyboard, so he can hear the difference in sound.

'I want to also press the pedals,' he whines.

'So grow up,' Mary-Ann huffs. 'Give me a scale.'

Mary-Ann doesn't believe in the fears that accompany performance. Rather give a small concert each term, put on the stage lights, and make the kids feel like stars. Invite their parents and let them show the amazed mothers and grannies what they can do. Fathers work and don't come to afternoon concerts. Some are too drunk to remember. But there is no fear in showing off to Mummy and Ouma. Just excitement.

So, after the initial plink plonk plank, there is a bow and another bow, and then back on the piano stool, small feet flailing above the silent pedals, for an encore. And the encore could just be that missing blaaa!

Benny's ma and granny are in tears. Mrs Brand leans forward and puts her hand on the coloured woman's shoulder.

'Congratulations, Betty,' she says.

'Thank you, madam,' says the old woman, proud of her grandson and happy that the white woman she's worked for for most of her life is also proud. Benny's mother grew up in Mrs Brand's house, and the Afrikaans woman has remained a friend of Betty's family ever since. Although she keeps saying 'Don't call me madam', old habits die hard.

Windgat is now lying on her favourite orange art deco chair, seemingly asleep. But the glint in her eye means that she's checking out the kids. The children are getting to know her better with each visit. Back home they don't

3

have time for pet cats. They would eat precious food. Cats are for white people who have the time and money to care. But here at the Perron, the eight cats are the heartbeat of the magic. And, with time, the kids have come to realise that Windgat is boss and not to be kicked, not even in passing. But Windgat would never succeed in catching a bird.

So where from this big feather? What kind of bird was this? A turkey? A peacock? A pheasant?

* * *

Sue-Ellen sits next to me in the fourth row from the back.

She looks at the feather in my fingers, twirling back and forth. We are waiting for the next small genius to show his scales. Sue-Ellen was probably named after a character in some American soap opera, as so many of our children are. From *Dallas*? No, that's too long ago. Maybe there was a Sue-Ellen in *The Bold and the Beautiful*, or *How the World Turns*, or one of the other ones. She'd been involved with the Perron since she was six.

She isn't enjoying the concert.

'Not as nice as last week,' she whispers.

'That was a real band from Cape Town,' I explain. 'This is just our children starting.'

'Ja,' she understands, 'but it sounds so kak.'

'Everything new sounds kak, Sue-Ellen,' I reply, trying to be serious and stern. 'You must start somewhere. But if you keep working hard, it will never be as kak as that first kak time. Each time it gets less kak.'

'You mean, all this kak playing will one day be nice?' She shakes her head, disappointed. 'Ja, I could do better.'

'Why don't you?' I challenge.

She shrugs.

'We don't have a piano-thing at home.'

No, she lives in one room with six other members of her family. No room for a piano. Or even a cat.

'If you want to, you can come and play on this piano here. Like the other kids.'

She sniffs. 'They small. I'm big.'

'So?' I reply. 'It will be less kak sooner with you.'

'Okay,' she sighs.

We wait for a small person to be smoothed out and readied to mount the stage and plink plank plonk.

Sue-Ellen looks around the wooden-walled venue. This was once the station, in the years when trains were the aorta of life for small towns like Darling. Johannes Abrahams, now in his late fifties and our irreplaceable Head of Perron Security, patrols the car park like the French Foreign Legion. He remembers faces and names like a lexicon and is the perfect welcoming spirit for all our guests, who never forget him either. Oom Johannes once carried suitcases at this station when he was Sue-Ellen's age. Now he is in charge of this building, known as the Waiting Room, which can function as a small theatre that seats forty people. Like now.

We call it Perron Number One.

The walls are covered with a treasury of memory. The pictures and signs, diagrams and flags, represent a particular past. Our worst nightmares. Symbols of the old apartheid days, when each picture had the power to frighten into submission. The symbol of Afrikaner nationalism, the Voortrekker Monument, features in many frames, some drawn in monochrome, others painted in colour. Some clumsily but lovingly embossed with silver paper.

'Die Bou van 'n Nasie'. The building of a nation.

And 'Wat is 'n Huis sonder 'n Moeder?' What is a home without a mother? God and the Son and the Holy Spirit of Racism go hand in hand, isolating us from the world for 360 years.

Pictures of the Battle of Blood River would hang in our classrooms like the Virgin Mary in Rome and the Queen in Windsor. In various depictions, the victorious Voortrekkers shoot the Zulus, who float face-down in the bloody river, slain and vanquished. And it was so, because God was on the side of the white Afrikaner. Ignore the fact that the Boers had the guns and the Zulus only had assagais. Also on the wall is the pompous, purple-prosed Vow to celebrate this day as sacred. A promise to God to keep the 16th of December as a day of thanks and prayer. In Afrikaans. In real life it meant that we whites were exonerated from the terrible deaths in our history.

And so it came to pass that on every Day of the Vow, we kids, imprisoned by the lies and legends of our faux history, sat uncomfortably in the Dutch Reformed Church to thank God for allowing us chosen few to win Die Slag van Bloedrivier against the barbarians. In my life as an Afrikaner Calvinist child, having to celebrate Dingaan's Day year in and year out made it the most boring day in the calendar! Until 1994, when that all changed forever. The barbarians were now in charge of the monuments and suddenly God changed sides and spoke fluent Zulu.

From Vrystaat to Amandla!

In the room there are also pictures of the piggy-faced, Dutch-born Hendrik Verwoerd, the architect of apartheid. White marble busts of his predecessors,

Dr DF Malan – my father's first cousin – and JG Strijdom – whose kids would come for piano lessons with my mother!

Smiling. Smirking. Staring. Stern. Sombre. Sinister.

A veritable museum of the past.

A true nauseum of now powerless horror.

Funny. Fabulous. Frightful.

And then the apartheid signs.

'Whites Only/Slegs Blankes.'

'No Dogs or Natives Allowed.'

From the small dressing room behind the stage, I can often hear comments from the people as they file through this exhibition of murky memories. Parents shuffle from one reminder to the next.

'O Mamma, kyk na hierdie kosbare goed!'

'O Pappa, dis te wonderlik! Dis ons lewens! Ons lewens hang hier!'

'Ja, Mamma, en daardie prent was mos in Ouma se huis.'

'En in my Oupa se voorkamer ook! O Pappa, ek gaan huil …'

And huilend they leave for Boerassic Park, as their children follow the route through the venue. They must be looking at the same picture.

'Jissis, check hierdie prente.'

'Fok my! Dis mos daardie een wat in Ouma se huis was.'

'En in Pa se foto's van sy skool!'

'Jissis, maar dis amazing kak!'

They laugh and leave for a smoke outside, as a family of black guests peer in.

The man sighs.

'You know, your mother had to clean that Blood River picture for Mrs Steyn every Wednesday.'

'Oh yes,' laughs the wife, once maid and nanny. 'And that Voortrekker Monument also!'

Their teenage kids ooh and aah.

'Let's have a picture with that one and also under the Whites Only sign,' says their father.

They take many pictures and there is much laughter.

As I powder my nose into Evita, I see the small handwritten sign on my mirror.

'Let us remember where we come from, so we can truly celebrate where we are going.'

*   *   *

Sue-Ellen is staring at the small sign in the room. White letters on a black background.

English words.

'What's that sign?'

'Whites Only,' I read.

'Ja, I can read: Whites Only. Is that an apartheid sign?'

'Yes.'

She hums softly as she studies the sign.

'Mmmm.' Then she laughs. 'Hey, it's so small?'

I look at the sign and agree. It is small. But then so are hand grenades. Small but lethal.

'Where was that sign?' she asks.

'On benches.'

'Park benches? Like our bench in Boerassic Park where the cats sit?'

'Yes.'

She gasps.

'You mean, that sign was on our bench? Whites Only? So only white people were allowed to sit on our bench?'

'Yes.'

'So a coloured like me wasn't allowed to sit on that bench?'

'No.'

'So who's going to stop me!'

Her chin is squared for a fight, her fists tight and ready for action.

I put my hand over her tense fist.

'Well, darling, for over forty years we were all too scared to sit together on that bench.'

'Because of that apartheid sign?' She sits incredulous, disbelieving. A bit disgusted.

'Yes,' I say.

She looks at me as if I've fallen out of a different age, grey, old and dusty.

She pats my hand sympathetically.

'Jissis, but you people were mad.'

The freedom of liberation.

When she was born in 1992, FW de Klerk had already driven a stake through the heart of legalised racism. Apartheid was already dead, although the stench would linger for a long time to come.

And here sits Sue-Ellen, a born-free, a child of the new democracy, not even interested in what is still regarded as the Struggle. Boring, gone, verby.

Her struggle lies ahead. Violence, crime, AIDS, rape, a job, a life, a future, a dream. A new madness probably just around the corner.

She touches the feather in my hand.

'Did Marilyn kill that bird?' she asks softly.

(Marilyn is a male cat with the name of a diva and the balls of a devil.)

'I don't know,' I say. 'I only found this one feather.'

'Oh.' She touches the grey. 'Not from a bird.'

I look at her. 'No?'

'No,' she says, convinced. 'Probably an angel.'

The next child starts his opus. Middle C and then five notes to the left and five to the right.

I stare down at the feather. A grey angel? An old angel?

Luckily, we still have our great guardian angels with us. Ageing, frail and still furiously alive, Nelson Mandela and Desmond Tutu protect the integrity of the Struggle and remind us of the truth.

2

HOMECOMING

There are two things left in life today that are truly live. The Theatre. And the Church.

The Church has a one-up on the Theatre. You go to hell if you don't go to church! I think you stay horribly sane if you never visit a theatre.

Everything else that attracts our attention as entertainment is in a tin. CDs, DVDs, recordings, tape, film. But Theatre is as real as the smells and the sounds. It's that remarkable moment of special treatment, sitting in the dark and watching real live people in the light do something just for you.

From their mouth to your ear.

Hopefully you leave on a cloud of inspiration. (Otherwise you leave at interval, and forget the whole experience.)

When someone asks you what you saw, you can show them nothing. All you have are the small tastes of a great banquet that remain in your mouth. And maybe a folded programme full of adverts. Just a menu of past emotions.

The Church preaches at you and makes you come to terms with your sinful existence and promise never, never, never to do it again! The Theatre challenges you and forces you to examine your membership of the human race, and you promise you'll never, never, never stop doing it!

*   *   *

I was hijacked by Theatre in the mid-1960s and have been imprisoned without any hope of parole ever since. Not even the hint of release in middle age due to good behaviour. It never crossed my mind that my life would be anchored in the world of dreams. When I left school in 1964, I spent a nine-month adventure as a sailor in the Navy of then Defence Minister PW Botha. My eyes were opened to many things there. Mainly the reality of the fantasy that one was just like anyone else. Of course no one was, but in the Navy one was meant to be. Meeting boys from other worlds down the road from where we lived in the Cape Town garden suburb of Pinelands, with other accents and lives, was confusing, exciting and in the nick of time. And during those few weekends when I could leave Saldanha Bay and go back to the safe cocoon of my family under the trees, the railway bus would stop in the early morning mist at the small railway station of a town called Darling.

I started my university years as a nervous Afrikaans-speaking BA student, focusing on English and History. I chose those subjects because of the inspiration of two teachers at school who opened so many doors for me. Meneer Fanie du Toit with Sosiale Studies, and Miss Aloise Nel with Engels. Du Toit dressed up the historical propaganda as entertainment and made the lies exciting and as fictional as a John Wayne movie.

Miss Nel once asked us to write a poem.

I said: 'No, Miss, I can't.'

She said: 'Yes, Pieter, you can. You can do anything you believe in.'

And so in 1963 I wrote a poem because the teacher said I could.

It was called 'Homecoming'.

> I see it there behind the trees
> The castle of my youth
> The tall red chimney marks the grave
> of tears of joy and grief
> The house is cold and ashen-grey
> the doors are locked up tight
> The windowpanes are broken out
> and filled with a musty light.
> A cat sits on the garden wall,
> looking at me with stern cold eyes.
> I see a message in their depth
> which reads: 'They did not wait for you.
> You went away a spoilt young man
> with great ideas in your proud head.
> You did not send a word
> of how you felt, or if you longed.
> You always wanted to be free
> and thought that they had wronged.
> To you they were a nuisance
> and a burden to your joy.
> You know now what you were like then –
> a selfish, hateful boy.
> You went alone into the world
> and left them on their own.
> They did not wait
> They could not wait
> They're dead, you know, they're gone!'

I wanted to be a teacher like Meneer du Toit and Miss Nel, because they had taught me to believe. So I enrolled against my father's wishes at the predominantly English-speaking University of Cape Town. It wasn't far from home, so I didn't leave my little room under the thatched roof, full of pictures of Sophia Loren and secrets and stuff that made up my private dreams. If I'd gone to Stellenbosch University, as Pa wanted, and lived in residence, my life would have been completely different. Staying at home just meant I became more isolated from real life and went deeper into fantasy and what-ifs.

I spent my first year at UCT passing my subjects okayly and leaving behind the Dinky Toys, *Angelique* novels and childhood baggage, and embracing cigarette smoking, parties and too-tight trousers. The smoking made me cough, the parties made me confused, and the trousers enticed unwanted interest and dangerous explorations. This boy was young and there was lots to learn as he caught up with the mid-1960s fresh from a childhood in 1875.

During my matric year at Nassau High School, Miss Nel took us to see a play at the Little Theatre. It was our Shakespeare setwork: *King Lear*. I still remember the heightened clarity of the colours on the stage, the intense brilliance of the lights on the actors, and the breathtaking excitement of the drama off the page. Suddenly dreary Shakespeare was real, interesting and just like the films at the Savoy.

At the end of my first year, which seemed to go well, as there was no extra frown on Pa's face, I was given a Christmas present from my parents: a three-month return ticket on the Union-Castle mailships, and a trip to see the world, staying in London with Ma's friend Betty Jones, meeting Pa in Paris, visiting Tante Friedel und Onkel Franz in Wiesbaden, and travelling to Italy in the hope of finding Sophia Loren! During this incredible journey, I was taken to see theatre in London by Betty Jones. With beating heart and throbbing hard-on, I sat and stared at a gay porno movie in Amsterdam, taken there by a boy called Jensch, who then wanted to try out everything we'd seen. I was paid for sex in Paris by two older men in their thirties, who never gave me their names and left me with a rash! And I found Sophia's apartment in Rome.

When I got back from that first world tour, a letter from her was waiting for me in Pinelands, starting our friendship, which I treasure to this day.

And I was hijacked by Theatre.

I met Phyllis Punt in the UCT canteen, over those legendary chips with tomato sauce, worthy of skipping an entire year of lectures. An Afrikaans actress from Pretoria who had decided to return to her studies, she wore a black beret, her pale face looked Garboesque in its pose, and the cigarette in the holder between her long fingers never seemed to get shorter. Phyllis was taking Drama! I wanted to look like that. So, inspired by her passion for acting, I joined the Drama course as part of my BA degree.

Once I stood in the light of a follow spot in the Little Theatre, the powers that be looked me over closely and told me what they found.

'You have no talent as an actor. You speak badly. You're too Afrikaans. You should go to Stellenbosch.'

I believed them, but decided to stay and find ways of becoming part of what Phyllis loved so much. The Theatre! I would find where they kept the berets and cigarette holders at the Little Theatre. Who did you have to smile at here to look like Phyllis Punt?

So I did whatever they said.

I was an Afrikaans Calvinist boy used to obeying orders. I studied stage management, which meant buying cigarettes for actors, cleaning floors, ironing costumes, setting up props, following the text to prompt lines during performance, doing all the dirty work and taking all the blame. Today the job description hasn't changed. This haphazard daily lucky-packet of experiences was the best training I have ever had for the job I do now. I've been doing it for forty years, and it's probably the same as it was then.

Fetch. Carry. Set up, structure, budget. Lock up when everyone is gone. Go home alone to be fresh for tomorrow.

The Little Theatre was little. But, in those early dream-filled days, it was the greatest auditorium in the world.

'How can people be heard here?' I asked myself while sweeping the small stage.

'Will I ever be able to act one day?' I murmured, as Mrs Helen Rooza, the legendary wardrobe lady of the UCT Drama Department, swept past with a 'Hey, stop day-dreaming and get on with sewing those sequins onto that hat. Luigat!'

Helen Rooza was classified as a coloured in those days. We white Afrikaner superpeople were not used to taking orders from a maid. But this was Theatre, where we were all slaves, workers and maids to the Madam of Drama! Mrs Rooza started cracking my granite façade of prejudice with her sharp humour, her professional focus and her great use of Afrikaans. She spoke it like a coloured and made it her own.

Lesson number one: it *was* her own!

Helen eventually left South Africa because of apartheid and went to Australia to live with her exiled son. I met her there when visiting Sydney with an Oz version of *Adapt or Dye* in 1987. We sat up in the revolving tower of the city's highest erection and laughed and cried and insulted the Ozzies in Afrikaans. She died far away from her wardrobe, and our Theatre has never been the same since she left. If the departure of one person made such a difference, imagine the effect of the thousands we lost during those years of terror.

I had no idea it was so bad.

I was white. I was Afrikaans. I had a car and a home and a family. And a dream that one day I would look like Phyllis Punt. I don't think I had any real acting ambition. But the world of Theatre was dazzling and sexy. Instinctively I knew that I would make it work for me through my commitment.

Helen Rooza taught me the hard way.

'It's all work. One hundred per cent work. Every minute you work. If you're late, you are rubbish. You insult your colleagues. You're an amateur. Go home and kill yourself.'

I've never been late in forty years. I'm now so early that the managements hate me, because they must unlock the doors three hours before the show starts. The Theatre has become the only place in the world where I feel safe. It started at the Little Theatre in 1966.

Eventually, I did act. A large production of the play *Volpone* needed extras to be roped in, and I was cast as Corvino. Following my raw instinct, I unleashed an over-the-top performance with much crude comedy and slapstick gesture.

The applause was shocking. The faces of my fellow actors backstage were perplexing. I had never confronted stage jealousy before. Having grown up in a family of performers, the pianists I called Ma and Pa, who didn't have time for temperament, I wasn't aware of the ugly face of rivalry and bitchery.

Performance was engrained in my upbringing. Not the applause and celebration of success – although that was there too – but the tension of preparing for an appearance on stage. The daily repetition of rehearsal. Going over and over three bars of hellishly difficult music. Repeating it all the next day. And the next. And the following week. All to be perfect for the twenty-three minutes of a Schubert or a Mozart or a Bach. The tension in our Pinelands home on the day of a concert in the City Hall had a particular smell. Like burning flesh. They stopped being parents. Their fear was tangible. The nightmare would repeat itself time and time again. Today my sister Tessa, who inherited all that was great from my parents in her musicianship and excellence, dies each time she relives the magnificence of her music.

Maybe that's why I don't have fear when I perform. Because I'm not a pianist. I'm just an entertainer. A stage performer. Mozart, Bach or Schubert didn't write my words.

I did.

I've been alone on stage over 7000 times.

People say: 'Are you nervous?'

I say: 'No, I'm excited!'

It's the same feeling in the pit of your stomach. You want to vomit and spend a year on the loo, but 'excited' means you can do it, 'nervous' means you can't.

And Miss Nel said: 'You can do anything you believe in.'

* * *

Backstage at the Little Theatre was a warren of passages and stairs, with graffiti on the walls from past productions, the names of their casts fading with time and their comments indecipherable. The smell of backstage was greasepaint. Make-up. Hairspray. Sweat. And always a toilet that never flushed properly.

It's the perfume of my life. The older the theatre, the more it feels like those days, as I sit at the stained mirror covered with lipstick messages from the previous week's triumph. Applying Leichner Number 9, with a lighter line above and a darker shadow below. Ending up like someone from the Wild West crossed with a samurai in a Japanese kabuki.

I played a woman, for the first time, in a kabuki drama called *Seppuku*, devised and directed by Robert Mohr, our senior lecturer. An Afrikaner who pronounced English like a pretentious foreigner, Robert was a remarkable man of the theatre who shared his genius with us with the passion of an explorer.

They created my alphabet, those magicians at the Little Theatre.

Professor Rosalie van der Gucht was Head of the Department, eccentric and never wrong. Though her name was Dutch, Van couldn't speak a word of Afrikaans. She could have been from a 1940s black and white Elstree film. Robert was always doing battle with Mavis Taylor, she of the blonde hair-helmet and cross-eyed make-up. A punk rocker before her time, combination bully and virgin, experimental Merlin and exploitative mentor. 'Fetch my ma from the hairdresser!' was more familiar from her than 'You have talent.'

And yet her interest forced me to present her with something interesting. Technique and experience weren't there yet. I was all new jeans, overlong hair, foreign cigarettes and permanent hard-on. I did sleep with girls in those days, because I didn't realise you could also sleep with boys. I liked sex with 'actresses', even though I didn't know what I was doing. They did most of the work. Usually older and often overweight, they were gentle and loving.

I often think of the Little Theatre. Standing backstage at the Utrecht Stadtskouburg in Holland during a tour in the early 1990s. Three thousand people in the auditorium. All Dutch. I knew no one. Why were they here? Had I come to the wrong place? Then I remembered how, in the huge vastness of the 120-seater Little Theatre, I had panicked about how to project my voice. And here I was doing it for 3000 without a microphone. I must have learnt something as a former stage manager who learnt how to act, direct, produce and drive the transport.

I feel safe backstage all over the world. Standing in the wings, waiting to go on, where Marlene, Marceau, Moreau and Shirley Bassey have also waited to go on. Sharing with them the greatest moment in our profession. Being ready to deliver the product.

Why was I not as nervous as tradition demands? The backstage jitters of the stars one reads about in biographies? No contest here. I'm just a stage manager from a small town at the tip of Africa. Let me show off and prove that even someone who was once backstage staff in a Third World country can present a theatrical night to be remembered.

*   *   *

Waiting for Godot was the first play I stage-managed at drama school. Robert Mohr directed it. It had just opened in Europe to glowing reviews. Two tramps under a dead tree are waiting for someone called Godot. They entertain each other and us while they wait. It was seen as a bleak testament that God is dead. Now, in the twenty-first century, it is a gentle love story about two old farts who can't live without each other and entertain themselves under an old stump while waiting for someone who probably wasn't going to come in the first place.

What God?

The Theatre is God. That inspiration never leaves.

I was nominated for my first acting award for my 'acclaimed' performance in *Volpone*. I was invited to have tea with one of the judges one afternoon. I wore a suit. She was naked under a transparent Indian silk cloth. I ran away and didn't get the award. I left my jacket behind. I never got it back. It had my favourite picture of Sophia in the inside pocket.

Then Prime Minister Hendrik Verwoerd was murdered.

I used to sing in my father's choir in the Dutch Reformed Church in Rondebosch. Prime Minister Verwoerd and his wife Betsie would sit in the pews and listen intently. They were fans. I have letters to prove it. Then I discovered Sophia Loren in the pages of *Stage and Cinema*, and she was prettier! When Verwoerd was killed, I think I cried, like so many others who thought he was the Boer Messiah. And yet there was laughter with the tears, because the coloured people I'd come to know during my years as a free person at UCT danced in the streets of Cape Town. The British satirical *Private Eye* said it all with their front page at the time. Dancing blacks. A headline: 'Verwoerd Dead. A Nation Mourns'!

My life was going one way and my soul the other. Theatre reflected truth and exposed the inhumanity of man towards men. But outside the theatre, the inhumanity of my so-called Christian society overpowered everything. Theatre was giving me a standard for life and proving that my own life was found wanting. My focus, outside the theatre, was simply being at home to sleep and eat breakfast. Talk to my mother and avoid my father. Then get to drama school and spend the day fully occupied. In the wardrobe with Mrs Rooza. Watching Keith Anderson build sets and train trapeze artists in the workshop. Watch rehearsals. Mark up my prompt copy of the play I was running. Go to the Hiddingh Hall Library and pore over precious *Plays and Players* that gave me a window into the world of Real Theatre Overseas. Finding the new texts of playwrights who had just carved out new detours through the granite of tradition. And then back into the theatre with Mavis. Helping her with make-up class for the first-year students.

That was the next window for me. The magic of eyeliner and lashes, rouge and lipstick. Laurence Olivier had just appeared in the film *Khartoum* as the darkly hued Mahdi. I found I could look like him by using the right Leichners on my own face. With a white sheet knotted around the head and eyes darkly kohled, I was Olivier's Mahdi!

Marlene Dietrich was performing her one-woman séance in Cape Town, and so one night I appeared as her in a crowd scene in Mavis's production of Kaufman and Hart's *Once in a Lifetime*. After a Groucho Marx and a Jean Harlow had appeared, to the delight of the audience, in came Marlene. Crossing the stage in her crabwalk, my Dietrich had recaptured in look and movement what local audiences had seen her do the night before at the Alhambra down the road.

Who had time for mere politics or even family relationships when The Theatre, Little as it was, demanded my full attention? I could borrow Ma's car and felt like a grown-up. My nights were spent sitting in coffee shops and steakhouses, watching people have fun. Making notes on scruffy pads. Smoking too many cigarettes. I had my own friends who, being drama students, all pretended to know about real life with more conviction than I could. Their worlds didn't make much sense.

I had nothing new to tell them about me. What was there to say? A talented pianist-sister going to London on a scholarship. A talented pianist-mother who supported my ventures into drama, and a hard-working pianist-father who didn't. The fact that my father's cousin had been the first National Party Prime Minister was admired by some. The fact that my mother was not just a German refugee from Hitler's Berlin was still unknown to me, for she only shared her Jewish heritage with us many years after her death in 1969.

Throughout it all was the need for a fix. My daily drug of Theatre. Watching other actors do it every night, play after play, rehearsal after rehearsal. Sometimes acting, mostly managing, often just watching. Then a moonlighting job ushering at Cape Town's professional Arts Council theatre, the Hofmeyr. That 'huge venue' seated 250 and became my Broadway. Watching those performers every night, trying to make something better out of what would never be great, was the training no textbook could deliver. These professional stars sometimes behaved appallingly, by making each other laugh and then trying to recover. Others would throw silent-movie tantrums backstage. I was easily led by example, and, happily, I noticed and learnt from the good ones.

Paddy Canavan had also started as a stage manager and was now an actress. She never forgot the basics of preparation and discipline and was happy to share it with me over many a glass of whisky. She inflamed me with her passion for Total Theatre and her fierceness towards anyone or anything that threatened that perfection. Val Miller, the Meryl Streep of our theatre in the sixties and seventies, was cast to play a princess opposite my prince in Mavis's production of *Once Upon a Mattress*. I was young enough to be Val's son, but she managed to make me feel older and treated me with love and care.

I was a terrible actor because I was Acting.

I didn't understand the concept of reacting. It took thousands of repetitions to make me realise that less is more. That theatre is just an impression of life and not the beginning or end of the world. What happens outside in the reality of daily life was far more important than mouthing words and setting props. Dramatic, pretentiously rehearsed moments on a safe stage have nothing to do with the real thing. But when you're up there, you are the real thing. You are the world, and nothing outside matters.

For over two thousand years, the cardboard horizon of the Theatre has been a special world. The stilted words are the only message, and if they are spoken as well as they are understood, nothing real can compare.

It's too late to wean me off this drug now. I'm an addict for life. And I'll die one. Every night.

On stage. And then rise up and acknowledge the applause.

3

A MAGIC SPACE

W/here did the mere clapping of hands become the oxygen of life? I found a space called The Space.

It all began without me. I was at the London Film School, forging ahead with my confused decision to be a film-maker while writing plays in my spare time. In Cape Town there was only one professional arts company, the segregated, government-subsidised Cape Performing Arts Board. Ironically, with CAPAB's experimental production of *Orestes*, Brian Astbury, who had taken all our photos during Little Theatre productions, started the process of creation with playwright Athol Fugard and Yvonne Bryceland. Brian was married to Yvonne. Theirs was the most powerful theatrical partnership in South Africa.

They were all in London at the legendary experimental Open Space Theatre one night. While I was probably down the road in Shelton Street locking up after a long night of editing, Brian, Yvonne and Athol came out of that evening inspired by the freedoms of an empty space! This led to chats and plans, the usual what-ifs and why-nots. Cape Town needed more than just the Little Theatre to counter official government culture in the form of CAPAB. And so The Space/Die Ruimte opened in March 1972 with a new play by Athol called *Statements After an Arrest Under the Immorality Act*. Meanwhile, in London, I was a stagedoor Johnny, sending notes to Ingrid Bergman's stage manager organising a meeting.

In this chapter I'll quote Brian Astbury from his book about the history of The Space. It has been out of print for years, but with the magic of the Internet, I hope the book will soon be available at the press of a button. Because so many people were involved with the success of The Space, I do not want my memory of involvement and nourishment to give the impression that I was in any way more important or significant than any other. I know Brian won't mind me inviting him here to put my thoughts in perspective.

'The idea had been planted by *Orestes*,' Brian wrote in 1979. 'If only we had a space to work in ... [I]t was Athol who articulated it: the right to fail.'

Having established himself as the best theatre photographer in South Africa, Brian now stored his cameras and became the leading energy. He found a building off Long Street and gathered a group of die-hard supporters, who painted, built and made coffee. There was one principle as firm as a foundation: anyone who wanted to be a member of the Space audience was welcome. Anyone could come and act.

Apartheid would not feature here.

So The Space's colours were nailed to the mast. The impossible was probable. It was the beginning of freedom of expression in local theatre.

Then came Fugard's *People Are Living There*, and the late-night dance drama *Gilgamesh*. Not enough cage-rattling to attract official attention, until *Othello – Slegs Blankes* caused an uproar. In those days, a black Othello would not be allowed to appear on stage with a white Desdemona. So in this version the Moor didn't show up. And that was the play! Othello for Whites Only!

Donald Howarth's *Scarborough* introduced nudity. A plainclothes cop watched the third performance with a hard-on. The next day the play was banned. The threat of official government censorship became the issue. Self-censorship became the fear.

Sizwe Bansi Is Dead was born, and John Kani and Winston Ntshona stepped out of the shadows of apartheid and started leading the way. This led to more police harassment. It also led to the stages of the world and Tony Awards in New York.

The Space/Die Ruimte became the conscience of a young generation.

I was still in London being Peter Ace, a fourth-year at the London Film School. Someone sent me a cassette of Afrikaner soprano Mimi Coertse singing 'O Boereplaas' as a joke. I cried all day and got on the next ship to Cape Town, the SA *Vaal*. As I sailed into Table Bay, with the perfect silhouette of the mountain and the range of bergs that led towards the tail of Cape Point, I saw for the first time the tomb that was there forever for my mother. Four years earlier, she'd thrown herself off the heights of Chapman's Peak. I could see it through the salty tears of the wind.

By now I knew about The Space. I had also written my first play and tried it out in London.

Faces in the Wall made no impression on anyone except me when I produced it at one of the Film School cinemas during the summer break of 1969. It did introduce me to the woman who is still my literary agent, Patricia Macnaughton. Marlene Dietrich wrote me good wishes. Sophia Loren sent a cable. I had copies of both in my hand as I popped into that space in Bloem Street on my first day in Cape Town after a two-week cruise from the world so far away.

They were waiting for me. Brian, Yvonne, Bill Flynn, Paul Slab, Peter Piccolo, Lynne Maree and Dawie Malan. A play was opening in five days, called *Skyvers/Jollers*, and they needed someone to play the harassed teacher. The director, Robin Malan, couldn't do it. So they smiled and looked at me with new eyes. My hair was too long and I looked too healthy, but I had my play under my arm that needed a production. Brian made me an offer I couldn't refuse.

'He walked into The Space healthy and bronzed to find Robin, myself and the rest of the cast waiting, script in hand,' Brian recalls. 'He thought we were joking. Five days later he opened – haggard and pale. It was not the first time that he raced to the rescue.'

It was also not the first time emotional blackmail was used at The Space. After acting in *Skyvers/Jollers*, I directed *Faces in the Wall* in the Upstairs Theatre, at the same time helping out by directing Joseph Heller's complex anti-war satire *We Bombed in New Haven* in the Main Theatre when that play's director, my old Little Theatre nemesis Mavis Taylor, contracted jaundice. I started learning how to burn my candle at all its ends.

Brian was at first not very impressed by *Faces in the Wall*. The structure was nothing more than a series of incidents in the London flat of a gay youth, who falls in love with a mysterious girl who reminds him of his goddess on the walls, Greta Garbo. Looking at it now, it's a meaningless exercise. It was more of a personal journey for me towards accepting gayness as part of life and not some kind of darkness, and a discovery of a flair for dialogue.

'I considered it to be a flawed play,' Brian writes, 'and our staging to be more for his benefit than ours. Owen Williams, the *Argus* critic, however, compared Pieter to John Osborne and the run was packed for weeks. Infallibility was never a strong point of mine. So Pieter was working on two plays at almost the same time. He didn't think he could do it. I did. Faith is a strong point. Pieter didn't let us down.'

I directed John Guare's comic-strip gangster spoof *Cop Out*. Then a lunchtime romp of a melodrama called *I'll Ring for More Toast*, followed by a tribute to the late Sir Noël Coward, comprising *Fumed Oak* and *Red Peppers*. I also attempted *Popcorn*, a one-act play of mine, as a lunchtime entertainment. Inspired by a recent foiled attack on Sophia Loren by robbers after her jewels, the play is about a famous actress who uses all her powers of seduction and guile to eventually kill her attackers in order to protect her baby.

The play didn't appeal to audiences or critics. In fact, to add insult to injury, one of the actors who played a robber actually fell asleep during one performance!

Some of us got together and compiled a late-night entertainment centred on kitsch. While this was being performed, John Kani and Winston Ntshona were back in the theatre below, dazzling in *The Island*, prior to another world tour. Our last sketch ended with the defiant and banned Black Power salute silhouetted against a back-projection screen. John and Winston would race up after their curtain call to do those amandla gestures, the clenched fist still being illegal and so liberating.

A national highlight was Yvonne Bryceland and Percy Sieff in Bill Tanner's production of *Long Day's Journey into Night*. It was by Eugene O'Neill and celebrated the first birthday of The Space. Meanwhile, noses to the grindstone, we delivered evening shows like John Guare's *Muzeeka*, Pip Simmons' *Superman* and, at lunchtime, Feydeau's *Don't Walk About with Nothing On*.

The Outer Space opened a second, smaller proscenium theatre with my new play *Pity About People*. Back to Brian:

'As usual – despite a lot of publicity – it took quite a while for the public to accept the fact that we now had two full-time theatres. Pieter did a very good job of directing the play and the acting was of a high standard. But it was not an easy "accessible" play. Its theme of catatonia, however, found much favour with the medical profession, and one evening the audience of eighteen included a party of twelve psychiatrists and psychologists.'

Because of the need to protect our multiracial audiences from prosecution and ourselves from being closed down, The Space Club was formed. Through this loophole, plays could be freely presented to its 'members', uncompromised and uncut. It didn't keep the censors away, but at least the police had to pay membership fees to get in.

Maralin Vanrenen and I were living together above the fish and chips shop, having a steamy heterosexual relationship, which didn't help our respect for one another as actor and director. She started work on a production of Jean Genet's *The Maids*, with me in drag as Madame and our two coloured company members, Bill Curry and Vincent Ebrahim, dragged up as the Maids.

Brian remembers: 'Maralin had expressed the desire to direct. She took the two actors who could only play before Club audiences – Bill and Vincent – added Pieter, and started working on an all-male production of *The Maids*. Extra ginger was added by the fact that the Maids were both black. At the dress rehearsal it was quite obvious that the production – done in full drag – was not working.'

The problem was elementary. Vincent was frightened of being seen to be gay, which he wasn't, while Bill was determined not to remind anyone of the fact that he was! So they both found it hard to be real. Instinctively, and maybe because I was already such a closet-case drag queen, my Madame was a close cousin of the later Evita Bezuidenhout.

There I learnt that the key to making an audience believe was reality. Play a woman as a man in a dress and it's a one-line gag. Portray a woman in all her glory and detail and you become that person. Theatre presents many ways to reach a destination. To this day, with Evita Bezuidenhout living in the minds of millions as a reality, that secret is still my trump card: let the women recognise the woman and the men forget the man.

Brian writes: 'Discussing it the next day, Pieter said that Maralin had actually wanted to do it straight, but was not sure if it would work. That night we cancelled the opening and they played it without props and costumes. The effect was electrifying.'

I'm sure it was enough for Jean Genet to sue us! We were in fact presenting what had already been written: the play by Genet set in a prison cell. My taste for pretentious experimentation without purpose or humour was pushed to its limits. Maralin and I broke up and went into separate beds and, eventually, separate streets.

Fugard's *Boesman and Lena* was never performed at The Space, even though Yvonne had initiated the character of Lena in the CAPAB premiere production some years before. But the saga of bergies and tramps usually happened outside The Space: in Long Street, Bloem Street and Buiten Street. And it was those pavement artistocrats that inspired in me so much of my alphabet of Cape sounds and laughter.

To celebrate The Space's twenty-five years, I wrote a piece called *No Space on Long Street*. With most of the old army in the audience, one of the characters I portrayed was Gracie, the old bergie who used to sleep on a newspaper in the doorway under the windows of the Main Theatre.

She stumbles into view, having been mauled and beaten, muttering to herself comfortingly.

'Gracie? You gotta stay clean. No excuse lying in the gutter like a piece of rubbish? So, if you're not rubbish, stay clean, Gracie!'

She wraps herself in what was once a blanket and lies down painfully on the open newspapers spread across pieces of tatty cardboard.

'But no wonder I can't sleep! This pavement is hard. Just here, specially here!' She taps at the ground accusingly. 'When I lie down here, I can also hear water underground. The pipes. Maybe a river? Spider [her bergie companion] said he learn at school there was a river under Long Street. Let me move before I drown ...'

With a soft cackle she moves her position slightly.

'That doorway there, it's softer. It looks like some sort of fancy marble? It's really just old Cape granite! Here's the nice little hollow for my hip!'

She lies down painfully, but can't seem to find a comfortable position. 'So damn sore, man,' she sighs, sitting up. 'First it's the traffic cop!' She mimics the Afrikaner bully.

'"Hey Gracie Goffel? Get off the streets!"'

'"Gaan kak!"'

'Gwa! With the back of the hand. On the ear. Now I hear the sound of running water, even when I'm lying down!' She rubs her ear gently. 'They make something go loose in my head. They klap me, tien, twaalf, twenty times. Meid! Goffel! Hoer!'

She nods her head wisely.

'Then it's the police in the green Ford Fairlane. Boere out of uniform. Young boys, smelling of beer and poes. Disappointed because they didn't have a lekker time with the fancy hoere. Makes my stomach turn. How can a hoer kiss a drunk who pays for poes? It's bad enough having to be pomped. The mouth should be private property. My mouth is my secret. No one gets in there. I wash it out every day. Purple mouthwash?'

She waves the familiar bottle and laughs.

'Meths.' She gargles and swallows it all. She shrugs sheepishly. 'Sometimes it slips past and just goes down. Hier af tot onder in my maag. Hot. Soft. But sore. Maar okay.'

She enjoys the warmth in her stomach. Then she scolds herself.

'Just don't skyf, Gracie! With all the meths in the maag, you'll go up like a Guy Fawkes.'

She shakes her head and addresses Spider.

'Spider, as true's God, mind your own bleddie business, okay? Look after your own problems! And God knows, you have problems. (a) You too young to look so old. (b) You got education. You know better. How can you live like me? I who know nothing? Just how to keep myself clean. And, (c) you are white, under all that shit and dirt and vuilis. And you break the law of the land, because you pomp me en ek is 'n meid!'

She smoothes the newspaper round her carefully and nods agreement with her thoughts.

'And who was here first? Me. Already so long, ou Mario Lanza [from the Italian restaurant on the corner] puts food here for me under his *Cape Times*. 'n Bakkie vol wurms bolognaise. Even when I'm not home. He knows. This is Gracie's place. But now?'

She points upstairs where the Space audience is applauding the play.

'My dear, the culture vultures has come to Long Street. God help us all! Every night the noise! Just when you settle down, the sore hip in the dent in the stone, cover your face with your dress, wind the doeke round your ankles, so no fokker can force open your legs and rape you when you sleep. Then it starts from up there. Always big words. In that unnatural voice.'

She intones grandly, booming the sounds without articulating anything. It sounds like Acting.

'Theatre? Kak man, it's unnatural. Who talk like this?'

Again she emotes pompously.

'I have to lie here and listen to all this? The mother says to the son: "Why you do this?"'

'The father begs the mother: "Stop doing that!"'

'The son to the brother: "You did this! You did this to Ma!"'

'"No I didn't!"'

'"Yes you did. Forsooth!"'

She howls with laughter, cutting it short with a fit of coughing. Eventually she gets her breath back.

'Watse kak woord is dit: *forsooth*?'

She shakes her head and looks up, listening for noise.

'Acting acting acting. So it goes on till eleven o'clock at night! I just stand up in my bed and scream: "Ag, jou ma se poes!" No, they hear me. They all stop acting and laugh! Mario Lanza says even he hears me down in his keffie without his hearing aid.'

Gracie enjoys her victory.

'Then Sunday comes and we all say: "Thank God, Long Street is dead. No one walks here. Even the birds sit like stale loaves of tired old bread." The day of rest? Not up in this windgat place.'

She intones sarcastically the rhythm of the performances.

'"What are they doing up there?" I ask Mario Lanza.

'"The Space," he says.

'"No, my space," I say. "I was here first!"

'"They practise acting on Sunday," he says.

'"Ja well, I sleep on Sunday," I say.

'"They build things and make clothes," he says.

'I wish they would just go away. Make some space!'

She touches her mouth carefully.

'Shit, man, I'm worried about my teeth. Still feels loose after they kicked my face. I don't want to lose my teeth, man. I never forget that drunk, lying in the gutter by the old Cape Town Station. Before all this; before I was here. I looked at her for a long time. She lay there with a open pink wet mouth.

'No teeth. God, man, it looked so horrible. Like her smile had been ripped out of her face. At least with teeth you could say, shame, she's sick. But with no teeth? Like a terrible black hole …

'When Spider buggers me up, I make him promise: not the mouth. Leave the teeth. He pretends to be tough, showing off, like he was once somebody. I say: "You don't have to try. You're here. Where you were is nothing. Where you go is nothing."

'He must keep himself clean, that Spider. He gets so drunk and comes and tears my clothes. Hurts me. Except sometimes. He holds me and cries. Like he was my child. My child would not be so dirty. No, not my child.'

She looks up again and listens.

'It's quiet up there. For a change. Maybe the police closed them down again, for mixing the races. Sis! Disgusting to see who wants to sit next to blacks. That Alex says it's all political. Just to be hardegat.' (Alex was a stage manager at The Space.)

A rush of applause and laughter from above brings her back to earth. She looks up and yells:

'And meanwhile decent people can't sleep!'

She tries to settle down. Then she remembers something with a start.

'Oh shit, I forgot to get some dagga for that Alex. I don't trust him. Last week, early one morning. I see him get out of the green Ford Fairlane. He doesn't know I'm under my blanket. I see it all. What's he doing with them? He knows the cops? But he asks me for dagga? Maybe he's a cop? Maybe I should warn the Space people?'

She considers for a moment, but the noise from above convinces her.

'No, man, I was here first. Let them all go to jail. But then maybe I get taken for the dagga? Maybe if I tell Mario Lanza? He's got the right words to talk to them with. He's from overseas. Like he said again last week: "Something's rotten in the state of Denmark."'

She seems to be impressed for a moment, then bursts out laughing as she screams down the street:

'Hey Mario Lanza? Jou ma se poes!'

*   *   *

Being an actor was not the most important job at the theatre, because everyone was that. It was the stage manager. The trick of conjuring up three productions and keeping them in the air at the same time, with no budget, too little rehearsal and too much democracy, made the stage manager worth his weight in gold. Not all of them were men. Beryl Berman was the Good Fairy of technology, and would replug seven lights into two adaptors while the play was going on, and we never sat in darkness that had not been preplanned. So not all the stage managers at The Space were suspected of being spies for the security police.

Take the Alex that Gracie mentioned. That was not his real name, although the name he gave us wasn't his real name either. Brian and I would sit at the Stuttafords first-floor restaurant with our tea and toasted cheese with HP sauce, planning the next twenty-four minutes, and we'd remark how lucky The Space was to have, say, Alex as stage manager. And then, inevitably, two days before the play's opening performance, Alex would resign. We would plead and offer him a R50 weekly raise! But he would go, frustrated by our lack of secrets. There was nothing to spy on. Whatever we did at The Space we did on stage and in the light.

We acted and directed, sometimes for the first time and often in more than one language. We wrote and rewrote and world-premiered something every week. We found and begged costumes, borrowed props and usually stole furniture from our parents' homes. We worked like slaves and felt like Caesars, all paid the same R22.50 a week, from the assistant stage manager to Yvonne Bryceland, who sometimes worked as assistant stage manager when not playing the lead.

The play that would be my 'big break', *Selle ou Storie*, only happened because there was no other option. A play for the Outer Space fell through, and over tea and toasted cheese, I suggested this Afrikaans play in the box under my bed. Let Brian take it from here.

'Pieter met Christine Basson in the Outer Space production of *Ooh La-la!* They got on famously and started looking for a vehicle for her. In another of those Space catastrophes, everything fell through and he landed with a cast of four, no play and thirteen days to go. Out came *Selle ou Storie*. I had first seen the script in its original English version. (It was then meant as a follow-up to *Faces in the Wall*.) We weren't interested, so he translated it into Afrikaans, moved it from London to Johannesburg and sent it to CAPAB. They weren't interested. Now he waved the script at me.

'"I've got the cast!" Who had a choice?

'*Selle ou Storie* is a legend in its own way – and my fallibility was well and truly established. Carried by a bravado performance of exceptional range, power, timing and courage by Christine, it smashed its way into the consciousness of many young urban Afrikaners as they heard themselves speaking onstage for the first time. The conservatives hated the mixture of English and Afrikaans and the swearing. But for the others, their playwright had arrived!

'We revived it later that year, when it began its battle with the censors. The first skirmish was the most reasonable, a No-Children-under-18 restriction, only when it moved away from The Space. Later the script was banned when the production reached the more uptight north, though you could see the production. Still, later, this too was banned. It became some ridiculous farce from which, with his usual quick sense of humour, Pieter made much capital.'

Ironically, my next play, *God's Forgotten*, was never deemed offensive or obscene, nor subversive in any way. It was, in fact, the most dangerous of my new plays, focusing on Afrikaner politics and the future of the Boer dream.

'*God's Forgotten* is probably Pieter's bleakest, strongest play to date,' writes Brian. 'A vision of South Africa after an unsuccessful revolution – totally cut off from the world – its prophecies started to come true with discomforting regularity. Pieter's overfondness for Chekhovian extracts led, in my opinion, to structural weaknesses which we never resolved in our production, but it is still my favourite of his plays.'

*　　*　　*

In the ministerial homestead, Excelsior, JJ Brand's sudden death is being managed by his eldest daughter, Tosca. Her sister Sarah is still suffering from a collapse and addictions. Her youngest sibling, Aliza, has just returned from abroad in secret, accompanying her father's body and his new, younger wife. His death puts them all in danger, and makes them aware of their irrelevance. The high-security walls block out the sun and terror outside.

Gudrun, the new stepmother, is out of her depth and frightened. Sarah has taken pills and is drinking. Tosca is convinced her father was assassinated. Seven hundred suspects have been arrested.

'But surely it will all come out in the trial?'

Gudrun glances at the rough wall outside the elegant windows. The sound of wood beetle in the stinkwood furniture makes her even more edgy.

Sarah smirks and smokes.

'If we had trials for every suspect in this country, we'd be like those beetles. We'd never stop. Having trials.'

Gudrun tries to stay calm and sensible.

'Can't they try and escape?'

Sarah cackles with laughter.

'You've been brainwashed by the late late shows. Where can we escape to?' She sees her sarcasm won't work. The young stranger in the room with her looks even more vulnerable. Sarah sits Gudrun down on the elegant sofa. She tells her story slowly, as if to a retarded child.

'Many years ago, there was a political prison near here, surrounded by water. All references to it have been deleted from the official records, because no one could believe that a political prison could survive in full view of a thriving Christian community. Even then there was no escape, but they were always in the public eye, so to speak. I think there is a God – with quite a devilish sense of humour too.'

Gudrun pulls away from Sarah's closeness.

'I see nothing funny in what you've just said,' she sighs.

'No, but look at the irony.' Sarah gets up and waves at the windows. The ash from her cigarette leaves a trail on the spotless carpet. 'Here we are, surrounded by walls to keep them out. We're safe and secure in our political prison, trying to escape through our so-called culture, our fabricated heritage, our desperate fantasy. Like blind stallions stampeding into the rusty barbed wire …'

*   *   *

Brian was right. The dependence upon *Three Sisters*, and the overuse of quotes from that play, smokescreened the clarity of the Brand family. But Chekhov helped me find a frame and anchor my people. I had structured this play instinctively, led by the drama of the dialogue. The words came easily. The characters were familiar. The isolation of the Afrikaner so often reflected in my own family, with my father's deep Nationalist roots which he also detested yet used to confront me, gave me enough mortar to secure the bricks. The death of my mother, leaving a rip down the centre of our canvas, was all part of the background to the action, with music by Debussy, which I used while writing to create the right atmosphere.

After the first chilling seasons at The Space and later at the Market during the terror and fears of the mid-1970s, all reflected in the actions of the drama, I stupidly listened to too much 'good' advice. I rewrote, restructured, reshaped and nearly wrecked the play. It was eventually published by Penguin UK in a collection of three of my plays and is unproducible. Somewhere there is a cleaner, simpler version of the play that remains in the minds of so many who saw it then. It's needed now, especially in this new century, where our lives have not turned out as predicted by Sarah in the living room of Excelsior.

Maybe because it had an English title, censorship ignored it.

The Outer Space season of turmoil through *Selle ou Storie*, *Karnaval* and *God's Forgotten* just proved once again that you could say anything in English. But beware if you dared whisper the truth in Afrikaans!

*   *   *

Aliza takes her sister's hand.

'What happened to us, Sarah?' she whispers, fighting back tears.

Sarah shrugs. 'I don't know … I suppose we became fat and secure in our comfort. We became dulled through our belief in our survival. Proud of our self-sufficiency, our arrogance, our power. As Christians we loved them, because they had no hope. And we hated each other, because we became our own rivals. We encouraged them to dance and rattle their beads, hoping it would make enough noise to warn us in time. And after we deprived them of everything that ultimately destroyed us, we bestowed on them the patience to wait for us to frighten ourselves to death. Do you still think of our token black friends?'

Aliza takes a sharp intake of breath. 'Mine were never token.'

Sarah nods slowly. 'Oh? And where are they now? Your eternal kaffir-buddies?'

Aliza controls her anger. She swallows loudly. 'I lost touch.'

'Well, that's what's happened to us, Aliza. We've lost touch.'

4

REACTING TO ACTING

Life outside the theatre influenced our passion and forced us to have opinions and act on them. The country was being strangled by the Afrikaner Broederbond's successful recipe for white supremacy called apartheid. The world called it apart-height, which easily became apart-hate. The small bleats of protest coming from our stages were often tolerated as irritating noises-off. The real dramas of life often made us feel ashamed of our creativity behind the safety of our theatrical 'fourth wall'.

Cape Town tried to pretend that life was going on as usual. The city prided itself on a liberal attitude, and, even though the roots of apartheid were anchored in 'the fairest Cape in the whole circumference of the earth', it was convenient to blame Pretoria for the reality of our politics.

In 1973 a city theatre festival was announced, at which drama, music and art were encouraged. It would obviously be within the structures of the law – in other words, for whites only. Because The Space was unashamedly 'non-racial', it was breaking the law by allowing blacks and whites to sit together in the same theatre. We decided to take part in this festival by presenting a piece of street theatre. Obviously no one in the tower of power down in Wale Street was quite sure what that meant. So we were officially included in the programme.

'The Space will present Street Theatre in Greenmarket Square!'

The public was fascinated. The production in the Main Theatre at that time was a new Tennessee Williams drama called *Outcry*, starring Bill Flynn and Michele Maxwell. While Greenmarket Square had not yet been given over to the colourful stalls of a daily market as it is today (it was illegal for the races to practise such business together!), the small, square men's toilet in the centre of the space – also for whites only – provided a perfect stage for our piece. It was publicised that Bill Flynn and Michele Maxwell would be doing an extract from their play on that 'stage' on a Saturday morning at 11.30.

The city would be full of shoppers, and workers would have time to have a look. Bill and Michele were famous and popular. Friends of The Space were concerned. Our enemies were perplexed. We were inspired.

Guerrilla theatre had always held an attraction for us. Even though we were never on the barricades fighting the monsters of oppression, the images of the Hungarian uprising, the Czechoslovakian bloodbath and the East German underground's attempts to puncture the façade of totalitarian power showed what could be done with the pen and the word. The American youth revolution against the Vietnam War demonstrated the power of the guitar and the song.

Saturday dawned, and Bill and Michele set off for their challenging experience. There was no amplification to help them, and they would have to project their voices into the ether, competing with doves and traffic, police sirens and drunks. While this was attracting the attention of a waiting crowd, the real presentation began to take shape.

Space stage manager John Nankin arrived on the south side of the Square. He was dressed elegantly, and so were those with him. They were part of a wedding party. He was the groom. There was a mother in a huge hat, a father with a fashionable moustache. There were best friends as best men, and a small page boy. They got out of their fleet of glittering, expensive cars, all lent to us by members of The Space Club, who were watching from a distance with fingers crossed.

It was nothing new for wedding parties to have their official pictures taken on Greenmarket Square. In fact, it was the ideal spot, with the historic buildings surrounding the cobbled area and the magnificent sweep of Table Mountain creating a perfect backdrop for that all-important moment in the lives of two young people, now joined as one.

Meanwhile, on the north side of the Square, the bridal party arrived. The bride was Toti Ebrahim, an assistant stage manager and aspiring actress, looking glorious in a shimmering white bridal gown. As there was happily no south-easter blowing, her three bridesmaids could arrange the long chiffon train behind her, while the small flower girls held their little baskets of rose petals in their gloved hands. The bride's mother was Cathy Zeeman from the Space Canteen. Her father was Bill Curry.

The two parties saw each other across a now crowded Greenmarket Square. They waved. People smiled with sentimental enjoyment. Weddings always make someone cry.

The wedding photographers arrived, Brian Astbury in the lead, with assistants who were ready to set up for the ultimate photo without fuss. The fact that there were more photographers than usual did not seem much of an issue. Yet.

On the roof of the whites-only toilet, Bill and Michele were passionately performing the great American dramatist. The crowd around them were fascinated. Very little of the dialogue was heard. Very few actually understood what was being acted, but this was Theatre and different from their daily lives.

As the two parties of the wedding group slowly walked towards each other, there was a slight parting of the waves. The crowd, who were concentrating on Bill and Michele on the raised platform, started taking note of the bride and the groom.

She looked so lovely. He looked so handsome. What a perfect couple.

But what was wrong here?

One by one the Capetonians in the multiracial crowd turned away from the official focus of their attention and stared at this everyday occurrence. A bridal couple and their families posing for a picture. It happened every weekend. Facing them, a handful of working photographers.

Then it clicked. As the cameras whirred, like a veldfire the ripple spread through the crowd.

The bride was coloured! The groom was white!

While actors from The Space were expected to be provocative and tap-dance on the crumbling edge of the cliff, their Tennessee Williams presentation was dull by comparison with this impossible sight. There was no way that a white man would be allowed to marry a coloured woman. If they attempted a relationship under cover of duvet and darkness, they would be arrested under the Immorality Act. The Mixed Marriages Act forbade them even to think of it, and the Group Areas Act made sure that, even if they managed to stay together, they were not allowed to live in the same place!

And yet, here they were, in the centre of the most public area of Cape Town, on a crowded Saturday morning? Holding hands? Smiling at the cameras? Kissing for a picture? He with her brown parents. She with his white father and mother. Black and brown mixing with white. Normally, delightfully, happily.

The reaction was nuclear!

White people took nervous steps away from the scene, coloured people pushed closer for a look, and blacks just stood and laughed. Fear and fascination mingled. The outrage of the normality of the moment far outweighed the simple fact that laws were being broken here and people would be arrested. On the stage the Tennessee Williams dialogue petered out as Bill and Michele stood transfixed by the happening.

My job was to be on the lookout for the police.

We had already seen some familiar slouches skirt the edges of the crowds.

Now photographers arrived who were not from the *Cape Times*. They were not just photographing the wedding party, who smiled sweetly at each camera with no hint of concern. They were photographing members of the public.

The bubble of fun could not last.

We heard police sirens approach. Because of the dense crowd, the trucks couldn't reach the centre of attention. On a signal from Brian, with casual smiles and supposed discussions on where the reception would be held, the wedding party split in two, making their way back to their cars. This time they were all mixed together. The white father in animated conversation with the coloured mother, the white best man opening the car door for the smiling black bridesmaid.

We held our breath.

The people of Cape Town started applauding. The swell of sound engulfed the entire Square. Bill and Michele joined them. The security policemen posing as photographers found themselves engulfed by a crowd of well-wishers who made it hard for them to take their snaps.

And then it was over.

We all stood around and looked at one another. I recognised some members of The Space Club. A coloured couple just shook their heads and shrugged. She was crying. The man was too moved to say anything. White friends were talking in low voices. The local bergies, already drunk on cheap booze, were now intoxicated by that brief vision of heaven.

'A white groom and a hotnot bride? Sies!' the toothless old hag screamed, and danced a wedding jig. Gracie and Spider had been watching from the steps of the church. Mario Lanza applauded with a flourish. Yvonne Bryceland picked up some paper flowers that a bridesmaid had dropped. All these things had to be returned. They had lent us everything: the costumes, the cars, the flowers. Even the shoes. Members of The Space Club had understood what guerrilla theatre meant in Cape Town in 1973.

Simple theatre in the street, reflecting the impossible.

*   *   *

My father, now living alone in Pinelands, was upset by my work. The use of bad language offended him. But it was my playground at the edge of darkness that frightened him the most. I didn't have the words to explain why I was doing what I did. I still find any logic difficult to pinpoint. At the time, there was no choice but to get on with the job. The alternative in theatre was deathly involvement with CAPAB, and all the hypocrisy and lies that went along with their safe Nico Malan Theatre productions.

The only solution would have been to close down The Space and bankrupt the business – and they nearly succeeded. But, because earning money was not an issue, for the simple reason that there was no money, passion and commitment kept the lights on and the words flowing.

It was one of those hot summer nights in the City Bowl. Very Tennessee Williams, although by now ten other plays had come and gone from the Main Theatre stage. During an interval, someone came rushing into the Space Canteen in a panic.

There was drama in Long Street!

We all ran out. The few doctors in the audience fetched their medicine bags from their cars in case help was needed. In the middle of the street, just in front of Carnival Court, stood a man. A young man, maybe, but after a life spent drinking at the Mountain View Bar, not so young any more. His eyes were wild, his face snarling.

In his hands he held two huge butcher's knives. He pointed them at us like a deranged Spartacus. We, the appalled, delighted Roman gentry, gasped.

'Don't come near me!' he snarled. 'Stay away!'

Of course, none of us rushed to wrestle him to the ground and disarm him. We stood entranced.

This was better than theatre.

The man wheeled round and thrust his blades out in all directions.

'Leave me!' he cried. 'Stay away!'

Then we saw a small figure come out of the shadows. She was crying, her bony arms outstretched. 'Johnny?' she sobbed. 'Please put down the knives.'

'Leave me, Ma! I'm going to die now. It's enough! Leave me, Ma!'

'No, Johnny, you can't die. What about me? And Auntie Kittie? And the others in Upington? Please Johnny ...'

She shuffled towards him. He wheeled round, and the knives nearly touched her tear-stained, wrinkled face.

'Leave me, Ma ...'

He started to cry. Sobs tore his pose to shreds. The knives lowered. She stood close to him and put her thin arms around him. Her head didn't even reach his shoulders. He cried against her wispy grey hair. Slowly, she shuffled him towards the kerb and the dark door of Carnival Court, murmuring motherly things to this large lump of unhappiness she called son. Then she turned and looked at each of us with a piercing stare.

'Good night, hey? The show's over ...'

* * *

The show was never over in Long Street.

Sitting in our kaftans on the verandah of our rented flat above the fish and chips shop, Maralin, Grethe Fox and I would look over at the balconies of Carnival Court and the activity among the residents. Those 'girlies' and their friends inspired my play *Karnaval*. I didn't have to use much imagination. I just had to look out of the window.

Karnaval was set in that very space in Long Street on a New Year's Eve in the mid-1970s. Auntie Dora is celebrating in her own lonely way. She advises the young girls who board in the building and hopes they will not overstep the mark. Meaning not having sex with coloured sailors for money! Like an old Medea who never had the children to kill, she represents an older generation exhausted by the demands of being special and white. Changes are coming. The sun will rise and bring another day. So enjoy the darkness of the night while it lasts.

I invited the residents of Carnival Court to a preview of the play in the Outer Space. We had built a set based on their home outside. The balconies with the broekie-lace surround, the washing line with the baby clothes dangling in the wind. Even the dartboard askew on the wall. Springbok Radio blaring from Auntie Dora's portable radio. There was no subtle attempt to pretend here.

Brian and I watched them come across Long Street. Dressed up for the theatre like no one did any more. Their hair had been done, their stockings were new. Auntie Dora had her teeth in, all of them! A special treat. I didn't want them to hear from others about *Karnaval* and think I had been making fun of them. I was quite prepared for their anger and hurt. Brian thought the tough with the boep on whom I based the character on stage, Boytjie, would donner me!

They came out of the play in tears.

'Ag, dearie me,' wept the old woman who had inspired Cornelia Stander's Auntie Dora. 'Those poor girlies. Haai, so tragic, maar ag, so brave. There by the grace of God go we!'

And they thanked Brian and hugged me, and I signed their programmes and they went back to their Long Street lives, without having seen any similarity with themselves on our stage. So much for theatre being the mirror of life. Maybe it was just a window.

The Publications Control Board thought it was obscene and blasphemous.

Karnaval was banned after ten performances. The censors were probably right when they saw my characters on the balcony, swearing, loving, laughing and living in Afrikaans. 'Ons mense is nie so nie!'

Our people are not like that.

The final character in my 1997 one-man celebration of The Space, *No Space on Long Street*, is Elsabe Lategan. Brian recognised her as one of the characters I had presented in a funny little drag show called *Just Hilda*. Then she was a cartoon of the offended moral minority. Now she was a member of the Censor Board. I dressed into her on stage at the Baxter, being very careful not to give any hints of Evita Bezuidenhout.

They could have come from the same school, but they did not share the same hairdresser, or IQ.

*   *   *

Dr Elsabe Lategan walks out of the Outer Space looking at the programme of the play she's just seen. *Selle ou Storie*. She stands at the lamppost waiting for her car to arrive. The sign with the street's name is broken. Just the 'LONG' has survived.

She looks angry.

'This time they've gone too far,' she says, confiding in us. 'I don't often say this, but I'm glad my husband wasn't here with me tonight. Herman would've been hysterical, to put it mildly.'

She gives a small laugh of enjoyment.

'He can't bear to hear women use profane language. Let alone Afrikaans women! Not that he would think of coming to the theatre, let alone this type of *alternative theatre*.'

She over-articulates the last two words as if they were some kind of foreign swearword. Laughter makes her look up. Through the large industrial windows of the Space Canteen, she can see members of the audience from the Main Theatre buzz with energy.

John Nankin, the stage manager for the Outer Space, closes the theatre doors.

'Can I call you a cab or something?' he asks.

'Thank you, no, I'm being fetched.'

She lights a cigarette. She has made an effort to conceal who she is: a powerful, conservative, intelligent woman, who confidently stands one step behind a powerful, stupid man. She has made her husband what he is. The country is now rewarding him. He doesn't like it when she wears slacks.

'I'm glad I didn't recognise any of my friends here tonight.' She rolls her eyes at the thought. 'Not very likely. I don't expect to, thank heavens.'

A couple come out of the Space building and walk past her. The young coloured man is excited about the play he's just seen, with Yvonne in the lead. His pretty white companion agrees.

'She's so great.' he says. 'Thanks for the treat. Nice there's one place we can have coffee properly.'

She laughs.

'See you at varsity!'

Elsabe watches them wave at each other and leave for their separate worlds. His, a silent black and white story. Hers, a loud stereophonic colour spectacular.

'The only time someone seemed to know me was last May,' Elsabe says, 'when the security police raided the theatre. It was during a performance of Tennessee Williams's *The Glass Menagerie*. One of my favourite plays. A wonderful production by Bill Tanner. I could've killed them! With Yvonne Bryceland at her most moving moment, suddenly, like the Gestapo, these barbarians storm in. And why? Because some fool phoned and told them there were blacks in the theatre and that is against the law!'

She sighs deeply.

'Dear God! If I had some boot polish, I would've smeared it over my face and dared them to arrest me! The lights went on, the magic was gone. Poor Yvonne became Yvonne and stood to one side. The young actors, Dunster and Flynn, stared.'

She nods her head slowly, remembering.

'I recognised the plainclothes man in charge. Ben Engelbrecht. Ambitious. Young. Ruthless. A killer. Someone, my husband said, one should watch. Cabinet Minister material, he said. Minister of Police no doubt.

'He stared at me for a long time. I pretended not to notice, but I could feel his eyes bore right through my disguise. I was dressed like this. Please – Mevrou Dokter Elsabe Lategan does not usually dress like this.'

She smirks and steps on her cigarette with an elegant shoe.

'Oh, yes, at the Nico Malan I merge carefully with the other tasteless matrons in their hideous Tini Vorster velveteen. But when I slip away from real life and get into my camouflage and come to The Space Theatre, I am … is the word … liberated?' She nods and shrugs. 'I can think again.'

A bottle breaks somewhere in the darkness off Long Street. A woman screams, then laughs. Elsabe Lategan checks her watch.

'I saw Engelbrecht again with Vorster some months later. He was in charge of the Prime Minister's security. On the ladder up to hell. He stared at me again. This time I stared back, secure in my crimpelene.'

She lights another cigarette.

'John Vorster was quite animated that evening. Strange to hear him talk about the theatre. Not the Nico Malan type of theatre, but this Space Theatre.

'"Elsabe?" he said, rasping my name between those thin blue lips. "What have you heard about this new theatre in Bree Street?"

'I said: "John, I have been well informed about what happens at The Space. And it's off Long Street. It's what they do on stage that's the problem ..."

'But Vorster had lost interest. His attention span with regard to culture was very small.

'Of course, as such a prominent member of the Censor Board associated with live theatre in the Cape, it is not only my job to be informed. It is my delight. I didn't say this to the Prime Minister, but, in my case, they had put the chocoholic in charge of the chocolate factory!

'I am truly privileged to go to The Space Theatre as often as I do. Of course, the next morning I want to ring up Astbury and his people and say: "Brian? Thank you for the wonderful plays I can see. Tennessee Williams. O'Neill. Orton. I love your theatre deeply, and the anonymous cheque you received in May was from me. But you are going too fast and we don't want to get to that destination of free speech and association. Be careful, Brian. We will not make a political martyr out of your theatre. We will just ban you for obscenity and blasphemy and bankrupt you! We know how to do our job ..."'

A stray cat stares at her from the middle of Buiten Street. Elsabe holds out her hand and makes comforting sounds. The cat walks away.

'My brief is clear. John Vorster gave it to me personally.

'"We must destroy them in any way we can. Plant drugs. Tap phones. Intercept mail. Harass the staff. Spread rumours. Frighten them to death." And then he frightened me to death by winking at me. "You see, Elsabe, we in power are also artists in what we do," he said, and left with Tini to go to Parliament. I was ice cold for hours afterwards.'

She looks up at the façade of the old building, with its op-art designs and colours.

'And here I am, back at the shrine. But this time I can assure you they've gone too far. When they subverted in English ...' She hears herself and starts again. 'When they criticised us in English, when they made us ridiculous in English ... it was manageable. It could be ignored. But this time they are telling the truth in Afrikaans.'

She looks back at her programme of Pieter-Dirk Uys's *Selle ou Storie*.

'By no means even a good play. Certainly nothing we haven't heard in English. But to have to listen to obscenity and blasphemy in Afrikaans? To see an Afrikaans woman my age claw her way to so-called love at the expense of her decency and self-respect? To watch pretty boereseuns naked in bed with other boereseuns?'

She closes her eyes for a moment, then shakes her head, as if to remove the image from her mind.

'Are they supposed to represent my sons? Is she supposed to be me?' The photo of Christine Basson as Ester Viljoen seems to laugh out at her from the programme cover. 'No! It cannot be allowed! I will write my report tonight and submit it tomorrow. I will insist that this filthy play is banned! I will demand that any new writing by this so-called dramatist be closely monitored and banned. I will see that he is destroyed. As I have seen other young passionate talents destroyed. Killed in the name of Kultuur.'

Her official car has drawn up. The white chauffeur opens the back door for her. She looks at the programme in her hand.

'Kak!'

She crumples it and throws it into the gutter. As the car roars away, the stray cat crosses Buiten Street with a dead mouse in its jaws.

*   *   *

If only I'd had the confidence to confront issues head on. After months of intensive work on the three productions, the crisis of *Karnaval*'s cancellation because of the Censor Board's interference, and working on a new revue that reflected the absurdity of censorship – and it was also illegal to make fun of the censors! – something went snap. It could have been resolved so easily. One of my actresses was married to a very sympathetic stage husband. She didn't get her weekly salary of R22.50. The excuse was, her spouse could support her. She was very upset and, being quite a feminist, threatened to walk out of the company and her parts in all three plays.

I could've just gone to Brian and said: 'Pay her, for God's sake!' And he would have found a way to do it. But after years of cutting the small cloth to fit the huge dream, there was no thread of common sense left.

We left Brian a curt accusatory note and took our plays out of that space into the real world.

I had support from friends who had been involved on many levels during my Space days: designing sets, building props, creating posters and programmes. Beni Stilborg and Maria Jensen took me into their circle of glamour and Danish charm and inspired me to think beyond the guilt of a small nervous breakdown – more of a speed wobble. We formed our own company to tour my work, called SYRKEL, and found a venue for the next performance of *God's Forgotten*.

It was in St George's Cathedral!

The idea of performing this dirge to Afrikaner power in an Anglican church was great. The reality was an echo-filled chamber of incomprehensible sounds. This independence wasn't going to be easy. I brushed aside the fact that The Space Club had commissioned the new play from me for R1000.

Doyenne of The Space Club, Moyra Fine, phoned some of her family and friends, mainly the lawyers among them, who suggested flatly that we get back to The Space, or else we would be sued! The use of words like that on Space Club letterhead was deeply shocking, but a contract was a contract. We decided not to fight Moyra's family mafia. We hired the Outer Space as a visiting company and completed the season, focusing on the premiere of *Strike up the Banned*.

Being back opened a minefield of problems. We were no longer family. We were the enemy! The atmosphere was terrible. Former Space colleagues avoided us, and we them. None of the sense of fun and challenge that had kept us together and going for so long seemed to remain. As soon as the contracted season ended, we ran away, never to return.

If I had been polite enough to apologise and get back on the job, my life would no doubt have taken a different turn. The Space needed a fresh injection of vision and ideas. While these were crowding the parking area of my mind, it was doubtful that I could have delivered anything through the fog of exhaustion. So I chose the wilderness outside. When, many years later, Brian and I could laugh about it, I said I was sorry for accusing them of exploiting us. He apologised for doing just that. What a lot of fuss about nothing. It's only fair to give Brian the last word here.

'Later in the season, Pieter split from The Space with much blood and gall being spilt. Working under the intense pressures exerted by our financial and spiritual realities, it sometimes seemed to be that there was no other way to leave. I wished it could have been different. Anyhow we made up later. And there was never any possibility of our denying the importance of Pieter's style and spirit to the growth of The Space. As The Space was, I believe, important to him.'

Amen.

5

THE CANCER OF RACISM

Racism.

There was no explanation for that word when I was a child, growing up with white supremacy the segregated oxygen of life. South Africa was a democracy for white people only.

'How many people live in South Africa?' the nine-year-old boy would ask.

'Four million people live in South Africa, Pieter,' his uncle would reply.

'But what about the other millions?'

'We're talking about people, Pieter.'

During the 1950s we would drive past the squatter shacks on the Cape Flats and look out of the window of our sweet second-hand Austin A40. Pa would mutter about the ugliness of it all, and that would be that. The small black piccanins standing next to the road staring at us were like dark cardboard cut-outs.

Everybody, including us, had a maid.

Sannie was in the kitchen, coloured and cheeky. Always good for a laugh. And always good to us. Watching over us like a hawk. Threatening to 'split' on us if we were naughty, and never doing so. She slept in the small room off the dining room with its outside entrance. I think it was a nice room, compared to the terrible hovels other well-off, decent whites squashed their black staff into. But then Sannie wasn't black. She was Cape coloured, a Christian married to a Muslim. Maybe that was the first hint of racism in my life as a kid.

Sannie would refer to blacks as 'die kaffers'!

Henry was our garden boy, although he was neither a boy nor black. He was an old coloured gentleman. Wore a hat jauntily perched on his head and thrilled us by speaking fractured German to my mother. Henry had been a soldier in the armies of the First World War, and he had fought battles. I was never clear where they were. Possibly nearby in South West Africa. But maybe even in Europe. Henry would kiss soft white hands with the charm of a Maurice Chevalier. He was especially attentive towards gruff Sannie, who would prepare his food on a tin plate. Like for the red-setter dog called Roger that we didn't own but which used to come and eat off his tin plate every lunchtime.

Sannie would call them both shrilly from the kitchen door:
'Rogerrrrrrr???? Henriieeeeee????'

I think Henry grew dagga in the garden. He always managed to look happy and contented. Or maybe it was because the Uys family treated him like a person.

The streets in Pinelands were always alive with the sound of black and coloured people talking, laughing, arguing. Loud, repetitive and familiar. The seller of fruit would have his cry, as he pushed his colourful little wagon down the road. The battered yellow bread van would announce itself with another yelp of Cape Flats dialect.

Xhosas sounded distinctly black and made me nervous. I could relate completely to coloureds and, after such a close relationship of trust and love with Sannie, even spoke with a coloured accent. Today, in my alphabet of sounds, portraying a coloured South African is comfortable and compatible.

*   *   *

My mother knew about racism.

Helga Bassel came to Cape Town from Berlin in the late 1930s. She was a concert pianist. She was Jewish. Her parents were already in South Africa. She met my father, Hannes Uys, on the stage of the Cape Town City Hall preparing for a double Mozart concerto. They played together often, and then got married and produced music and me and Tessa. We lived in a thatched-roof cottage called 'Sonskyn' in Pinelands, with its huge garden at the back. There I created my life around imagination and Dinky Toys.

Ma never talked about her life in Germany, other than the occasional description of snow in Charlottenburg and the ice on the Lietzen See, where she would skate as a child. Racism was the reason she left Germany. It was leave now or die in a concentration camp. And only after she committed suicide in 1969 did Tessa and I realise that we were Jews.

Today, the details of our German roots are so much more dense and extraordinary. Tessa does far more research and homework than I do. I suppose I still have a fear of too much discovery of the past. Whereas my mother was a victim of racism, I don't want to acknowledge that I was racist for most of my childhood.

Today the accusation of racism is an easy way to win an argument. Usually a black South African will accuse a white fellow citizen of racism. The white will argue: 'I'm not a racist.' It's the first giveaway and leads the conversation nowhere.

How can I – and so many of us – brought up in a racist society, strengthened by racist education and, in my case, a racist Dutch Reformed Church that preached and taught the superiority of a white skin and a Eurocentric heritage, pretend not to be in complete understanding of the strength of prejudice? And so, like an alcoholic who doesn't drink any more, I have to start my day admitting: Yes, I am one. I am a racist, therefore I will not be a racist. And it is a full-time job to fight the ease of prejudice and the casualness of inflicting pain through careless words.

I now try to use the stage to highlight the dangerous power of words like 'kaffir' and 'nigger' and 'hotnot', not to celebrate their use as an example of free speech, but to underline the danger of giving them their cutting edge by banning them and treating them not as mere words but as contentious issues. The sooner words become powerless through humorous usage, the closer we can get to defusing the terrible effect they can have on the lives of insecure people, be they of colour, physically disadvantaged, or just foreign.

Laughing at the unmentionable has always been taboo. But laughing at fear can make that fear less fearful. Never less lethal. It can still kill and destroy, but at least one is more in charge of it and not its victim. Racism needs to be outed with brutal humour and then hung there from the tallest lamppost for all to see. Only then can we realise how flimsy and pathetic it is. And how destructive it was when it was kept secretly in the dark, usually by politicians who knew how to use it to their own advantage.

Early in my work, it became important to trap the authorities with their own tricks. To be censored by the Publications Control Board for using the obscene words they themselves had created to establish legalised racism was a surreal reflection of our particular madness. Most of the bannings of the 1970s happened because the work in question 'set the racial groups in disharmony against each other'. As if the politics of apartheid did the opposite. The use of words like 'kaffir' was condemned for 'encouraging racial tensions', even though those words had been enshrined by the very people who now banned them.

The comedy of prejudice.

Reflect the racism in your audience, let them laugh at the familiarity of it and so give themselves away. And maybe next time, instead of automatically using those words to feel superior and demolish the dignity of others, that memory of laughter could defuse the moment. Because apartheid was based on the very essence of racism – the white skin being superior to the black skin – an understanding of racism was essential to being able to fight it with its own weapons.

Having been sexually attracted to young men of colour since my teenage years certainly helped me realise the evil and futility of racial postures. Having intimate sex with a body that's a different colour than yours, and knowing that someone has deemed this not only illegal but against the Word of God, certainly put many things into perspective. Once you conquer the fear of questioning the authority behind these laws and decrees, and find them wanting, your freedom becomes personal and precious and you can celebrate your liberation by feeling less guilty about everything. Especially sex!

*   *   *

Whereas it was illegal for people of colour to go to whites-only places, it was also illegal for whites to go to places reserved for blacks. I had the extraordinary experience of spending the night with a coloured youth in his small outside room. Like Sannie's room, it was what his white employers gave him as his home.

We meet at the birthday party of a friend from drama school. There are a few people of colour there. This boy is funny and sharp. I stare at him till he stares back and winks. We speak Afrikaans and share a cigarette. I suggest we drive up the mountain. I know a place where we can park and do something nice in the car. He says it's too dangerous, and he's right. I am relieved.

He says, 'Come home with me.'

I have my father's car, so I can drive us out of town, to the coloured townships. He diverts me into a white suburb. As we cruise into the road where he lives, he slides down into the seat, making himself less visible. This happens without explanation. It makes me nervous too.

We park well away from the gate that leads to the luscious garden and large house.

He puts his finger to his lips.

'Shhhhh.'

He gets out of the car and closes the door gently, making no sound. I slam mine out of habit. He is horrified.

'No man, are you mad?'

I hide in the hedge-bushes near the driveway. I watch him go to the door of a little one-windowed world. Once he has detached the lock and slid back the rusty bolt, I wait until I can see the small flame of the match lighting the candle. Not for romance, but because of the reality: he has no electricity in his room.

He is the garden boy!

I swiftly pad across the damp grass he cut yesterday, praying there's no garden furniture in the way. Or the horrible surprise of a large dog. Then I'm in his room and he closes the door, finger on lips, listening.

My heart beats like a naval band. The only sounds we hear are the noises of the city. Police sirens. A train shunting. A dog barking. The candle casts our shadows against the roughly painted green walls of his room. It smells sharply of cleaning fluid and him. I am so used to my friends pulling faces and referring to the stench of blacks. I never do. His room smells sweetly of him, and it is sexy. The candlelight makes his brown skin look lighter than mine. Colour seems to drain away as I look at him, etched against his dancing shadow on the wall. He is nineteen. His parents live in the township. His father sells scrap metal. His mother is a char. His sister is pregnant. His other brother was killed. I don't ask how.

His curly hair is no longer fuzzy. His mouth not dominated by 'thick kaffir lips', but a sensual curve like a boyish Sophia Loren. He touches me, not like a servant, but with the interest of a lover. We kiss. I taste his mouth, which is sweet and so similar to the mouth of an Afrikaans boy I tasted last night. I take off my T-shirt and my jeans and bundle them in a heap on the floor. There is no carpet on the stones.

His white shirt is a hand-down from the white madam. It belonged to her son, who is now in the South African Army of Defence Minister PW Botha, fighting terrorists who all probably look like this young man working in his mother's suburban garden. The boy folds his shirt carefully. He looks at my clothes, crumpled on the floor. He picks them up and folds them too. Then he looks at me and shrugs. He looks embarrassed. Is it because he is behaving like a maid, folding the white boy's things?

His body is so beautiful and strong, sculpted like that statue in Florence. He unbuttons his trousers, also once part of a white boy's school uniform.

'Sorry, Pieter. My underpants are not as nice as yours.'

Even in the wobbling light of the candle I can see why. How he has used needle and thread to darn the tears and salvage the once-fashionable striped scants. They have been bleached by many washes and scarred like a refugee from a serious soap-sud war. But once we have both discarded the uniforms of our class, we are the same. Teenage boys erect and glistening in the candlelight. Exploring each others' bodies and playing. Holding and heaving, doing what randy gay boys do. Except here we are breaking the law of God and Land.

I wake up later. His taste is still in my mouth. The sun forces a glare through the small cloth that acts as a curtain over the little window. For a moment the chipped and watermarked ceiling is unfamiliar. I look down at the curly head cupped in my arm.

Suddenly he sits up, shocked to find me there.

'You must go!'

'Don't worry,' I smile, 'I'm only due at varsity at nine.'

'No! You must go now! They will find you here with me. I will lose my job. I will go to jail!'

He is terrified. I'm shocked at my sudden feeling of fear.

I dress quickly. He pushes my shoes and socks into my hand and waves me to the door.

'Go go go!'

I want to kiss him goodbye, but he is not playing any more. He opens the door slowly and peers out, holding his breath. He whispers.

'Go round the back, behind the washing line. Behind the garage. There's a hole in the fence. Go through that. And be careful that the neighbours don't see you either!'

'Can I see you again …?' I try to plan a relationship.

'God man! Please Master Pieter, go!'

I never saw him again. I saw many other curly heads sleeping in my arms. Every time it would end in terror. For them to be caught with me was worse than me being caught with them. The warm nights were so normal. The mornings so chilling in the shocked reality of illegal love.

Fuck apartheid! It worked! And those who perpetuated it knew how well it worked.

So don't ask me about racism. I wouldn't know, because as a racist it never affected me. Ask me about my relationship with the boys of the Cape. Then I can tell you about racism.

*   *   *

And so relationships between ordinary people became the focus of my writing. Because they were South African people set against the background of a very specific South African political system, most of my plays in the twentieth century were seen as political statements. They were regarded as comments on the political upheavals and social earth tremors of the moment. That immediately dated them. But, looking at the plays now, the stories remain strong, without the politics being of much importance. Relationships are universal. Love is as rare in a political hailstorm as in a romantic sunset. Pain and betrayal don't always breed the support of disapproving politicians.

But because each was a South African story, and love and relationships were always in focus, every play would reflect the reality of that terror of discovery. Breaking the Immorality Act. Crossing the colour bar. Not just going to jail, but also going to hell!

Love your neighbour. But don't get caught.

Before the seventies made way for the next decade, I wrote a column for a Sunday newspaper.

Berlin 1933.

The eyes of a depressed world are on this glittering capital of a mighty nation. Consciences of those free societies are puzzled and confused by the sudden self-assurance and inner strength shown by these people who were, only a decade or two ago, shattered by contempt and searching for an identity.

An identity has been purchased through power. They are the Master Race.

Warm magical evenings add to the legends that have grown around this jewel of the North. At a sidewalk cafe, well-dressed young lovers sit, laugh and enjoy their prosperity. Groups of elderly folk sip drinks at gaudy tables set around the foot of a large bronze statue of yet another superhero from their generation of heroes.

This is a city with a past and hints of a future. The people are prepared for an evening out. Expensive German limousines purr past the flashing lights of the busy social metropolis. Gorgeously gowned women float by on the arms of their escorts on their way to the opera, or the theatre, or an exclusive dinner.

Colourful posters fence the crowded pavement. Tantalising hard-sell pushes products and tells where the fun is. And about the future. The daily headlines brand *Crisis! War!* and *Death!* into the brain, but nobody notices the pain. Who cares about the propaganda forced onto the front pages of a controlled press by decree? They all know the truth is also banned by law.

All is well in this Reich.

In his brownstone bunker surrounded by flowers and flags, the Führer plans for a greater tomorrow. Uniforms are here and there, but not yet everywhere. The boys with pink cheeks and happy smiles in brown, the men in blue – they have become part of the urban colour scheme.

Civilian fashions are not as daring as the tourists from the South had hoped for, or even as dull as the rivals from other cities make them out to be. This is the capital of a strong military might, a bubble of complacency. Here the decisions are made that will affect the rest of the time left. People walk their dogs carefully among the leafy trees that line the boulevards of power. They pause as lumbering army vehicles sneak past, and don't even bother to glance up as yet another military aircraft flies over the glittering city, nestled among the hills of the Fatherland.

The Zoo is still the centre of this urban planner's paradise, with animals from near and far entertaining the viewers from far and wide, with bored faces carefully borrowed from Noah's Ark.

A group of shadowy figures are stopped by men in uniform and their passes checked. Most shuffle on, invisible to the rest of the unconcerned populace. One or two are roughly pushed into the darkness of a police van.

Keep your City clean!

Clusters of young men, fresh from military service, loiter on street corners, smoking cigarettes and laughing among themselves, healthy and eager for the next challenge. They do not need luck. They have the weapons to win. Their present targets mince by shyly, eyes averted, high heels clicking, hearts beating, egos praying.

Love is as elusive here as eternal life. On Sunday the church is full and the prayer thunders through the echo chamber of God: You must love your neighbour! And everyone nods and tries to forget. The silent monuments to bureaucracy stand and watch over the City, their lights still shining over countless empty desks, their floors being silently cleaned by countless empty-faced people. A burst of music erupts from a nearby cellar where people allow themselves to slum it.

A siren screams by. The police cruise in search of yet another fugitive.

The noise of another military aircraft.

A train far away wails.

Glass breaks.

Another siren, a laugh, a lull. The nights eats up the waiting crowd, promising to keep them entertained and happy and feeling important.

Somewhere on the university campus, a group of educated thugs breaks into a lecture theatre and viciously assaults a leading academic because of his outspoken views on their common background and destiny. He is tarred and feathered for criticising the politics of the day. No official action is taken against his critics. The thugs plan their next attack on privacy and opinion, knowing they have the upper hand over law and order, because of the very sensitive essence of their protest.

The survival of their race, their creed and their culture is the ultimate issue.

In a prison a few blocks away, a young man is hanged for the same reasons: the survival of his race, his creed and his culture. He lost. He wasn't Jewish. He was black.

They weren't Nazis; they were white.
It wasn't Berlin 1933.
Just Pretoria April 1979.

6

WHEN PARADISE
STARTED CLOSING DOWN

Paradise is closing down my friends
and only soldiers and police and one frightened voter
pitched up for the final sale
locking up and cocking guns
and in the only sunbeam somewhere on the sand
lies a little child with a bullet in his head
and a stone in his hands
while back in the Mother City
round dinner and TV
with wine and food and fashion
we frightened angels of death
beat our wings in time to the requiem
but the sun is gone forever
and the birds will cry till they die in the dark
and the empty landscape of shame and anger
colours the soil red and the sky black

Miss Nel didn't ask for that poem. It came to me about the same time
I realised that things, as the song goes, will never be the same again.

The year 1976 closed down the dreams of many South Africans. Many
died in the hail of bullets. The country had to go into the valley of death to
get through to the other side. And many of us didn't even know what the
man looked like, the one who would lead us to hope and fairness. Nelson
Mandela existed only in legend. His picture was forbidden. Not many of us
whites searched for one either.

I'd left The Space in 1975 and started my own company, SYRKEL. The
decades of official unemployment were nigh. With the support of a few
actors who knew my work, even those that were banned, we toured small
towns and performed at festivals, breaking the mould of expectation. The
plays were mainly in Afrikaans. The banned one had an English text so that
the show could technically be run. There was a lot of frisson and gasping,
but generally even the enemies with brains realised that what they were

seeing was just a portrait of what they – what we – were going through. We even played Bloemfontein with *Selle ou Storie*, and they survived!

My chronic lack of confidence made life very hard. I found it impossible to ask favours or negotiate better deals. I just didn't have the vocabulary or the cheek. Sometimes I was lucky when people in the business cut me some slack and a better percentage than 5 per cent, but even friends turned into unsentimental businessmen when it came to rentals and fees. It didn't matter that there was no money to be earned. It made sense to stay poor and unbeholden towards management. The play was the thing. The simplicity of production was another key ingredient.

I was criticised for directing my own plays. For years I felt guilty about it, but my instinct forced me to get on with the job. It was practical. Beside the fact that I couldn't afford to pay a director, I knew that what the plays needed were not directorial flourishes and interpretation, but radical editing and rewriting. I have never been sentimental about the written word. If it doesn't work, change it, tighten it, cut it. Move it around. Take it out and keep it for the next play. Never waste what could work in the right bracket of a future drama.

By the first week of a run the play was usually ready. In a normal society there would have been plans to publish the text. This was never the case in South Africa. The first play to appear in print was *Die Van Aardes van Grootoor*, probably published more as a 'fuck you' to the establishment than as a guide to study and future productions. But I kept a copy of final texts neat and ready for use.

Writing a play is still the most satisfying, sexy experience. The privacy – some call it the loneliness – of writing means no one need see it. It can remain your secret and you can burn it and no one will know. Many of my attempts should have gone that way. And yet to talk about a planned project was to let the cat out of the bag, never to return. I'm sure bouncing the drama off colleagues could have solved many issues, but then that's what rehearsals are all about.

When it came to creating a play, democracy wasn't my ideal way of working. I loathed the fashion for improvisations, usually favoured by Mavis Taylor. Hours of waffling usually just led to uncontrollable giggles, especially when the text had not yet been allowed to become the framework for the improv.

I realised that I needed to be available for each new idea in search of a dramatic hook, and after two hours of writing, I would break the dry moment with a cooldrink or the start of a Bette Davis video, and, ignoring the terror of 'nothing left to say', the next inspiration would be knocking on my door before Bette had climbed those Warner Brothers stairs for the sixth time to the magnificent Max Steiner orchestration.

The seventies were my decade of discovery and confusion.

First and foremost, I realised the power of the theatre, the extraordinary effect it had on people who had not even seen the work. The value of humour to diffuse the tension of embarrassment and horror at something best left forgotten. The Space had given me a blank page on which to write. There were no expectations. Just something to rehearse today to open next week. Usually the first draft of a play would start a rehearsal period and then develop with the production to open as *Selle ou Storie* or *Karnaval*.

The Space was the womb for the daily invention of the alphabet that would become known as Protest Theatre. I don't think there was a conscious movement to create such a thing. The political plays of the time usually focused on the worst around us and were seen as a protest against apartheid. But they were all stories about people set against a fearful background. Of course there were the noisy, sweaty amandla-gumboot sessions with angry, usually black performers and cowering, usually white liberals in the front row. Cries of 'Free Mandela' and 'Stop apartheid' made for a short show, and the rest of the time was taken up with toyi-toying and copious subversive sweating on the wealthy.

Not many South African plays were being written at the time, besides by Athol Fugard, who occasionally popped into The Space Theatre to rehearse a new work. Then suddenly the cosiness of the family was over. We minor members of the company had to walk round the block to get to the canteen, which was on the other side of the building. You couldn't walk through it. Fugard's rehearsal was out of bounds to mere mortals.

I knew I couldn't compete with his work. But I didn't like it enough to want to copy it. I felt all the plays should have been in Afrikaans. Besides, his early plays were so familiar to me in their structure and dialogue that there was no need to repeat them. I acted in his *People Are Living There* opposite Yvonne, playing the seemingly unplayable part of Don. They say the character was based on Fugard himself. I found it quite playable. What wasn't helpful in the text, I imagined.

Isn't that what acting is all about? I've never found a character to be unplayable, and later, in the years of the instant sketch, giving a personality in a punch line, this lack of pretension helped. Some actors never stop talking about how impossible parts are, and as a result either don't deliver or make you so nervous that your lack of delivery makes them stand out as brilliant.

I suppose acting is a very specialised calling.

To be given words to say, thoughts to think, motivations to link emotions – to be told where to move, when to sit, how to react – is to be assembled like a plastic robot out of a million pieces. To repeat it all night after night takes a special kind of dedication. As time went by, I started realising that acting was not my cup of tea. Reacting was more fun. And harder and so much more dangerous. It was never the same, night after night.

My first South African play was *Selle ou Storie*, followed by *Karnaval* and *God's Forgotten*. *Karnaval* will probably survive the test of time and fashion, as the story and the charm of the setting have a universal appeal. *Selle ou Storie* found its way back into the line of fire in 2004, when I unleashed Evita Bezuidenhout into the role of Ester Viljoen. The stronger version then was the English translation *Same Old Story*, which had never been produced before. It was rewritten for 2004, and it tingled. The leading part of Yvonne Godard was played by Evita's sister, Bambi Kellermann. Of course.

God's Forgotten was a play for the 1970s, as it reflected the terrors of where politics could take us. My few non-South African plays were the first one, *Faces in the Wall*, and then *Pity About People*, both produced at The Space, as well as the operatic *Rise and Fall of the First Empress Bonaparte*, which I directed at the Little Theatre with the drama students in 1976. The play was eventually professionally produced by PACT in the 1980s, lavishly costumed and boringly directed, with a scintillating Empress Josephine from Jacqui Singer. It's an ideal play for training, as there are many women, much style and period behaviour, and damn good fun at the expense of the cursing Corsicans. It also made critics sit up in surprise.

'My goodness, he can write plays and not just political slogans,' headlined one twit.

It was extraordinary being back at the Little Theatre.

The building was more or less the same. Robert Mohr was now Head of Department, and Mavis was still leading a left flank against his regime. Helen had gone to Australia. The small theatre held no more surprises. It looked more like a double garage than the London Palladium. I had already been to the Department a year earlier to direct Gorki's *Enemies*, a Russian play which reflected much of the iceberg of South African politics. By ending the play with the banned Soviet anthem while the iron fire curtain came down to obliterate any speech on stage made no impact on anyone, from critics to security police. But I liked it and I think Robert did too.

My love affair with Josephine de Beauharnais made the production a pleasure, seeing her come to life and react with the other extraordinary women in the life of Napoleon Bonaparte. That first production had a linking series of small sketches featuring the char lady at the Tuileries Palace. They had been written into the script for my assistant director, a senior student who didn't get much chance to assist in direction except to take mindless word runs. Inspired by the Carol Burnett character we were seeing on television at the time (a fatal error, as it became satirical and topical, which it wasn't supposed to be), it also managed to ground the melodrama of the ups and downs of the Bonapartes into the small reality of the life of a working mother, whose son is killed in the Russian campaign. She receives the official letter with the news of his death, but, as she can't read, grovellingly requests that Eliza Bonaparte read it to her. The coldness and casual manner in which the former tart, now queen, informs the woman of her loss, and the shocking gratitude shown by the servant, made an impact. The character was later lost in the PACT production. She's somewhere in a box – I must bring her back.

One of the tours took our SYRKEL group to the Grahamstown Festival, which was still centred on the English language and culture, and was mainly supported by speech and drama teachers. To hell with the English focus; we did the Afrikaans *Selle ou Storie*, the bilingual *God's Forgotten* and *Strike up the Banned*. Here my later celebrated character, Jewish African princess Nowell Fine, was born in a sketch about her liberal subversions and her illegal passion for her black garden boy Nimrod, and was performed by Michele Maxwell. The woman portraying the 'woman' was interesting, but not as sharp as the later performances of Nowell by her male creator. There are some things real women just can't do, and I suppose one is to portray a fictitious female monster as 'real'.

The Grahamstown Festival asked me for a new play for the next year.

It was to be *Paradise Is Closing Down*. The taste of the drama came to me on an overcast Cape Town day. The sky hung low and angry. Thick air made it uncomfortable to breathe. Smog? Pollution? It reflected what was happening in the townships outside Johannesburg, where schoolkids were rising up against the authorities. They rejected Afrikaans as a language of tuition, but it went far deeper. Anyone over the age of twenty had been so indoctrinated and ironed out by the apparatus of government propaganda and fear that only someone young enough not to care could care. This Soweto uprising changed the future. It also gave me the inspiration to write a play about Cape Town caught in the grip of similar terrors.

The play centres on Molly, a middle-aged kugel, now single, still alone but desperate for companionship and love. A man. Her friend Anna, Afrikaans, confident, in charge, is suffering from the same needs. Their gofer, Mouse, a Rhodesian refugee and as small and timid as her nickname, becomes the focus of their frustrations and power trips. They plan to go and have good time in the town. The fact of township unrest doesn't seem to affect their plans.

* * *

Molly is furious. Everything seems to be going wrong. And now that Mouse has been burgled, she knows it will take even more time before they can get to the restaurant. She doesn't want to lose the booking.

She looks at Mouse, hunched up at the kitchen table, tearfully sobbing into her damp handkerchief. Anna gives a dangerous sigh.

'Mouse, is your passport safe?'

Mouse nods and holds it up. Anna seizes it firmly and takes it to the drawer in the kitchen dresser. A safe place. When she opens the drawer she sees the gun. She is about to ask Molly about it, but she is on her special hobby horse by now.

'My grandmother knew the writing on the wall when she saw it,' she patronises Mouse. 'She'd laugh today, let me tell you.'

Anna is worried about the weapon in the drawer.

'Molly, do you keep a gun?'

Molly looks at her confused.

'What?'

'A gun,' Anna intones slowly.

'Next to my bed, why?' Anna shakes her head and closes the drawer slowly. Molly focuses back on Mouse. 'My grandmother was an incredible person, let me tell you. Of course I never knew her. She was killed by the Nazis. My father's cousin was murdered by the SS. My father's oldest sister was massacred by the Russians. My second cousin on my mother's side was accidentally executed by the Americans. My relatives have in turn been killed by everyone, and here I am. Molly. Molly Mashuga, with, as her best friends, a Boer and a shiksa. Where? The southern tip of nowhere. Why? Because it's heaven and it's mine and I love it.' She stops. 'They took everything?'

Mouse sniffs. 'Hey? Oh yes: my shampoo, the suitcase, which was real leather, the alarm clock, those shoes I got last month ...'

Molly doesn't need all the boring details.

'Yes, yes, yes, well go and find something in my room. We must go now!'

Mouse builds up enough courage.

'Molly? Anna? I'm sorry, I just can't face a party tonight. Really ...'

The two women stare at her, Anna recognising Mouse's courage, Molly wanting to hit her.

Anna smiles. 'We quite understand, Mousie ...'

'Rubbish!' snaps Molly, taking control. 'You're both being menstrual about tonight. Tonight has been booked for weeks.'

Mouse tries to get up. 'But ...'

Molly holds her down in her chair.

'Tonight is Christmas! Tonight is Easter! Tonight is the end of the world!'

Anna puts it all in a nutshell.

'And we're going to have a party!'

Molly applauds her logic.

'You're damn right!' She pushes Mouse out the kitchen. 'So get your arse in there and find yourself a suitable skin and smile!'

*   *   *

Things go from bad to worse. They don't get to the restaurant because there are police roadblocks on the way. When they get back to Molly's cottage, they surprise a young man who says he is the son of Molly's maid. We never know for sure. The threat is defused – or heightened – by sex play and flirtations. Molly plays games with him, Anna plays white with him, and Mouse is honest with him. And the gun in the drawer is there for a reason.

Paradise Is Closing Down has gone through many stages of maturity. The original production, based on the first draft, didn't give the young man a name. It was illegal then to have blacks or coloureds acting with whites on the same stage. The fact that this play pitted a sexy young coloured man against three sex-starved white women was in itself a grenade waiting to explode.

When the play travelled internationally, the young man was called William, the name of the actor who originated the role. At the Edinburgh Festival in 1979, the play had to explain the reality of the madness of our politics, so British audiences could appreciate the danger of the relationships. They would automatically be prejudiced against Anna the Afrikaner, and their sympathy for William the black would overshadow their common sense. The danger of the 'good non-white character' and the 'bad white racist' was a constant easy way out.

In Grahamstown I had Val de Klerk, Christine Basson and Melanie-Ann Sher as the trio of women. William Meyer came from the Cape Flats, an exquisitely beautiful young man with more than just talent. Illegal lustings throughout the audience were the order of the day.

At Edinburgh we had Helen Bourne, Barbara Kinghorn and Naomi Buch as the trio. A British man of colour played William. The play was later filmed for Granada television, with Estelle Kohler replacing Barbara Kinghorn, who had been contracted to the Royal Shakespeare Company on the strength of her performance in the play as Anna.

I did the adaptation for television, and, listening carefully to advice, wrecked the play. By cutting it down to the right length we forfeited all the moments of repose. The pauses, the spaces between the lines, the breathing essential to the balances of tension. All that was left was a garbled race for a comedic finish.

In 1992 I rewrote the play for men. This *Paradise* was still set in Cape Town, but now after the end of apartheid, in the transition to democracy. It reflected the fear and uncertainly that gripped the audience watching the play. Very close to the bone. We meet the three gay men dressed and ready to go to a drag party in town. Molly has been reconceived as Mervyn, Anna as André. They too are turned back by roadblocks and find William at home. The same games are played, but now the playing field is level. The humour is more vicious, more dangerous. The sex will now be legal but possibly lethal, as the shadow of HIV/AIDS added a jarring new colour to the rainbow of sexual intrigue.

*   *   *

Mervyn is Jewish, gay and not a queen to be trifled with. He planned to go to the club as Tina Turner. Mouse is slim-hipped, pretty and permanently bullied, while André is an Afrikaans moffie with a bag of chips on his shoulder.

They're back at Mervyn's cottage, having been stopped by riot police from going to their party at the gay club. Mervyn has changed back into civvies, but André and Mouse are still in costume. Mouse looks pretty in a kimono. André looks terrifying, his Cher-blonde fright-wig topping an all-leather outfit worthy of an S&M bar. His beard sets off the huge false eyelashes.

Mervyn has bought them Chinese food as a stand-in treat. No one wants to eat.

'Mouse?' Mervyn says through clenched teeth. 'Come and eat something before I really start throwing it around.'

Mouse recoils from the chop suey.

'I'm not hungry ...'

Mervyn slams it down on the table. Chinese food splatters on the floor.

'God, you make me sick! Both of you! You bore me to death!'

André laughs and drains his glass. He leans across and grabs the bottle of wine.

'Boredom, our national disease! The symptoms are all the good things in life, without the need to pay for them in blood!' He searches for the corkscrew and finds it under Mervyn's arm. He pushes Mervyn to one side. 'I think I caught the virus from you, because here I am again spending valuable time in order to forget, in case I look down and see my real face reflected in the pools of blood at my feet.'

Mervyn sighs and turns his back on André. This is familiar, unwelcome territory. André's drunken aria gains momentum.

'At least in the good old, bad old days of Boere politics, there was something to live for, eh Mouse?' Mouse shrugs, uncomfortable and nervous. 'Such fun playing dodge the purple water and getting home in time to watch it all again on TV.' Mouse doesn't want to be reminded of the day he was caught in a Cape Town riot, when police hosed protesters with purple spray. André pours the wine. He spills some on the floor. 'God, all you had to do was wear an illegal T-shirt and get locked up without trial as an investment for future international martyrdom. But that chapter is now closed.'

The newspapers lying on a chair trumpet the remarkable changes as FW de Klerk dismantles apartheid and prepares to free Mandela.

'So here we are!' André raises his glass. 'Relics of a bygone barbarian age, dying pathetically of boredom. Life we shun, because we've never been taught how to live it decently. Rather hide behind our armour: God, degrees, debts, investments – because it's the reality of survival. The colour of our money is now our sex, and the trappings of fear our appeal!'

He drinks his wine, emptying the glass noisily. Mervyn gives him a slow clap.

'Welcome to the club, André!'

André leans towards Mervyn and gives him a grotesque pursed-lip kiss.

'But the death-defying difference, between me and you, is that me and mine went through it all here and stuck to it and fought for it, and even changed it before going rotten' – he kicks at the face of De Klerk on the paper. It falls to the kitchen floor – 'while you and yours went through it somewhere else and lost and ran.' Mervyn sighs and pretends to be bored. Mouse gets up, but André pushes him back in the chair roughly.

'But there's still a lot of room left in our laager, Mervyn, if you can bear the smell. So, welcome to the club!'

He pours more wine.

Mervyn glowers at André.

'You're drunk!'

André doesn't argue.

'But now that you've both got rich and fat on the evil laws of my land, remember that yesterday, because of me and mine, you two also had a soapbox to stand on, and tomorrow, without me and mine, where would you be? Back in a ghetto behind barbed wire? And somehow I don't see you taking that last train to Manenberg with a smile on your face. So cheers, meide.'

He lifts his glass and takes up a camp pose.

'I drink to us and what's left of our orange, white and blue heaven. Let's enjoy it while it lasts. Very quietly!'

*   *   *

This version, too, played at the Grahamstown Festival, in the freezing winter of 1992, before opening at Johannesburg's Wits University Theatre with a cast dying of flu. The play also died, universally massacred by the critics. We closed after a week, and Mrs Bezuidenhout came to the rescue and took over the rest of the run. Looking back now, it's easy to understand why the reaction was so violent. This new *Paradise* was too soon, too near the scene of the crime, too close for comfort or opinion. The original play was now safe. Those three 'normal' women and their 'normal' apartheid woes were a relief. No one wanted to see the reality of the street outside reflected on stage. The gay critics were the most demeaning. It was obviously too close to the story of their lives as well.

Today, both plays have a different impact. The original play about the 1970s women has the feel of a sitcom episode, while the gay 1990s play is closer to *Will and Grace* than to *Angels in America*. And yet the stories of lonely needs and brittle friendships remain topical and universal. The fears of failed relationships and lost youth have not changed. Only today there is no place to hide.

7

GROOTOOR, O GROOTOOR

The darkness of the fifteen years after 1976 would cover my most formative years in the theatre. The everyday fears grew dangerously familiar. One stopped being on the lookout and became careless. It was good for the work, but bad for one's life. Not meaning sudden death. White performers don't die because of their politics. They die because of the quality of their box office appeal. And success constantly threatened to paint me into the same corner with the safe brush.

Success inevitably meant people wanted more of the same. And you could never deliver the same, otherwise the magical element of surprise would be gone. The reaction would be disappointment.

'He's not as good this time round,' headlined another twit.

Soon I would have only four successful recipes in my repertoire, each carefully tested to perfection. But they had to be disguised in a new menu each time so that the element of surprise was always there.

That was the challenge: always to be ahead of the audience. Let them be confused and not quite sure. Force them to think and work things out. Because the day you hand them a plate and they nod in agreement and point out the ingredients, you've lost the precious jewel of surprise.

Surprising yourself is the first step. Don't always feel you have to understand everything you create. It thinks for itself. Just be a gentle shepherd, a good stage manager, and don't panic. Always know that you can't please everyone each time. So the one person to please is yourself.

But still the confidence to confront my own fears and needs eluded me and I was easily swayed by advice and criticism. Too often I would cut my creative foot to fit another's critical shoe. Too often I would take comments and notes from a casual observer to heart, believing they knew what they pretended to know. The Market Theatre would be full of them. I attracted know-alls like moths to a flame!

Until I met Dawie Malan.

One of the ways to stay solvent in Cape Town during the 1970s came from being offered small parts in Afrikaans films by local film-maker Dirk de Villiers. A rough-diamond, conservative, charming old Afrikaner, Dirk didn't suffer fools gladly, often because he saw the joke first. He was a confusing personality of shock and awe mixed with a gentleness and generosity that defied his John Wayne image. He employed us liberal lemmings from The Space in bit parts in his films – chauffeurs, hotel receptionists, doctors, policemen and diplomats – and allowed us to practise our multitude of accents and false-moustached, bewigged and sometimes bedraggled impersonations, inspired by Peter Sellers and Woody Allen.

We had free reign for those precious forty-five seconds of screen time with a director who was more interested in the tits of the script girl than the tensions in the script. The fact that, politically, we didn't even meet on the same page gave Dirk's kindness a special meaning, and if he will not be remembered as the Leni Riefenstahl of the Celluloid Boere Baroque, many of us will never forget that R245 job that saved our lives.

I wrote him some screenplays too, probably worse than the films he made. *Dingetjie en Idi* and *Die Spaanse Vlieg* sometimes see the light of day as the afternoon matinee on television. I pray everyone is working when they're on. But the experience of having produced such crap somehow freed me to be able to comment on the crappy work of others. And there was a lot of crap.

Dawie Malan also commented on the crap, but usually in front of the wrong people. He acted for Dirk, but not as a romantic leading man. How do I describe him? The obvious picture is easy. Dawie Malan was a dwarf. He was deformed by scoliosis at an early age. He could have been surgically repaired when he was young, but that didn't happen. He always told us he would die before he was forty, and he did.

Dawie, with his short crooked legs, a hump on his back, strangely beautiful long zigzag fingers, and a large head with an unruly mop of curly hair, had the face of an angel when he was smiling, or a snarling devil when he wasn't. He was dangerously intelligent, and had studied at Stellenbosch University and graduated with a drama qualification. He was known for his fearless, vicious tongue and a violent temper that, if he'd been taller, would have resulted in him beating us all up. We mortal normals just got on his nerves. Us well-formed sexy blond boys, lazy and spoilt. Taking everything for granted. Dawie had to fight for the front row in the stalls of life, and yet, at the end of a night on the town, he always took home the blond boy with the prized bubble-butt.

Dawie was theatre in crisis. He would never get a job as a leading actor. No one thought of him as a director. His extraordinary instinct and vision were tempered with an insane sense of humour. He would attend opening nights with his hump exposed and covered in glitter. Mascara turned his blue eyes into lasers. He would go up to those colleagues who maligned him and insult them brilliantly. He would solicit sex from young husbands within earshot of their wives and then invite the wife to join them. He was the court jester and the poisoner of the chalice.

I had met Dawie at The Space, which was the right place for him. We were all misfits in one way or another. He was in the cast of that play, *Skyvers/Jollers*, in which I took over the part of the schoolteacher at the last minute. This would become routine during our next three years. We understudied each other and could take over a role at a day's notice. Dawie sometimes acted in two plays at the same time, which I was directing, in the different theatre venues. I wrote plays and he swept the stages, as we gossiped and intrigued. He had sex with boys while I fantasised. There was a lot to be said for 'doing it yourself' and hoping for the real thing. And when the real thing happened, Dawie was always the first one to tell us what he did and how he did it, and we believed him.

We talked about theatre all the time, because it was the breath in our lungs. We laughed at ambition and ego, because we didn't have time for either. And we soon realised that we both loathed the same things. That makes for great friendship and undying trust. When Dawie came up with an idea for a piece of drama, we listened. This small giant could make a mountain out of a molehill. He could conjure up truth from a trivial comment and manage to make his theatre live without a budget.

Together we drank red wine and talked our way into *Die Van Aardes van Grootoor*.

This play had started life as a revue sketch in *Strike up the Banned*. It was a spoof of a radio serial, in which Trix Pienaar and I read all the parts, with an underlying war of tugs and shoves around the mike. It reflected the reality of the never-ending Springbok Radio soap operas that constipated the Afrikaans ether day in and day out. We decided to extend the idea into a play.

Because I had left The Space some time before, and Dawie was constantly turned away by the Afrikaans fascists down at the Nico Malan, we both needed a job. And we knew that to wait for a job in the legitimate theatre was to grow old in a queue. So we became our jobs. We listed our group around the table in Dawie's kitchen, sipping red wine from a box and chewing peanuts: Lida Botha, Antoinette Kellerman, Bill Curry, Mary Dreyer, Marthinus Basson, Chris Galloway, Pieter-Dirk Uys, Dawie Malan. And, in the doorway, staring at us with huge eyes like a baby rabbit on his first excursion into the French kitchen, Nico de Klerk, fresh from college. One would direct, one would write, one would design. The rest would act.

I took that recipe and wrote the most successful Afrikaans play of the seventies and eighties.

Die Van Aardes van Grootoor retained the conceit of a radio serial. Of the never-ending 780 episodes, we would 'show' a selection of five during the play. Starting with Episode 4, set on Christmas Day in 1928, then Episode 110 in 1948, followed by Episode 400 in 1958.

This took us to interval. As the climax to Act I, we killed everyone off, with the exception of the daughter Elana. She finds oil on the farm Grootoor, and, as the lights fade, swears to carry on, like the heroine in *Gone with the Wind*.

* * *

Tragedy has smitten the Van Aardes of Grootoor. Most of them are dead! But, at the last moment before interval, Aia, the faithful black nanny, has taken the blame for all the deaths that litter the stage with bodies.

'Ek, Aia Witbooi, het die Baas Fanie gesteek, die Nooi Mimi laat verdood, die Baas Tertius laat verwilder and die Nooi Dolla bedonner. Dis alles ek. Sorry.'

She plugs her hearing aid into the electric mains and dies magnificently.

Pretty Elana, bereft of family and maid, launches into her curtain aria.

'O my bruin suster, lê rustig in my arms, want daar's niemand om te sien nie. Dis die einde vir jou, maar die begin vir my. Totsiens, ou vriend.'

She folds Aia's black arms over her still body, stands up and becomes the Boere Scarlett O'Hara.

'En nou is ek werklik alleen, sonder geld, familie of toekoms – maar ek lewe, en ek lus vir die lewe. O Grootoor, hoor my toekoms-koor! Die bloed van vandag sal bly kleef aan die rand van my beker van geluk en voorspoed en my laat onthou! Ek sal nooit trou, net leef vir jou! Gee my net 'n teken, O Grootoor, my plaas van verlange, my plaas van verdriet, my plaas van verderf! O Grootoor, gee my jou oor!'

She sinks to her knees and claws at the ground. With a rumble, bubble and whoosh we hear oil explode into the sky in front of her. She smells it, licks it, covers her face with it so that it, too, is black.

'Olie! Dankie Grootoor!' She stands with intent and grandness. 'Die wêreld sal nog van my hoor – ek, Elana Caltex van Aarde van Grootoor!'

* * *

In that blackout we had to get all the bodies offstage. There was no curtain. When *Die Van Aardes* opened the new Laager at the Market Theatre, the size of the stage could barely hold four people standing. There was no space even for a second stool. Also no dressing room, just a screen behind another screen. The play ran there for two years.

When Act II opens, we see the children of the dead characters, who look just like them. Economically sound, as we used the same actors to play their own offspring. It also made for wonderful comedy, seeing that the son of the father looked just like his neighbour!

Son Tertius van Aarde looks just like the hated English landlord who had appeared at Grootoor in 1928 to turf the family off the land.

How did this happen?

Fanie van Aarde had the idea on that Christmas Day in 1928. In Act I, he convinces his wife Dolla and her sister Mimi to make themselves pretty and seduce the hated Rooinek, forcing him to put the farm into their names! John Firestone Junior is all buck-teeth and no chin. When the two sisters appear in their Sunday best, each capped with a Voortrekker bonnet, he is instantly smitten.

'Goodness gracious!' he gasps.

Mimi sees him and falls in love, but Dolla wants to kill.

'O moerbei!' whispers the younger sister.

John holds out his hand stiffly. The problem of language looms loud and clear. He cannot manage Afrikaans. They cannot understand English.

'Hello!' he splutters. 'John Firestone Junior. Pleased to meet you.' They look at him blankly. He attempts a feeble translation. 'Lekker te vleis jou!'

Fanie butchly introduces his wife and sister-in-law.

'My wife Dolla. Her sistertjie Mimi.'

Mimi overarticulates like an Eliza Doolittle.

'How doooo youuuuu doooo?'

John is charmed.

'Charming. Very well. And you?'

Mimi blushes.

'Thank youuuuu toooooo.'

Dolla hisses from the corner of her clenched, chapped lips.

'Mimi, gedra jou!'

John feasts his eyes on Mimi's youth and freshness.

'Well,' he decides, 'we were just getting down to business, but I'm sure that can wait.'

There is a pause now, as they all stand around trying to find something to say. The wind blows a dry bush across the sunbaked land.

Mimi nods gravely and points.

'It. Is. Very. Very. Dry.'

John agrees.

'Indeed.'

Dolla doesn't follow this. Fanie explains and indicates a turning of the wheel with his hand.

'Iets draai ...'

Another pause as Mimi looks around for something else to say. A chicken clucks off somewhere to the left. Mimi nods gravely and points.

'Ja. Our chicken is also ... giving us ... some very bad lays.'

'Frustrating,' clucks John.

'Ja.' Mimi nods in agreement. John stares at her throat and the fullness of her breasts. He crosses his legs with the intention of hiding his rising interest.

Dolla watches this with an expert eye.

'Mimi, wat sê julle?'

'But our little goat is fat with milk. Want some?'

John has seen the mangy goat.

'No!'

He sits on the bench near to Mimi. While they stare into the distance, aimlessly waiting for something to be said, Dolla edges towards Fanie.

'Ek voel belaglik. Ek voel soos die Hoer van Babylon!'

'Dis alles vir Grootoor!'

'Ja, maar sê nou die Dominee kom doen huisbesoek?'

John has now touched Mimi's leg.

She is excited.

'Hey Mister Fireplace! You somaar touch me on my bone!'

And so the story continues, filled with passion and confusions, based on hatred and revenge. A very familiar tale of where the Afrikaner came from and where he was going.

After interval, two more scenes were played out for all they were worth. Episode 600, set in 1968, sees a masked garden party at Grootoor, where Elana, the richest woman in the world, entertains the world and rediscovers her brother and her past.

The final episode, Episode 780, is simply titled: Farewell to Grootoor.

Banned three weeks into its Johannesburg run, and then restored, Dawie Malan's production of *Die Van Aardes van Grootoor* broke the stale mould of traditional Afrikaans comedy. It was irreverent, vulgar, suggestive, camp, shocking and politically explosive. When it opened in 1978, the first four episodes brought the house down. The element of surprise was held for the last scene, the farewell. Here the great farm Grootoor is sold to a black woman, who turns out to be the granddaughter of the very same Aia who looked after everyone in Act I, and then sacrificed her life for her Miss Elana. Suddenly the jokes were on us. It was very close to the bone. This chilled the audience. Some were unhappy. They said it was from another play and didn't fit in with the fun.

*   *   *

As the rest of the family plunder the remains of the magnificence of Grootoor, Elana van Aarde is left alone with the black guest. Madame Quazilesi is dressed ethnically, but with international trimmings. Elana is in black, frail, pale and trapped.

She looks the other woman in the eye. Here the play swerves into English, after an orgy of luscious Afrikaans.

'And the name, Madame Quazilesi? May I take the name: Grootoor?' Elana purrs.

'Of course.' The black woman's white teeth dazzle. 'I have a new name, naturally. Kwalimbia.'

Elana laughs softly.

'Of course, how silly of me. You should be happy here, Madame. This land has everything. All you need is that something to make it work. We had it. Once. It was good while it lasted.'

Madame Quazilesi is impressed by the statuesque Afrikaans icon.

'You amaze me, Miss van Aarde. You're so calm. You're a squatter now, and yet you still manage to play the Empress. Can anyone be that arrogant?'

Elana is not fazed.

'I am dying, Madame. I have terminal cancer and few sunrises left. But I still have everything, in spite of you. My arrogance, my achievements, my contempt. Everything.'

'Except your health. You can't buy it, you can't bribe it, you can't steal it.'

'But I can dream it!' Elana gets up with difficulty. She stands where she can look out of the window at the vista of her land. 'My dreams are all I have left, and they will keep me alive.' Madame Quazilesi joins her, and they look towards the blue mountains, the sparkling seas, the rolling vineyards. 'I have always lived with wild hopes and that maddening vicious thirst for truth and survival! And now suddenly my greedy hunger has become a bloated handout and my Technicolor dream a monochrome nightmare. So what is left for me but the scorched earth that was once my paradise and now will be yours?'

'I will respect your memories.'

Elana smiles sarcastically. 'How sweet of you.' She has an attack. She can't breathe. She coughs. She flails out with her hand. The black woman gently helps her back into her chair. Elana pulls away. 'Forgive me ...' She puts a handkerchief to her mouth and then looks at the blood on it. 'Do you find me disgusting?'

'No, Miss van Aarde, I find you attractive, very brave and somewhat futile.' Elana stares at her and then slowly nods.

'Yes.' She stares at the black woman again, trying to place a face and a name. 'You so remind me of someone I once knew. Her grandmother gave her life for my survival. Maybe I should blame her for everything. If she hadn't been so bloody loyal, all this might have died a natural death.'

'And I remind you of her granddaughter?' Madame Quazilesi says with a smile.

'It's silly, really.'

'I don't know. You people always say we blacks all tend to look alike.' Elana points at the dazzling smile and frowns.

'She also had that same infuriating habit of smiling. Always smiling. I always knew she would come to a bad end.'

'Miskien is jy reg, Mies Elana.'

Suddenly the grandness of Madame Quazilesi dissolves into the familiarity of Siena, who was once the maid. Elana is delighted.

'Siena!! Maar ... maar dit verander alles. Waar het jy skielik oornag alles aangeleer? Ons moet planne maak. Ek sal aanbly en Grootoor namens julle bestuur. Sienatjie! Ons was mos altyd vriende. Ten spyte van alles wat jy in die verlede gedoen het, is ons nog vriende?'

Madame Quazilesi reclaims herself, echoing Elana's earlier sarcasm.

'How sweet of you.'

'Saam kan ons Grootoor nog groter maak!'

The black woman confronts the white woman.

'Madame, you are now trespassing on my land.'

And with that she leaves the room. Elana tries to get up to follow, but can't. She calls.

'Siena?' Then again with the tone of voice from the past. 'Sienatjie??' The snarl of reality. 'Kaffer!'

*   *   *

Today that final scene makes the play. Whereas Elana van Aarde finally chooses to detonate a nuclear device and take all with her, rather than share it with a black, mercifully this didn't happen when the National Party leadership had to make a similar choice with South Africa in the early 1990s.

As *Die Van Aardes van Grootoor* has developed through the decades into the new century, the only adaptation has been due to technology. The structure has been changed from radio serial to TV soap opera, a local *Bold and the Beautiful*. So instead of radio commercials dividing the episodes, they are now shown on TV monitors as send-ups of familiar television spots. And, at the end, videos of multiple nuclear explosions illustrate the farewell to Grootoor, while soprano Mimi Coertse sings her famous Afrikaans ode to the Boer homestead: 'O Boereplaas, jou het ek lief bo alles.' The same song that in 1973 convinced me to return to South Africa from London.

The next reinvention of *Die Van Aardes* could be as a feature film. There were requests in the 1980s to extend it into the format of a television sitcom/soap for South African TV, but happily it didn't happen. The few instances where I did get involved with television during those years were all a disastrous compromise between censorship and stupidity, and hopefully forgotten.

Now when someone says, 'I saw that 1980s piece of yours on TV last night,' I can tell them they've obviously confused me with Jamie Uys!

PDU as Corvino with Caroline Spence in the
UCT production of *Volpone* by Ben Jonson

Peter Kruger and PDU as Lady Kyo in
Robert Mohr's UCT production of *Seppuku*

Giving Marlene Dietrich roses on the stage
of the Alhambra Theatre in Cape Town

Living in the trenches of alternative theatre
also meant dressing for the part!

Farce about Uys director Dawie Malan and
Thoko Ntshinga as Evita's faithful Sophie

Chris Galloway (Sersant Uys), PDU (De Kock Bezuidenhout)
and Thoko Ntshinga (Madame Quazilesi) in *Farce about Uys*

With Dr Piet Koornhof during the shooting of *Skating on Thin U...*

Evita Bezuidenhout shows off her cup as
'Koeksister-bakster van die Jaar' for the National Party in Laagerfontein

NICO MALAN THEATRE
ONE WEEK ONLY! 2 - 7 MAY

Ending its 150 performance sold-out world-tour of South Africa!

PIETER-DIRK UYS & CHRIS GALLOWAY in

REARRANGING THE DECKCHAIRS ON THE S.A. BOTHATANIC

directed by RALPH LAWSON

THE PRESS SAID:

"Cheeky bugger. He gets away with it — splat on target!" SUNDAY STAR

"God bless this ship and all who sail in her." SUNDAY TIMES

"Pieter-Dirk Uys op sy beste" RAPPORT

"Superb... Uys is never better..." NATAL WITNESS

"'n Treffer." VADERLAND

BOOK NOW AT COMPUTICKET
Monday to Thursday 8.15
Friday & Saturday 6.00 & 9.00
Matinee Wednesday 4th at 2.30

Dear Minister Botha

This is to Complain that CRY FREE MANDELA by P-D UYS at the NICO MALAN THEATRE is a) offensive b) blasfemous c) permissive d) anti-ons mense e) promotes the ANC f) is subversive, disgusting, rude and true. I hope you BAN IT or else I vote for the C.P.

Annonoumous.

CRY FREEMANDELA
– THE MOVIE

a true story
within the
framework of the
present state of
emergency

★★★★★★★★★★★★★★

PIETER-DIRK UYS
CHRIS GALLOWAY
SELLO MAAKE KANCUBE
as
Sir Richard Attenborough
Mrs Margaret Thatcher
Members of the SAP
Ronald Reagan
Joan Collins as 'Mrs Winnie Mandela'
James Coburn as 'Nelson'
the Clapper Boy
and
Donald Woods as himself
with
Sir Laurence Olivier
Marlene Dietrich
Michael Caine
Orson Welles
Richard Burton
and
a cast of thousands of dead bodies
and millions of angry people

Flyers for *Rearranging the Deckchairs on the*
SA Bothatanic and *Cry Freemandela – The Movie*

Ruphin Coudyzer

As Captain PW Botha in *Rearranging the Deckchairs on the SA Bothatanic*

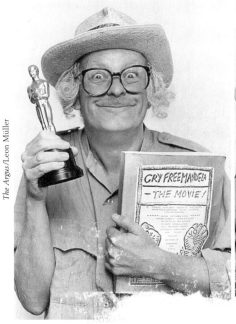

As Richard ... director of *Cry Free* ...

...agan and Margaret Thatcher

As Miss Joan Collins,
who must play Winnie Mandela ...

... and the ... as ...
performe...

The clapper boy
and the police...

...he clapper boy,
...ugh and
...ald Woods

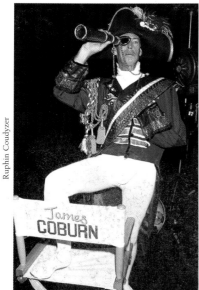

Chris Galloway as James Coburn
playing the wrong Nelson – Horatio!

PDU as Margaret Thatcher as Steve Biko's
doctor, watched by a tense Donald Woods

Chris Galloway (Mervyn), Stephen Raymond (Mouse) and PDU (André) in the 1990s' reinvention of *Paradise Is Closing Down*

Twenty-five years after meeting at The Space Theatre,
PDU and Lynne Maree retrace their long walk to freedom in Long Street, Cape Town

8

POEP, ETC.

There was no censorship during my early work. The creative freedom that The Space gave me was never compromised by what was deemed politically correct or socially acceptable. Let us not forget that most of our work was illegal. People's safety was constantly compromised by the things we said on the stage. No one ever asked me to be careful for their sakes. Or even for mine. I don't know why we were so fearless. Did we not take our work seriously? Oh yes, sometimes more than sufficiently. Did we not believe the power of the enemy? There was no reason not to. People were dying because of apartheid.

The only criterion was: does it work? Rehearsals were always the most creative and exciting part of the writing process. It was here that the actor took the word that was familiar in my head, as spoken by my image of the character, and often made it something different and often better through their interpretation. And after discussion and experimentation. I very seldom argue with an actor when they want to change a line. It's not to remove meaning, but purely to make the rhythm of the words more comfortable and effective.

Christine Basson couldn't say 'kak'. As a child, her mother had washed out her mouth with soap, and she still found the word impossible to articulate. So she said 'stront'. I think this sounds worse, but it didn't matter to Christine, because it wasn't a familiar swearword to her. Some actresses didn't feel comfortable saying 'God' or 'Jesus', for Calvinistic reasons. I learnt early on that in Afrikaans theatre the culture wouldn't tolerate the use of words like 'kak' and 'poep', or the mention of God. By all means tell the truth about what we do to each other. Torture, maim, kill and orphan. But leave God out of it. Very logical for a Calvinist society.

My biggest slip-up was my carelessness in using words like 'poep' and 'kak' and 'fok' and 'moer' and the occasional 'For God's sake' or 'Jesus!' Because that hint of raw meat attracted the scorpions of government censorship.

The word 'fuck' was an easy way to wake up an audience. During the sixties the use of the word on television usually created the aura of controversy that the utterer was hoping for. Freedom of speech and the right to say what needed to be said became the slogans on the T-shirts of the time. Today it is the opposite. The use of four-letter words is so dull and unimaginative that the more you use them the less effect they have. Other than to make your work sound like an old episode in a long-running television sitcom. The word 'motherfucker' is now more familiar on our screens than 'compassion'.

The more I wrote for the theatre, the better my work became and the more intense my determination to survive. *Selle ou Storie* came from a translation of *Same Old Story*, which I had written in London as a sequel to *Faces in the Wall*. The moment it embraced the sounds of Afrikaans, the play became a time bomb. For me there was only one target: the Afrikaner and that product of Afrikaner 'compassion' – apartheid. Or to put it bluntly: anything to piss off my Pa.

Could one actually summarise my development as a satirist with the childishness of that idea? That it was all just to irritate the older people in my life? The former teacher and the dominee, the oom and the tannie? My father was never happy with my writing, and I think it was because of the political echoes of anti-establishment attack. Maybe it was because of all the 'poep' and 'kak'. Maybe he saw the carelessness and my lazy homework. We never talked about it. We fought. He threw me out of the house in Pinelands and I started my sojourn in Long Street among the bergies and whores and actors. All the stuff of legend and Piaf songs.

My first brush with censorship was a crossroads in my life. My first reaction to the official letters from Pretoria was predictable. Terror. I have always been terrified of all authority, bowing down meekly to the uniform, the rank and the experience. Pa was very specific about having respect for those 'who knew better' – in this case, the uniform, the rank and the experience. It kept my inner voice silent till after my fortieth birthday in the last years of the previous century. The only voice I allowed myself during the sixties, seventies and eighties was through the mouths of characters. Peter in *Faces in the Wall* could say what I wouldn't even allow myself to expose. *God's Forgotten*'s sisters in Excelsior were aspects of my roots that, on the one hand, wanted to flee the land and condemn it, while on the other stay and embrace the few aspects of goodness that remained.

A love/hate relationship is nothing unique in a writer, or any creative person. My nemesis was not my family, nor my affair of the heart. It was my land. My country. A passion so strong that instinctively I knew that no matter how hopeless things felt, the good would win and eventually we would be allowed to be illegal and therefore free.

Criticism of apartheid was not tolerated and was seen as anti–South

African. It was regarded as a denial of Afrikanerdom's sacred place in the outstretched hands of God and a communist-inspired lack of patriotism for Land, Volk en Taal. All of it crying out for a devastating slap of 'poep', 'kak' and satire. And once these feelings were encased in the puff and powder of theatre, could the upholders of the crippled status quo actually find that rusty blade in the camp cottonwool ball that was drawing their blood?

*   *   *

It was 'poep' and 'kak' that got me into shit.

Stupidly, I had given them the reason to close me down. Instead of forcing them to give themselves away politically by fingering me for being that communist, terrorist or whatever label helped make their point. *Selle ou Storie* was the means to that end. Through my fifties play with its sixties message, banned in the seventies, I found the love of my life and the way to become famous.

The Publications Board of South Africa.

The law made it clear that they could act on an anonymous complaint. And so, after receiving one with regard to the production of *Selle* in the Outer Space, the typed official letter arrived on Brian's desk, only demanding an age restriction of 2-21. In other words: no children. That suited us fine, and the small hiccup of publicity added some spice. But once we took the play out of the cocoon of subversion and performed it one weekend at the minute Libertas Theatre in Stellenbosch, we were shitting on the Broederbond's stoep and knocking for toilet paper.

We then moved to Johannesburg, joining the Company at the Blue Fox Theatre, situated in the hotel of the same name and the future Market Theatre's first home. Christine Basson won the Dalro Award for best actress, angry letters were written to the press condemning our existence, we received death threats and, worse, were prevented from playing in any theatre in Pretoria!

Then the script of *Selle ou Storie* was banned.

Somehow we could still perform the play with its present cast, but training a new actor meant we were breaking the law by looking at the banned script.

So I translated *Selle ou Storie* back to *Same Old Story* – set in Hillbrow, Johannesburg, among Afrikaners, but all in English. This was legal. Works were banned according to their title. This was not just another title; it was another language. And so we could run an Afrikaans play on an English text! *Same Old Story* was therefore not the same old story as *Selle ou Storie*! By now the absurdity of the actions outweighed the sinister implications of police action and prison. People started laughing at the nonsense, and it *was* funny!

Thanks to my Pa getting onto the censor board as a censor, I started laughing too.

He couldn't believe what arseholes they were. He invited me for lunch. We started reconciling. He said: Don't be scared of these people. Make fun of them.

The weapon had been found. Humour is the ultimate sword of revenge.

Within a week of its premiere, *Karnaval* too was banned. I thought we had become immune to such actions, but this was bad because it put us out of business. Actors lost their jobs. The depression felt sinister and darker. But then we realised that I now had a play that you could see but not read – *Selle ou Storie* – and a play you could read but not see – *Karnaval*!

The PCB became my public relations department. The strangled media breathed a sigh of relief. Fun was to be had here. They wrote glorious articles about all the nonsense of our impending cultural suffocation. But does culture suffocate when the victim can still laugh?

*   *   *

The official letters in their windowed brown envelopes started streaming in, carefully typed, telling me what I done wrong.

> Dear Mr Uys,
>   a) Whereas the following words are deemed offensive in terms of section 47 (2) (a) of the Act, the following words are hereby banned: kak, poep, tiet, drol, stront, slapgat, kakhuisvloer, kaal hol, glinsterende stront, moffie-mond, die ou verlepte doos met die kesh en contacts, draadtrekker, starstruck-sodomist, fokkin' teef, opgefok.
>   b) Whereas the following phrases are blasphemous in terms of the Act, the following phrase is hereby banned:
>   'En die Engelekore skree: Poephol Poephol!'

Imagine how my filth had corrupted the poor, white, Afrikaner Calvinist typist! She then even corrected my spelling:

> Meneer Uys!
> Die woord 'fok' spel u met 'n 'f' en nie 'n 'v' nie!

The fun of fucking with the ooms and tannies cancelled out any fear. This was better than a publicity stunt. All one had to do was tell the truth and let them do the rest. But make sure that when you say 'kak', 'poep' and 'fuck', it's the only word that will work in that context. Don't add noughts or shocks for effect!

The next clash with the armies of apartheid happened in Johannesburg in 1979, when *Die Van Aardes van Grootoor* opened at the tiny Laager in the bowels of the Market Theatre. Within three weeks it was banned.

The poor corrupted typist was at it again, swearing and cursing:

Beste Meneer Uys,

a) Die refrein in die advertensie vir KAKS is ongewens. [We sent up the familiar LUX toilet soap adverts to underline the use of KUX. We spelt it KUX; they read KAKS!]

b) Die karakters betas mekaar se borste.

c) Die gebruik van die woorde: naaimasjien, koeksister, boerewors, krimpelene drol, genotskrots – is ongewens.

d) Daar word deurentyd op aanstootlike wyse verwys na: Rooinekke, Jode, Kaffirs, Meide, Plurale, Boere, Afrikaners en Nie-Blanke toilette.

To translate this into English would be to lose something: we experienced such liberation hearing it all in Afrikaans. Suffice to say everything they banned was what they had created, 'Nie-Blanke Toilette' being the obvious. Frankenstein had challenged the Monster, and the Monster had exposed its obscenities.

*   *   *

The funny thing is, there were no real swearwords in *Die Van Aardes*, just ordinary Afrikaans words like 'naaimasjien' and 'boerewors', meaning sewing machine and farmer's sausage. But the Afrikaans word 'naai' is also slang for 'bonking', and farmer's sausage … well, what can I say? They meant one thing, they echoed another – all in the mind of the beholder. I also made up words that sounded truly gross, like 'trawantgetras' and 'genotskrots'.

By the time of the Johannesburg banning, I'd become more confident in fighting the authorities. I also had friends and legal minds on my side. If we kept our tongue firmly in the media's cheek, we could only triumph through the goodwill of the press. We could also afford to appeal. This had been impossible after previous bannings, when we didn't have any money to pay for an appeal. But Mannie Manim and the Market Theatre rallied the troops and we decided to beard the censor lion in his own den.

There was no legal procedure here. We had to appeal to the same people who had banned us, and they would decide either for or against themselves. At the time, the new official building that would house such wisdom was still being completed in the centre of Pretoria, and the floor set aside for the courtrooms was still in disarray. We held our appeal case in the passage.

All state buildings of that time seemed to have very wide passages, as if one could expect to see them park their new Mercedes Benzes outside their office doors.

There we sat, in the passage. The proceedings were opened with a prayer in Afrikaans, them knowing that God was on their side, and us a sight for sore eyes in our suits and ties. We were suitably dressed for the occasion. At no stage dared we meet each others' gaze. Giggles here would be uncontrollable and fatal.

The official table slowly voiced all the complaints, and to hear them articulate the obscene Afrikaans for tit, shit, fart, arse, cunt, turd and fuck was an unforgettable treat. They then came to the words that had no meaning.

'These words are also obscene,' the professor in charge slowly explained, peering over his bifocals at 'genotskrots' and 'trawantgetras'. 'They are not acceptable ...'

He looked up at me with a benign smile. 'Eh ... Mister Uys.'

Our legal team of one had prepared us for this.

'Professor,' I said, 'may I ask the esteemed prosecution to give the meaning of these supposed obscene words for the edification of the learned court?'

With the same smile he nodded to a clerk, who proceeded to page vigorously through a huge dictionary. To G. To T. Then back and forth. Then the clerk shrugged, defeated.

'Neither word is in the dictionary, sir.'

They all looked at me. The guilty party. As if I had committed the ultimate crime of using my imagination.

'Mr Uys? This word "genotskrots"? What does it mean in the context of your usage thereof?'

As if it would start meaning something if one could put it in the right context.

I felt like a minor character in a Hitchcock courtroom drama, the warm-up for the star to come in and win an Oscar.

'Actually, you won't find the word in the dictionary. It doesn't exist.'

'It does exist, Mr Uys. It is obscene.'

'It sounds obscene, Your Grace, but believe me, it doesn't exist. I made it up.'

'You made it up?'

His Grace, His Honour, Her Worship looked horrified.

'Yes,' I admitted meekly. 'That's part of what we do in theatre.'

'And yet it has no meaning? Even for you?'

'Oh yes, it does mean something to me.'

They all leant forward in anticipation.

'What does it mean?'

There followed a wondrous theatrical pause. Our lawyer came to my rescue.

'My client does not have to give meaning to a word that doesn't exist. Or does he?'

They conferred. They mumbled. They smacked their lips and clenched their thighs. And then they fixed beady, watery eyes on me.

'Very well. Under the circumstances you can have the words back. But don't do it again!'

So we won the battle, more or less, even though they prolonged the war.

Die Van Aardes reopened at the Laager to run for two years with suitable, accepted replacements for the original offences – words and phrases with hidden meanings that sounded worse than actual obscenities. And assuring us of more publicity than money could buy.

The Publications Act stated very clearly that the censors needed only one anonymous complaint in order to carry out their mandate. Since *Die Van Aardes* I sent them complaints about every new work – four letters from various post offices, some sprayed with cheap perfume, some in English, most in Afrikaans. All anonymous. All bitterly complaining about the blasphemous tone and obscene content of this latest communist-inspired work by Pieter-Dirk Uys.

In the beginning the censors fell for it and arrived, banned and suffered.

It started with *Info Scandals*, a minstrel-style revue we performed in a small room in Pretoria to parallel the Information Scandal that was rocking the foundations of government and would result in the firing of John Vorster – meaning he was kicked up from the Prime Ministership into the State President's job – and the rise to megapower of PW Botha.

The sketches all lampooned the stupidity and arrogance of the Pretoria regime. Doing it on their doorstep added to the flavour and delight. Sybil Coetzee, blonde and beautiful, stripped from her staid Voortrekker dress to bra and panties in front of a huge projection of the sacred Voortrekker Monument to a traditional Afrikaans song 'Afrikaners is Plesierig' and made the whole thing look like pornography. The censors salivated, came and blew their tops.

Part of the so-called appeal against their banning was to perform the show for them. I added an old sketch from an earlier show about censorship:

I hereby exorcise the powers invested in my person as a censor and in terms of the Publications Act declare the following things as follows as far as my Government is concerned:

a. Whereas – because of the obscene nature of their shapes, the following objects are deemed undesirable: Candles, Cucumbers, Boerewors and Plural Orbs formerly known as Nigger Balls.

b. Whereas – the following place names have been declared indecent and/or obscene, the following places will hereby cease to exist: Kakamas, Holfontein, Nigel and Donkergat.

c. Whereas – tomorrow has been declared undesirable, because of the obscene phrase: 'the crack of dawn'.

d. Whereas – the following are also banned: photographs of any prison in South Africa; media coverage of any unrest in South Africa; quotations from the utterances of any banned person and/or persons; the wearing, flaunting, displaying and/or circulating of the banned ANC flag, colours and/or any other communist slogans.

e. Whereas – because of the obscene insinuations as perpetuated in the 'Koek' and 'Moer' in Koekemoer, the 'Shitz' in Lipshitz and the 'Tiet' in Tieties, the telephone directory has been declared undesirable.

f. Whereas – all Afrikaans universities have been closed because of the 'Fak' in Fakulteit.

g. Whereas – all nudity – other than that of large kaffir girls in the home-lands, which is regarded as officially natural – all other nudity is declared offensive and undesirable. If we were meant to walk around with no clothes on, we would've also been born black.

On the night they allowed us the show back, but insisted that we cut Nigel. Naai Jill?

*   *   *

I look back now and realise how easily we all fell into the trap. While black writers were exiled and black artists were imprisoned or isolated, intelligent white artists and writers, and most of the talents in theatre and writing, wasted their creative energies fighting for the right to say 'poep' and 'kak'. While that made sure the media would be in attendance, PW Botha marched our army into Angola and South West Africa, the Department of Education under FW de Klerk successfully completed their lobotomy of a generation, and the National Party took parliamentary democracy and stuck it up the hairy arse of the convenient arch-enemy, communism.

Whites were seldom stopped for political reasons. Gordimer was only banned once. Fugard was not forbidden. But then, in the early 1980s, two crazy white boys did a crazy tatty show in which, dressed as Blues Brothers clones in fedoras and shades, they presented a duologue about the architect of apartheid, Hendrik Verwoerd. Matthew Krause and Robert Coleman were blazingly subversive and shocked us to the core. They were young and uncompromisingly angry, Verwoerd's Children who were now losing their lives and sanity on the perforated borders of the bloody republic of racist supremacy. Fuck it all, they spat, with obscene laughter and blasphemous cheers their main encouragement. They were banned instantly. Police threats came with the letter.

I met with Lauren Jacobson and Edwin Cameron, who were defending these boys and their right to write. They asked me to be a character witness at the appeal. That cracked us all up for a few hours, but once we realised the seriousness of the matter and the need to fight the darkness that was racing towards us from the right, we prepared to go to Pretoria.

The building had now been completed and the courtrooms were ready. The Verwoerd family were in attendance, led by Anna Boshoff, whom I remember teasing on a beach in Hermanus when we were all teenagers. This lady was no longer for teasing. Her offspring reflected the granite impassiveness of her expression. No clues. I think our eyes met, but there could have been a cement wall between us.

Once I was on the stand, having sworn to tell the whole and nothing but the whole, the issue was a scene in the play where Verwoerd's parents, travelling in a Dutch train, submit themselves to some sex play. The sight of the two sombrely clad, portly actors in fedora and shades, impersonating Verwoerd the Father being sucked off by Verwoerd the Mother made even the prosecution clones whimper in suppressed amusement.

The question to me was simple: 'Mr Uys, did you think that scene was obscene?'

I said: 'No.'

They all looked at me with one word on their lips. Liar!

'You didn't think the scene suggested some sexual deviation?'

'No.'

'Are you sure?'

'Yes.' Then I added: 'But again, Your Grace, could you just explain what you mean by obscene?'

With deep breaths and squeezed sighs, the prosecution explained the complicated scene.

'Mr Verwoerd ... Mrs Verwoerd is practising oral sex on her husband.'

The family sat numbed and probably oblivious to what had been said. Can't imagine them indulging in a taste of cunnilingus or a slurp of fellatio.

My gasp was the loudest.

'What are you saying? Is that what you saw?' I trilled.

The prosecution now looked perplexed.

'But what did you think the scene was about, Mr Uys?'

'I thought Mrs Verwoerd was merely sewing a button onto the trousers of Mr Verwoerd and biting through the thread ...'

I might be wrong, but I think Anna Boshoff gave a slight smile. It was truly terrifying!

The case was not won, but there was one little victory: the judgment allowed that in future it would no longer be illegal to make fun of politicians. The boys never performed again. I was never called as a character witness again. Lauren Jacobson became my legal advisor, and Edwin Cameron eventually became a Supreme Court judge in the future democracy and a leading AIDS activist, being honest enough to admit to having the virus, and living an active life in spite of it.

We celebrated our guerrilla victory over mundane thought-control as a major step forward, even though we all knew it was too late. We were sliding into a terrible twilight.

That darkness was called the 1980s.

9

BETWEEN THE ROCKS
AND A DARK PLACE

The 1980s separated black from white, good and evil, and exposed a great divide in South African society.

On one side was the devil, in the shape of an all-encompassing government machine, present in every aspect of life: church, school, entertainment, law, sport, leisure, life and death. On the other hand was the deep: the enemy, the communist, the terrorist, the subversive, the dangerous anti-us that had to be eliminated. Anything from that dark place was illegal. The writings of the black leaders were banned. The pictures of the political prisoners were not allowed. Some of us didn't even know why they were in jail.

The trouble was, very few of us actually cared.

White South Africa was happy to be led by fear and comply with every demand to perform self-lobotomy. The few who managed to break the mould of propaganda secretly informed us that in the twilight zone of non-existence dwelt people of compassion who loved the land. That not all were enemies. That not everyone who was against apartheid was for chaos.

Television only came to South Africa in 1975, and whatever we'd seen during the past five years was carefully fabricated behind an official's desk in Pretoria. Especially the news. It was public knowledge that PW Botha, after recreating himself in the image of State President, had telephoned the SABC after a newscast had shown a coloured leader in a favourable light. He demanded the news be rewritten and replayed to show the Rev. Alan Hendrickse as a subversive. The good boys and girls at the SABC did just that. Today, many of them are still there. And of course they were all part of the Struggle against Apartheid.

Amandla.

That word was also banned. The closest we got to it was when Afrikaans cabaret artist Amanda Strydom drunkenly raised a clenched fist and screamed 'Amandla', and was forced to apologise or be cast out into the wilderness. Winnie Mandela was the Scarlet Bitch of Liberation. Nelson Mandela was the Phantom of the Island. To most whites, the initials ANC were short for 'ante-nuptial contract' rather than the African National Congress.

Every time I managed to get myself over to the United Kingdom, I broke the law by meeting an untouchable. Starting in the mid-1970s with a holiday in London, then later that decade for the TV shoot of *Paradise Is Closing Down*, and into the early 1980s en route to my first discovery of New York, the occasional meeting with members of the banned ANC filled me with inspiration. And terror. Just to be seen with a representative of the Afrikaners' enemy was enough to make one lie awake at night with beating heart and fearful dreams. Was there no place left to hide? A pub? On Hampstead Heath?

I couldn't understand why the ANC exiles were so ordinary. So emotional. So in need to hear Afrikaans. I was horrified that I could not detect the bomb-maker and grenade-thrower beneath the tatty duffle coat and the worn-out hat. Black men and women cried when I told them a Van der Merwe joke in Afrikaans in Leicester Square. They embraced me and called me Comrade. It was horribly unsettling. Someone was wrong. My instinct told me it was me.

While The Space had given me madness as a survival kit during the 1970s, the Market Theatre gave me a commitment that saved my life. Arriving in Johannesburg in 1978 for the season of *Die Van Aardes van Grootoor*, which had been tried and tested (and ignored) at the Baxter Theatre some months before, I moved into digs in Melville and reported for duty in Newtown. The Market Theatre was based in the old Indian fruit market and has retained all the splendour of this magnificent colonial heap. Mannie Manim and Barney Simon were the leading energies, creating a space for so many of us, including John Kani. Political correctness today encourages the uninformed to credit Kani for starting the Market Theatre. Mannie Manim and Barney Simon did that. The whiteness of their skins might not allow them full acknowledgement in the future annals of our theatre, but the fruits of their labour can be seen today. There is a vibrant theatrical tradition in South Africa whose roots can be traced to the work done in Newtown during the 1980s.

I plunged head first into the inviting, crocodile-infested water.

Strike up the Banned was the first resident production I did, still in the old Market Café, before it was transformed into the Laager and became home to *Die Van Aardes* for so long. Censorship had hit the hull of the Market like an iceberg, but by now we knew most of Pretoria's dirty tricks. Their modus operandi held no surprises. The constant run-in with authorities about mixed audiences in our theatres no longer seemed a priority. Gone were the days when, at The Space, we would stop a play and ask the few black members of the audience to accompany me to the wardrobe where we would sit out the police raid that we'd been forewarned about. Maybe the regime realised that blacks and whites sitting together in a small theatre didn't spell the end of their world. Pretoria had other priorities. The unofficial civil war had become a reality.

One night, driving to Pretoria to perform *Info Scandals*, we passed a military convoy going in the direction of Johannesburg. Not just ten or fifteen trucks – the motorised column stretched almost the entire thirty-nine kilometres from Pretoria. It was obviously not a manoeuvre. Probably on its way to Soweto. We could catch a glimpse of small, tense white faces peering out into the night from under huge, uncomfortable combat helmets. Could have been our brothers, cousins, friends or lovers. Going off to shoot the children of their maid.

At the beginning of the new decade, *Die Van Aardes van Grootoor* was transferred to the Main Theatre of the Market. We took a deep breath, wondering if this Boere-epic could survive the move from a small 120-seater room. It just got better. The sweep of space and the high roof of the old Indian fruit market gave the play a new dimension. I was playing the part of Tertius van Aarde, the supposed romantic lead, who then turns out to be a closet drag queen, transvestite and eventual President of South Africa. Echoes of Bapetikosweti Baroque.

The Market was not The Space. But the Cape Town experience had paved the way for new experiments in theatre. Mannie Manim was an inspired theatre manager and friend, but also a canny businessman who had to cut our expectations down to a bare minimum. One was simply not paid at the Market for what one did. And we all knew it and gratefully took what we could get. At first, after we took over the derelict former Market Café, which we transformed into the Laager, the Market management promised us rent-free occupation for the first two productions. They gave us no money to renovate or produce the show, but we managed with nothing, led of course by Dawie Malan and his inspired vision.

Magda Beukes, our first glorious Elana, put on higher heels and more lipstick and went to ask for money from her Afrikaans contacts. She came back with R1000 from Louis Luyt. We were speechless. He was the last person we'd have approached, with all his obvious Broederbond connections. And yet the breathtakingly beautiful redhead managed to get a cheque out of him! No one asked how. When Mannie heard, he didn't bat an eyelid.

'Should we give this tainted money back?' we asked, worried that we were compromising the integrity of the Market philosophy.

'No,' said Mannie. 'Cash it immediately, spend it and don't tell anyone where it came from!'

Needless to say, after a sensational first six-week run of *Die Van Aardes*, the Market started charging us full rental. So much for promises and commitments. It was up to us to commit to the Market, not the other way round. It didn't matter. We had the freedom to speak and the inspiration to create. And, with no money, we created without money. And it was better!

The thinking public needed the Market Theatre now more than ever before.

We would be playing to a converted audience. The enemy didn't come and see what we did – well, at least not in the light. So we realised that even though the size of the theatre was smaller than a church, the impact of what happened on our stage rolled across the suburbs like thunder.

Even though *Die Van Aardes* ran for all those years, I had no income to speak of. Luckily I was living in a small house on 2nd Avenue in Melville that cost R79.50 a month to rent. My days were spent at the theatre, so it was just a place to sleep. And to write. Out of this came a new play called *Scorched Earth*. It was in the style of *God's Forgotten*, a serious epic about home and family, crippled by politics and compromise. We did a reading of the play in my little house, with an inspired cast of actors who agreed to come and give my play life. Mannie listened. The reaction was very promising. Then it died. Because I didn't have the courage to pursue a production. Because, as always, I just cowered back into the comfort of silence. I missed that chance, and when the play was produced at the Market some years later, it failed. The timing was wrong. These things don't repeat themselves. The lesson was simple: if it feels right in the theatre, do it. There will be no second chance.

*   *   *

One of the most exciting things about working in South African theatre during this time was that there was no time for the luxuries of discussion and reflection. Decisions had to be made immediately, casting had to be completed within days, and a production moved into high gear within hours.

I went to London, within a few days of the Royal Wedding, for the telecast of *Paradise*. The truncated, melodramatic, confusing production failed miserably and depressed me. Being polite and grateful was no way to ensure quality work. I should have been more helpful in making sure that British directors and creative people would understand that not all South Africans sounded like lower-class tarts from Brakpan. English was also spoken here by some educated Afrikaners without a rugger-bugger accent. I should have said that we were all pretty similar to the people living in London.

I didn't. The fact that British actors couldn't manage the South African accent and all sounded as if they came from Birmingham, which most of them did, didn't help either.

My use of humour to lighten the burden of tragedy and fear didn't work in the UK in those days. The accepted standard was a Fugardian dirge with meaningful dramatic insight into a bleeding society. Today, ironically, it's the other way round. The only way to put across the tragedy of a terminal world is to find a way to laugh at that fear.

So after pretty Diana married her unfaithful Charles and my pretty sister married her first hideous husband, I left London for New York for the first time, spending the most exciting holiday of my life in the city that never sleeps. Nor did I. My old friend from drama school days, Maggie Soboil, took me to all the magic places, from Chinatown to Little Italy. Gay pals escorted me around the squalid fleshpots of Christopher Street and introduced me to poppers and porno. I was like a starving Biafran at a Jewish wedding.

When I got back to 2nd Avenue, Melville, the culture shock was enormous. Not because I struggled to get back into the swing of South Africa after the merry-go-round of Manhattan, but because of what was missing. I realised we had nothing. Apartheid Kultuur had its fingers tight around the creative throat of the people. Sanctions made certain that our lack of inspiration from the rest of the world showed up as bald spots on a spotty head. Except for what we had in the Market Theatre. On the one hand it was terrifying; on the other, the realisation demanded braver action and taking risks.

I was writing a weekly column in the *Sunday Express*, which was my first forced discipline in 'less is more'. My weekly story had to fit within the permitted number of words and the requirements of topicality and news. There was so much that one wasn't allowed to write about, and so much that wouldn't be understood by a reading public who were in the dark about what was happening in their own backyards because of censorship and control.

The difference between a play and a revue was obvious: plays told a story, while revues gave the smell and suggestion of a story. Having tasted the fun of reflecting topicality in my newspaper column and seeing my cat get thinner made me think of other ways to earn money. During this time, Prime Minister PW Botha announced another general election for whites only, and I toyed with the idea of standing as an independent candidate against Pik Botha, then already Minister of Foreign Affairs and head of the SABC. Happily, through good advice and common sense I changed my mind, and the structure of what would have been my very theatrical political meetings became the backbone of a one-man political cabaret. 'Adapt or die!' PW had spat out at us from the television news. And so the new show was called *Adapt or Dye*.

*   *   *

It started small-small. Maybe just for a few evenings. Late night.

When US President Ronald Reagan survived an assassination attempt the day before we opened, I saw this as an omen. Not sure if it was good or bad. The show was a collection of sketches reflecting the political icebergs floating in the tranquil sea of mundane news. By now the woman I had created in the *Sunday Express* column, already called the Evita of Pretoria, was well known enough to open the show. Apart from the fun of doing drag, that kind of extreme acting – a man playing a woman – had its drawbacks. It was seen as homosexual and probably against the law. But while a man in a dress pretending to be a woman resulted in some gay friends ending up in jail on their way to a Friday-night party, my excursion into the world of high heels and handbags went from tentative to successful.

Nowell Fine the kugel, who had emerged at a Grahamstown Festival, was another dazzling blonde in the chorus line. Pik Botha appeared as Hamlet, as he'd carried theatrical spears in local National Theatre productions in his youth. And Barbara Woodhouse was training dogs on TV – and so did the same to Progs. The show ended with my PW Botha, already tried and tested in *Die Van Aardes* when Tertius appears in the final scene as the President of South Africa. Although PW was still PM, the comparisons weren't lost on anyone.

Adapt or Dye moved from a small venue in Durban to a new cabaret space at the Market, playing late-night to Janice Honeyman's sharp Afrikaans kabaret by Hennie Aucamp, *Met Permissie Gesê*. It all added up to a night of very significant comment on our belaagered world outside: the fear, hypocrisy, absurdity, beauty and hope. As the weeks of full houses and generous reviews went by, I realised I had a product here that could live. This time there was no need to depend on someone for help. I was on my own. I made the phone calls, wrote the letters, produced the tour and drove the transport. It was the start of the rest of my life in theatre: the one-man band.

Adapt or Dye performed sold-out seasons at the Baxter Concert Hall, going from an 80-seater in Natal, to a 130-seater in Johannesburg, to a 690-seater in Cape Town. The audiences stood and roared, the critics triple-starred the show, and my friends hugged me and said: 'We're so happy for you. It couldn't have happened to a nicer person.'

What was *Adapt or Dye* other than light-hearted fun at the expense of a few loutish politicians? No major onslaught against the system. It gently tickled and coyly blushed. It used 'poep' and 'kak' to flex its muscles of free speech. It stabbed occasionally in the direction of political incorrectness. Possibly it stepped over the line once or twice. But the focus of the attention was not on so-called satire. It was on theatricality: I stayed on stage throughout and changed into character in front of everyone. With a collection of stacked cardboard boxes filled with props and costumes, one character would be peeled off while another was added. A woman became a man, became an Afrikaner, then a kugel, then a minister, then a leader. The one I hid carefully was me.

By then there were the odd calls from people who didn't leave a name. Whether they were meant to be threats, I don't know, but they were not friendly. I put it all in the show. The linking voice was the security policeman, Sersant Swart. He was bugging the theatre and commenting on the illegality of the material. While the audience laughed at the absurdity and stupidity, the fact was: it *was* illegal. But maybe putting it on stage somehow diverted attention from the need to stop it.

There was no censorship of *Adapt or Dye*.

Only when we put it on video and it appeared in the video shops that seemed to mushroom up in every suburb overnight did the PCB quickly slap an age restriction on the show. How do you control people under twenty-one from watching a rental video? Delightful nonsense like this just added to the publicity value, and *Adapt or Dye* became the most popular video at the time. My small theatre audience grew to millions who were introduced to me via the television screen in the safeness of their homes. Exiles and political prisoners watched the videos too. When it came to payment from the company that distributed the video, 'hidden costs' took the majority of the profit and I think my share was minimal. Nevertheless, I was now earning cheques of R15 000 a week, a big leap from R22.50. I had more than enough money.

What a horrible reality that turned out to be. For the next ten years, the fact that through so small an investment of funds I could make a fortune weighed heavily. It felt wrong to be rich. I felt guilty and unworthy of success. Happily, though, I could support my sister and Pa. A cheque for a few thousand each month softened his resistance to my work. He could at last follow his dreams of travelling the world, which he did, going up the Andes and down the Nile. After all, if Pieter's communist filth made that sort of money, it couldn't be all bad!

Usually shows have large production budgets to balance before profit.

Not *Adapt or Dye*. I was alone in this production with its four cardboard boxes. Those could be harvested in any alley within sniffing distance of a theatre. Props and costumes were bare essentials, and expenses were virtually nil. Because it was obvious where my material came from, I gave credit to the National Party government for being my scriptwriters.

'I couldn't make it up it I tried!'

I also said that I didn't pay taxes; I called it royalties.

During the two-year tour of *Adapt or Dye* through most provinces and cities of the land, with countless return seasons to the Baxter and the Market, the show changed constantly as the politics changed. New characters were added and less successful ones given the boot.

It was not usual to be serious in shows like this. When I introduced a few sketches which, although encased in wry humour, dealt with the deaths of young soldiers in the Border War and the inhuman treatment of blacks by so-called Christian whites, there was a general sense of discomfort.

*   *   *

The businessman sits at his desk. He picks up his phone and speaks to his secretary.

'Yes Suzanne? No, it's your lunch hour. You can finish the letters this afternoon. No, I'll wait for their call. Good.'

He replaces the receiver and carefully lays his pens out in a neat parking area.

He confides in us.

'Like so many families in our street, we also have a son in the Army. He completed the first year of his service without any cause for complaint or celebration. He saw much of the country from train windows and picked up things here and there that he couldn't even explain to his own father! He also quickly lost that puppy fat for which we called him Rolly for so many years.'

He picks up the framed photo of his son and smiles back at the smiling boy-face.

'Grew so tall that his mother began to cry when she stood beside him on his first weekend pass, looked up and suddenly felt like an old woman.'

He sighs.

'I'm afraid she's become one since. She never recovered after the car crash: reverted to a routine of sleepless nights and weekly visits to the chemist for her precious prescriptions.'

The phone rings.

'Excuse me.' He holds the phone to his ear. 'Hello? Ah yes. Good. No, I've postponed the preliminary meeting until he's rested ... Yes, there will be a representative from Armscor sitting in. Good.'

He hangs up.

'The telephone ... Rolly would always phone from one or other obscure place and yell out the number of the payphone so we could write it down quickly in order to phone back and have a nice long chat. That evening he called to tell us he was coming home for a short while.

'We were all so excited. Just babbling together to give and receive news. My wife spoke about her health. His sister about her love life – but then what can one really say over a telephone?

'When it was my chance to talk to Rolly, I sent the women through to the TV room where truths were dispensed about the United Nations and Beirut and rugby and the terrible fact that Aunt Sally from Brakpan was bitten in the backside by a bulldog! You know, our usual old world news.

'"Dad? I'll be home again in a few days' time; I have a few weeks' pass," Rolly told me from far away in his bush war, somewhere north of Pretoria and south of Luanda, where he was protecting us from the terrorist-sons of our maids and gardeners.

'His news was nearly too good to be true.

'"Rolly? Your mother will be so pleased to have you home again. She really needs you now ... Oh no, she's much better, of course ..."

'My white lie stuck in my throat.

'"... but she now needs all our love and attention. You'll see what I mean ..."

'In the lounge the TV news made place for the glossy advertisements showing fat-cat South Africa sweetly licking her credit cards.

'It was then that Rolly asked if he could bring a pal home with him. I was just going to agree how nice it would be when he said: "It's a buddy of mine, Dad. You know, Dad, he's been through a rough time ... I just want to warn you people in time, Dad."

'Warn? Drugs?

'"No, Dad, it's just ... this guy was in a landmine explosion, Dad."

'The telephone line echoed and crackled. Landmine explosion?

'"Yes, Dad. He lost both his legs, Dad ..."

'His legs?

'"No, but Dad, he's absolutely okay. Really, Dad, it's amazing what the medics can do these days. Dad? It will be good for him to be with us, won't it, Dad?"

'My son the Samaritan.

'But me? I didn't feel sorry for that kid. Just felt immediately irritated that a victim wanted to use my family to feel better. Where was his own family? His people? It was unnecessary, inconvenient, and, above all, without legs … uncomfortable. I couldn't say these things to Rolly, of course. I just told him directly that his mother wouldn't be able to handle something so awful, so ghastly.

'I thought my son would understand. It seemed he understood too well.

'Two days later his friend was dead. Suicide. You see, even without his legs, he could get at the pills …'

The phone rings.

The businessman sits for a moment composing himself. Then, with a deep breath, picks up the receiver.

'Hello? Yes, hello, welcome!' He is cheerful and wants to be heard as such. 'How was your flight? Good, yes, I was saying to your Ambassador only yesterday, we can look forward to great cooperation between our countries – of course, only if there is stability … and there is … yes, great changes taking place … very exciting, yes … let's meet in an hour? Good …'

He replaces the phone and stares ahead.

A small toy tank comes rumbling out of the darkness and crosses the stage into the light.

*   *   *

There were many well-meaning words of advice.

'This has no place in a comedy show, darling.'

'Poepie, no man, what do think you're doing?'

I didn't know what I was doing, but it felt right. The people who inspired me to carry on were parents of sons who had died and families from black areas who knew what it was like to be a 'kaffir' in this Calvinist heaven called Home.

The minefield of life became more familiar, and I found a way to tiptoe through the dangers. My 1980s felt like one long year.

I never stopped moving, travelling from town to city. Three-month seasons in Cape Town. Visits to Grahamstown for the festival. Maybe staying on the move was the closest to being on the run. They couldn't catch me if I was faster than they were! It was also possible to live out my dreams in an atmosphere of danger because there was no family at home, no emotional relationship to protect. Just my cat, Peeps. And I always had someone in Melville to look after Peeps!

Looking back twenty years later, from the vantage point of a free society, that year of living dangerously has the feel of a damaged black and white film in my memory. Scratchy, with faulty sound and missing bits.

Adapt or Dye started a career in one-man shows, with titles usually inspired by the words of PW Botha. *Adapt* was followed by *Total Onslaught*, and then *Beyond the Rubicon*. The shows were similar in structure: simple, easy to transport in the backseat of the Volkswagen (first Beetle, then Kombi), and adaptable to the daily political merry-go-round.

Dawie Malan directed me in *Total Onslaught*, and again we tangoed where professionals feared to dance. He gave me a great piece of advice: always cut, but never lose. There's always another show. The box under the bed became a favourite reference point. Dawie also didn't believe in agonising over problems in text and production. We'd work intensely and then both lose our energy more or less at the same time. Flat. Uninspired. Irritated.

Then we'd get into the car and go to the movies. Halfway through the popcorn, the solution would usually pop up from the subconscious and we'd race back to work. We laughed through the whole nightmare of trying to create something out of nothing. We always delivered something. It was magnificent.

After video-taping *Adapt or Dye*, I realised the importance of using this medium to establish an audience. Even if the theatres were full, the size of the audience couldn't compare with the number of viewers watching a video on their TV sets. So *Total Onslaught* was filmed in the State Opera House in Pretoria in front of a thousand officially white people.

The opening line was: 'Pretoria. The State Opera House. This truly feels like doing *Fiddler on the Roof* in Nuremberg.' And this was 1984 – a constant reminder that George Orwell's world was about to happen. Ours had already happened in 1976 but no one noticed.

When Botha made his infamous Rubicon Speech in 1986, snuffing hopes for a democratic solution, the gift of such material almost made up for the darkness of the political reality. We were moving into states of emergency, arrests without trial, killings in township communities. There was massive censorship. Any word sympathetic to the enemy was fatal. Any suggestion that South Africa's future lay in a democracy for all its people was suicidal. And so that's where the material had to take me. Doing the tango in front of the firing squad.

In *Beyond the Rubicon*, Evita appears at the end in a 'futuristic South Africa' where the tables have been turned. Nelson Mandela is now President. Oliver Tambo is Minister of Justice. The former Ambassador is living in what was once a famous black township, but under house arrest. Afrikaans is banned. Whites carry passbooks. They are treated the way we treated blacks. Looking at the sketch today, it chills with its prophecies of what might have happened. At the time, none of us could even pretend that our problems would end in a party of reconciliation. We were marching towards a bloodbath. That, we felt, was certain.

My material became dangerous.

By 1986 Evita had established herself as my alter ego. *Farce About Uys* and the film *Skating on Thin Uys* made her a household personality. Everyone wanted her at their party. The SABC invited her – live on TV – while Pieter-Dirk Uys was persona non grata. This was because Mrs B never swore or blasphemed. Same old story. When it was said that she was taking over my life, that she was all I could do, that she was Frankenstein's monster devouring her creator, I decided to experiment with new work that did not feature my major clown.

Chris Galloway and I sat down and rehearsed a new show, directed by Ralph Lawson. Called *Rearranging the Deckchairs on the SA Bothatanic*, this cabaret, as florid as its title, became a play about the last voyage of the *Titanic* of Afrikaner politics. PW was the captain, and his cabinet were the motley crew. The passengers were a collection of us citizens, wallowing and drowning in our luxuries and our fear of too many icebergs in the scotch.

On board are two security policemen on vacation, who demonstrate torture techniques to one another on an unsuspecting passenger.

*　　*　　*

The SA *Bothatanic* is sailing under a blazing sun. An announcement over the ship's intercom alerts the passengers.

'We've had a record number of passengers entering the competition, in which the ship's course was to be correctly predicted. Most of you predicted that the ship would move rapidly ahead, then veer confidently to the left. However, you were all wrong. The ship hasn't moved at all. We are drifting in circles to the right. There were no winners. Try again tomorrow. Thank you. Dankie.'

PDU and Chris Galloway enter as the two holidaying policemen, relaxing on their deck. They wear suggestions of the SAP uniform, with peaked caps and mirror-lensed sunglasses.

PDU swaggers to the ship's railing and spits over the side.

'Hey Chris,' he asks, 'what did the seagull say when it flew into Table Mountain?'

Chris is reading the daily newspaper. He quotes from a report.

'"One of the accused had his medical drip ripped out before being questioned and was whipped with a hosepipe."

PDU is taken aback. He repeats disbelievingly what Chris has just said.

'One of the accused had his medical drip ripped out and ... what?'

'"And whipped with a hosepipe."'

Chris points to the report on the second page.

PDU nods.

'But before or after?'

'It doesn't say.'

PDU shrugs.

'It's a crucial piece of information. Was the medical drip ripped out before or after he was whipped with a hosepipe?'

Chris scratches his head.

'What difference does it make?'

'A big difference!' PDU explains.' You have either two things: (a) a medical drip and (b) a hosepipe. Or just one thing, that was first the one, and then became the other.'

Chris doesn't get it yet.

'So what?'

PDU patiently starts again.

'You've seen a medical drip?' Chris nods. 'It's delicate, right?'

Chris agrees.

'Ja, I suppose so.'

'And a hosepipe is ... well, a hosepipe.'

Chris laughs.

'Okay.'

PDU makes his point.

'You get someone to hit you first with a medical drip and then a hosepipe. You'll suffer more under the drip. It's like a whip. The hosepipe is ... well, shit, I wouldn't use a hosepipe on a dog!'

PDU likes dogs. Chris waves the paper at him.

'You did on the accused.'

'I never used a hosepipe on the accused.'

PDU tries to control his temper.

Chris refers back to the paper.

'It says here: "One of the accused had his medical drip ripped out before being questioned and was whipped with a hosepipe."'

PDU sneers.

'Bloody communist paper ...'

He spits over the side of the boat.

Chris rereads the report.

'"One of the accused was whipped with a hosepipe and another smashed to the floor."'

'Do they say he was beaten to death?'

Chris checks the report.

'Ehhhh? No.'

PDU tries to convince his companion.

'Ja.' He closes his eyes and quotes from the regulations. '"Assaults on detainees, as long as they do not result in death, are justifiable."'

Chris shrugs and reads on.

'"One policeman's policy was: You thrash him until he cracks, until he points out what has to be pointed out."'

PDU has been there. He sighs.

'Ja.' He looks up into the sun and takes a stretch and a deep breath. 'It's so ... what's the word? Sexual.'

Chris looks at him, surprised.

He nods and repeats it. 'Ja, sexual.'

PDU steps behind the deckchair. In it sits the figure of a dummy, legs crossed, beach cap at an angle. It is another passenger snoozing in the sun.

PDU has found his victim.

'He's got something you want. He knows it. He knows what he's got and that you want it, that you would kill for it. But he doesn't give it to you. He doesn't open up. He plays hard to get. He plays the coquette. So now you have to woo him.'

Chris watches with interest. PDU demonstrates on the dummy as he takes Chris through the process of the torture.

'You take it slowly, so that you don't spoil the climax. You are tender in the beginning. You stroke him gently with a live wire, avoiding the sweat pools of his terror, so that you don't blow a fuse and put the whole place into darkness.'

The dummy doesn't have a chance. Chris watches with intense interest.

'Then you feel the skin and touch it and pinch it and squeeze it with the tips of your fingers.' The dummy writhes under his terrible touch. 'Now he's getting hot. Hot and sweaty, and he tries not to scream because that would spoil it for him. Because he's playing hard to get! But you don't let up.

'You take parts of his body and mould them together ... and stretch them ... and then, just as it looks like he's going to crack, you take out your gun and slide it into his open mouth!'

The dummy has the gun in its open mouth; it flails with arms and legs, but PDU doesn't let up.

'Feeling the teeth chattering against the cold metal. And then you pull him up towards you and whisper sweet nothings in his ear.' He has his mouth close to the head of the dummy. His voice drops to a rasp. '"Talk to me, boytjie? Tell me everything I want to know. Or else I will have to come to the end of my wooing." And then your finger tightens on the trigger and he feels your pressure against him and then the gun goes off in his open mouth!

'Click!

'Not bang. Not the climax yet.

'But the bastard has cracked up by now and spoils all the fun, because now he blabs and blubbers and tells you everything you want to know. The names. The addresses. The secrets.'

PDU drops the lifeless dummy to the deck.

'And you know something?'

Chris snaps out of his trance of fascination.

'What?'

'You never feel satisfied, man. It's like being with a woman with no heart. There's no heart in the thing.' He gives the dummy a final, fatal kick. Looks back at Chris's newspaper. 'Well, at least they put in a nice picture of us.'

'Yes, but what came first: the hosepipe or the drip?'

PDU laughs.

'You'd better watch more carefully next time.' He checks his watch. 'Which is in about twenty minutes. See you down in steerage?'

Chris nods.

'Okay. I just want to shave and change my shirt.' He moves off and then stops and turns. 'Oh, by the way? What did the seagull say when it flew into Table Mountain?'

He gives a seagull's cry.

'Fuuuuuucccccccckkkkkkkkkkk!!!!!!!'

*   *   *

With our two deckchairs and ocean-liner bunting, it was an easy show to tour, and the recorded soundtrack of shipboard effects gave the occasion a reality that took everyone back to the harbour, waving at Union-Castle ships and saying goodbye. At the end, the *Bothatanic* hits something in the sea and sinks, while Captain Botha makes a speech from the lopsided bridge. There is, he tells us, no crisis. Everything is under control.

We opened at the Market Theatre in Johannesburg on the night of the general election of 1987. After the performance, we gathered at my house in Forest Town. I'd moved to a rambling mansion next to the zoo, while letting the Melville house. We watched the election results on TV and saw the opposition PFP almost disappear overnight. The terror of PW's Total Onslaught had won. Whites closed their eyes and let the Bothas steer the ship of state into the whirlpool of fear.

Again, no censorship.

It had become a running gag that the empty four seats in row C were kept for members of the PCB who hadn't turned up. Possibly they'd lost interest.

An interviewer asked me about *Rearranging the Deckchairs on the SA Bothatanic.*

'Pieter, what is your message?'

'There is no message. It's just entertainment.'

The fact that it was entertainment seeped with blood and lies just made it real and truly South African.

10

CRY FREEMANDELA
– THE MOVIE

It was on my way back to Johannesburg after a season in Toronto with *Adapt or Dye* in November 1987 that the unsolicited new show emerged. We were to make a return visit to the Market with *Deckchairs*. It would open in three weeks. In London I had seen the Richard Attenborough film *Cry Freedom*, about anti-apartheid newspaper editor Donald Woods and his friendship with Black Consciousness leader Steve Biko, and his flight from South Africa after Biko was murdered. The film worked well in London. It was made for a middle-class white English audience, who came out horrified that such terrible things could happen to black people so far away. It convinced them not to buy South Africa's Outspan oranges or drink wine from the Cape. Donald Woods's flair for extremes and his theatrical swim across a raging river in flood made for exciting cinematic drama. That it had actually taken place in the drought-ravaged Lesotho border area was another matter.

For me the target was clear: the liberal world was discovering the struggle against apartheid as a glamorous way to make money, to win awards and to rewrite the facts to fit the fantasy. American and British accents tried to disguise themselves in ridiculous attempts at South African sounds. Blacks were cast as blacks, meaning soon-to-be dead bodies, and foreign box office stars became the heroes of a struggle that had been restructured on the drawing board.

I planned my own onslaught on the plane, oiled by glasses of red wine poured by supportive SAA koffiemoffies. It would be about the making of a feature film called *Cry Freemandela – The Movie*. Chris and I would play the various parts, me starting as 'Dickie Attenborough', gushing 'lovey' and 'darling' with each breath. Chris would be Donald Woods. He would also play 'Nelson', as played by Hollywood star James Coburn, to whom he had more than a passing likeness. Winnie Mandela was to be cast. The actress had to be box office. A star. So Joan Collins would play her, and I would play Joan Collins. The first time Ms Collins realises that Winnie is black is when her two babies turn out to be dolls that aren't white! British Prime Minister Margaret Thatcher, who had recently branded Nelson Mandela a terrorist and was therefore a friend of PW, impersonates all the SA Police, wearing huge boots and a rubber pig snout over her face. In the end she transforms into her hero PW Botha, resplendent in Caesar-like laurels and a deep red velvet cloak. PW then turns the cloak inside-out to show the banned ANC colours, which he wears! He ends the show by suggesting that he will go down the road to Pollsmoor Prison, unlock the cell door and invite Mr Mandela for lunch, so they can talk together like normal people and solve the problems of our land. This was a devastating ending: so obvious and, at the time, so impossible.

The first reality check was being told it was illegal to print the words FREE MANDELA as part of the newspaper adverts. The show had to be known as CRY FREEMANDELA – one word – in order to be allowed!

Chris and I rehearsed for ten days. The setting was four panels, each depicting the background of a major scene. The border hills and river. The prison for Biko and Winnie. We cast a young black actor in the third role – that of clapper boy and general gofer, not an unknown job description for blacks in South African and international films. He had no name. He would do the menial jobs for these white stars who were representing his struggle. The actor, Sello Maake ka Ncube, also portrayed Buthelezi in the final scene of the 'film' – causing the leader of the Inkatha Freedom Party to react with fury and indignation.

Ironically, while Evita was nowhere to be seen during those two years of *Bothatanic* and *Cry Freemandela*, people kept saying how much they enjoyed her performance. She was on video, she appeared on TV and in the press. There was no way I could pretend she didn't exist. But without her involvement I think I produced my best work. And another thing was sure: Mrs Evita Bezuidenhout would not come and see *Cry Freemandela – The Movie*!

*　　*　　*

Go to Cape Town's windy Foreshore and put yourself into the Nico Malan Theatre in early 1988. A bastion of what was legal and correct. In other words: white and Afrikaans. The only reason I had this space to perform in was because I'd learnt to go into the CAPAB office a year before, with the full rental in advance, in cash, and sign a contract that says: An Evita Bezuidenhout Show.

By the time you arrive with a cabaret about the end of the world, it's too late. They've taken the money. The contract is signed. And if Evita's not there, but Pieter-Dirk Uys is? Who will take whom to court?

There they sat for the first performance. Five hundred and fifty people. Looking at the stage while bland local music played in the background. Nothing threatening on stage, just the four framed pictures and a figure in a chair, his back to the audience. The chair has a name on it.

RICHARD ATTENBOROUGH.

Sir Richard wears his familiar panama hat. He is reading a newspaper, probably the *Guardian*. The muzak stops and suddenly the theatre is filled with a magnificent version of 'Nkosi Sikelel'iAfrika', the ANC anthem from the soundtrack of his film *Cry Freedom*. The anthem is banned in South Africa. The audience must sit through the whole four minutes of it.

Do they stay seated? Do they stand in respect? Do they walk out?

Dickie turns to the audience as the anthem ends. His huge spectacles are framed by greying sideburns. He enthuses and gushes in character.

'Hello my darlings! I am Sir Richard Attenborough, Oscar-winning director of such masterpieces as *Oh What a Lovely War*, *A Chorus Line*, *Gandhi*, etc. etc. etc.'

He applauds himself, then stops.

'Thank you for not applauding. No, my loves, there is a time for clapping and cheering and compliments, but it's obviously not here and now. No, darlings, this is a most profoundly deep and meaningful moment.'

He stands up and lowers his voice. The audience leans forward.

'Here you are, sharing with me the birth of a new and great masterpiece, and, frankly, if I'd known you were coming, I would have rehearsed some really splendid tears ...'

He clicks his fingers and the black clapper boy steps forward.

The boy announces gravely:

'Sir Richard breaks down. Take 320.'

He claps the board and Dickie breaks down in familiar sobs and tears.

'I humbly feel such profound depth of emotion that I'm in floods of tears, darlings, floods of tears.' He calls sharply: 'Props!'

The clapper boy hands him a large handkerchief. Dickie blows his nose.

'Cut. Print. Keep that for my appearance at the United Nations. Now, where was I?'

The clapper boy prompts him.

'"... a profoundly deep and meaningful moment ..."'

Dickie takes up his pose.

'Ah yes. The scene that you are going to see being shot today is part of my latest film *Cry Freemandela – The Movie*. Some call it a small film. Others a mere trifle, but, in its own dear way, it is a great personal statement of commitment to freedom, and a commercial indictment of the universally accepted intrinsic evil of apart-hate. And if it doesn't get me another Oscar, I'll make a musical about the life of Hendrik Verwoerd starring Michael Jackson.'

The clapper boy presents him with an Oscar.

Dickie takes it tearfully.

'Oh, thank you, my darlings, but really, I'm not worthy of this. After all, I'm just an old-fashioned British liberal Mary Poppins when it comes to the old underdog, but I'm moved beyond words ...'

He is moved beyond words, which leads to the first pause, during which he weighs up the Oscar shrewdly and mutters:

'A bit light, isn't it?'

He pulls himself together and gushes forth.

'My darlings, what you're about to see in *Cry Freemandela – The Movie* are the facts: the lives of men and women embroiled in their struggle for freedom. The eternal heartbreaking story of bloody sacrifice and never-ending love, of unbridled, unchristian, unspeakable evil and repulsive, vicious, menacing Afrikaners.'

He takes a deep breath in order to rhapsodise further.

'South Africa – where the repressed black heart beats with the shining light of hope, while the pasty white skins of their oppressors ooze and ejaculate the stench of their racist Nazism – and because they wouldn't allow me to talk on their pathetic SABC-TV when I was in South Africa some years ago, South Africans won't see my film, so fuck them ...'

The clapper boy holds up a newspaper poster: BIKO FILM PASSED. Yes, it had been banned, but then was allowed to be seen in selected cinemas.

Dickie is slightly taken aback by this.

'Oh? So South Africans will see my film! But fuck them anyway.'

He glares at the clapper boy.

'Right, is that everything?'

The boy nods. Dickie beams at the audience.

'Now remember, darlings, don't get carried away. What you see here is only the recreation of the facts. What really happened was far worse than you can ever imagine.'

The clapper boy attracts his attention and whispers: 'The list of people to thank?'

Dickie remembers.

'Ah yes, there are always people to thank. Let me use this opportunity to thank Dr Malan, Advocate Strijdom, Dr Verwoerd and John Vorster for their tireless brutal dedication to institutionalising apart-hate and therefore creating the raison d'être for this film. And without whom *Cry Freemandela – The Movie* would never have needed to be made in the first place.

'Also, thank you to Mr PW Botha, who could've released Nelson Mandela before we released this film, thus making me horribly irrelevant and the film rather old hat. But, bless him, quite predictable to the end.

'Thank you also to the hero of my film, Nelson Mandela. Thank you, Nelson my love, for staying exactly where you are, because we all think you're seven foot tall anyway.

'Then, of course, I must thank some of my old chums who dropped everything just to be in my wonderful film. They are all acting for free – yes, my darlings, they have all donated their huge salaries to the ANC Non-Violent Education Fund to keep comrades in Scotch whisky and Havana cigars for another year.

'Thanks to Ronnie Reagan, who brings his great gift for turning tragedy into farce.

'Thanks to beautiful Joan Collins, who has agreed to leave the cast of *Dynasty* to portray another great legend, Mrs Winnie Mandela.

'Thanks to James Coburn, who has come out of retirement in B-films to play the great Nelson himself.

'And to Maggie Thatcher who, as a great authority on South Africa and Law and Order, has offered her services without even having read the script!

'What a splendid cast! What a spectacular explosion of talent! Of course it goes without saying that I spent months auditioning thousands of extremely talented blacks for the leads in this film, but alas we could find no one.'

The clapper boy tries to attract his attention. Dickie ignores him.

'And of course, last but not least, a deep thanks to the author of the book on which my film is based. Donald ... eh ...'

He can't remember the name. The clapper boy helps.

'Woods?'

'Donald Woods, who plays himself throughout *Cry Freemandela – The Movie*.'

There is now a title sequence accompanied by dramatic music, with Dickie narrating what we see. Slides of South Africa, showing the locations for the film.

Dickie conducts the drama from the side.

'Cannon Films ... Casspir Pictures ... Twentieth Century Hippo proudly presents ...' We all read the title of the film. 'A true story within the framework of the present State of Emergency. Long shot of the surf crashing onto the rocks. Seagulls. Table Mountain. All right Larry, take it away.'

*   *   *

The clapper boy presents his board and announces:

'Sir Laurence Olivier narration: introduction. Take 1!'

On the soundtrack the familiar voice of the Great Olivier.

'South Africa ... the soft sensual underbelly of the tough and tortured continent that is Africa ... the paradise of the wild and the playground of the free buck and antelope, the lourie and the dove.

'It is still ... quiet ... time ceases to exist. Life is a mere buzz track to existence.

'And then ... suddenly ...'

In strides the policeman in his familiar blue uniform with guns and attitude.

'Okay, you fucking communists and kaffir bastards! Move your arses! Die Boere is hier!'

He threatens the audience, who recognise him with gales of relieved laughter.

'This is your final warning under the present State of Emergency. There is too much liberal multiracial undercurrents here. Everybody will listen to what I has to say, and, if you don't, we will take you to Caledon Square Police Station and kick you in the balls, or smack you around the tits if you're a meisie, and/or throw you out of the seventh-floor window, which is anyway your own fault, you bleddie communist bastards!'

He goes into a frenzied dance, aware of the lights and the action.

The clapper boy has been watching and now applauds the effort. The policeman regains his threatening pose.

'And what's so funny?'

The clapper boy bursts out laughing.

'You. You think you'll get a part in this film as a policeman?'

The policeman nods confidently.

'I've been practising for months, in and out of the townships. I'm perfect for the part.'

The clapper boy agrees.

'Ja-nee, but they're just getting people from overseas to act in this film. They didn't want me and I'm perfect for some of the parts too.' He acts with powerful Black Power intensity. '*Amandla!*'

The policeman warns him.

'Hey, don't become a riotous assembly!' Then he sighs. 'But my pa is a policeman and so is my uncles and my grandpa. I come from a long line of sersants.'

The clapper boy is sympathetic.

'Listen man, anyone can play a sersant. Try for one of the leading parts, my bra.'

He shows the depressed policeman the script. The cop mouths the names of the characters.

'Mandela ... Biko ... Woods ... no man, these are all banned people! They can't be quoted. Nothing. Only we can quote them to prove how dangerous they are. Hey!' He brightens up. 'Here's a nice part: Captain de Wet, SAP. Who is playing that part?'

'Sylvester Stallone.' The clapper boy has another idea. 'Listen man, you must try and attract the producer's attention. Jump the queue.'

'Who do I beat up?' the cop asks, looking around.

'No man,' soothes the clapper boy. 'Don't be violent. Don't be obvious. Tell a joke! Make the producer laugh. That's how I got this job. I told some jokes.'

The policeman looks pleased.

'I'm good at that.' He takes a deep breath and starts: 'Why did the chicken cross the road ...?'

'Political jokes, my bra! This is a political film.'

The policeman is perplexed. He thinks for some time. Ponders.

'Political? Political ...' Suddenly he is inspired. 'Why do black people have such flat noses? Because they do so much window-shopping.' He laughs. And so does the audience.

The clapper boy just shakes his head.

'Listen man, let me help you. What is a zebra?'

'A zebra?' The policemen visibly thinks, worried that he will be trapped. 'Type of bok.'

'A zebra is a victim of enforced racial integration.'

The policeman is confused.

'Oh. I thought it was a bok.'

The clapper boy tries again.

'What is a guerrilla?'

'Easy,' laughs the cop. 'Your grandpa!' He laughs alone. 'Okay, what is a guerrilla?'

'A South African soldier in Angola,' is the confident answer.

The audience doesn't laugh either.

The policemen shakes his head. 'No, that's too hard. Can't I attract the producer's attention some other way?'

'You could hide in the back of a truck and then jump out of the packing cases and shoot at the school kids.'

This had happened recently in a local black township not far away from the Nico Malan Theatre, when security police hid in a delivery truck and opened fire on marchers. The audience is very quiet.

The policeman looks unhappy.

'They've stopped that. Spoilsports. No man, I want to be a film star. Or on TV. I'll do anything to be world famous.'

The clapper boy pats him on the shoulder.

'You are world famous,' he smiles. 'Just keep on being yourself.'

* * *

The familiar dulcet tones of the British Prime Minister are heard.

'No no no, I've said it before and I'll say it again ...'

Margaret Thatcher walks on, dressed in familiar Conservative blue suit with black bag and big blonde hair, slightly stooped. The bull in the china shop. She is speaking on the phone.

'My stand on sanctions is final. The Boers are reforming. They're now allowing people of different races to marry, on condition that they promise not to live together.'

The policeman gets into professional mode.

'Where? I'll kill the bastards!'

Maggie is not pleased. She booms into the phone.

'Hang on, the place is teeming with overkeen extras. It's just like the House of Commons. Now don't worry, Nancy, I'll give Ronnie the message when he's ...'

She looks at the canvas chair with Ronald Reagan's name on it. In it sits a small ventriloquist's dummy dressed like a cowboy. It looks just like the President of the USA. Ronnie is asleep. The audience sees this too.

Maggie tells a lie.

'... when he's free. He is deep in conference at the moment. Goodbye.'

She hands the phone to the policeman.

'Please take this phone and tap it, will you?' She looks at his outfit with interest. 'What a splendid uniform you're wearing. Made in Birmingham, no doubt.' She checks the label and is pleased. (Mrs Thatcher had recently flaunted her contempt for sanctions by allowing the South African Police to buy their uniforms from a factory in Birmingham.)

'You see how wrong sanctions would be?' she purrs. 'You'd be naked!'

'No, sis!' gasps the policeman.

Maggie looks out at the audience.

'What a splendid multiracial crowd.'

By now the Nico Malan Theatre complex had given up trying to keep its audiences white. There was always a smattering of black and brown faces to be seen.

The policeman also looks out and pulls a face.

'It makes me want to vomit. Sis. Multiracial.'

Maggie pats his arm comfortingly.

'Yes,' and she quotes: '"... multiracial, all races welcome, right of admission reserved ..." It's an old British trick.'

She looks around and sees the canvas chair with her name on it. Calls to the clapper boy.

'Would you please bring madam her chair, you poor suppressed black bugger.'

The clapper boy brings her chair and the British Prime Minister sits.

The policeman is impressed. He asks the black man.

'Is she the producer?'

The clapper boy laughs.

'The producer, the director, the censor, the critic – but not of this film. But tell her a joke. Practise!'

The policeman goes over to the future Lady Thatcher.

'Hey, Lady? What did Adam say to Eve?'

She keeps the smile on her bored face. So he tells her.

'"Stand back! I don't know how big this thing gets!"'

Maggie just smiles. The policeman shrugs and leaves dejected. Then Maggie slowly looks out at the audience.

'What thing?'

As the audience roars with laughter, she shades her eyes from the lights and calls out into the dark. 'Sir Richard, are you there?'

His voice booms out from the speakers. It is on tape, as I'm playing both parts at this moment!

'Thank you, Maggie, but you're not in this reel of the film yet, my darling. This is still the 1970s. I'm trying to establish South Africa, the realities of the brutal policies of John Vorster and his thugs, and then move to East London, introducing the Hoods.'

He gets the Woods' name wrong.

Maggie is perplexed.

'Aren't the hoods usually in Pretoria?'

Dickie corrects his slip.

'... the Woods family, and Donald Woods's friendship with the black man.'

Maggie is apologetic and yet not subservient.

'Oh, Sir Richard, I don't know any black men. I don't care for Robert Mugabe and Kenneth Kaunda. Well, he reminds me so much of a monkey!'

Dickie decides not to go there. He carries on regardless.

'You come on in reel two ...'

'Yes, and that's my point, Sir Richard.' Her honeyed tones hint at a cobra ready to strike. 'When I said I would assist in the authenticity of this film, I didn't expect to be cast as a brutal Afrikaner policeman. Surely there are some of these extras who are just dying to play the part?'

She looks into the audience and asks.

'Is there anyone here who could play a white South African with a clear conscience?'

No one offers.

'I thought not. I'll just have to do it. But, Sir Richard?'

She looks deep into the darkness beyond the lights.

'Is there any chance of me portraying someone nice?'

Dickie's had enough of her whining.

'Maggie, don't be so picky! Of course there were nice people in South Africa then. I'm sure there are now. But history will never give them a thought. The world is bored with Nazis and Auschwitz. Thank God we now have Afrikaners and Soweto.'

'But surely it's not that simple ...'

Dickie cuts her short.

'Get back to Number 10 Dressing Room, Maggie. This is my film and I'm in charge! And by the way, Maggie?' Mrs Thatcher stops on her offended exit. 'You look gorgeous on the monitors. Ten years younger at least and prettier than Princess Diana's mother-in-law.'

Maggie leaves the stage flattered. Dickie smirks.

'Silly old bitch!' He calls for attention. 'Stand by please. Next scene is East London, the mid-1970s. Is Donald Whatsisname standing by?'

The clapper confirms.

'Standing by!'

'Settle down please.'

'Silence on set,' calls the clapper. 'Silence ... silence ...'

'Stand by for a take!' calls the director.

'Stand by for a take ... stand by ... stand by ...' echoes the black assistant.

'Mark it!' commands the Sir.

'The Woods House in East London. Scene 1. Take 1!"

The clapper claps and the focus is on the backdrop of the house in East London.

Richard Attenborough calls:
'Action!'

* * *

Suburban muzak fills the air. The lights are warm and familiar. We all feel at home. Donald Woods appears in his cardigan and cravat. Chris plays him, having changed from the policeman. He holds a large black toy cat.

Donald beams out at the audience and, as the music fades, confides in us.

'The name is Woods. Donald Woods. My wife is called Wendy Wood [Wendywood is a suburb of Johannesburg] and we live here in East London where I run a newspaper. This is our cat Natalie Woods [the American film star had recently drowned]. Our children are called the Vienna Woods.

'We're just an ordinary, happy, white liberal South African family who live in a spacious, architect-designed house with a swimming pool, two cars and a live-in maid called Evalina.'

He stops and peers into the dark.

'Sir Richard? I changed the script here a bit, added some funny bits, you know – universal references: Natalie Wood, a live-in maid ... Sir Richard?'

The director is not pleased.

'Just stick to my brilliant adaptation of your dreary book, Thingummy, my darling. Stand by: Take 2!'

The clapper boy claps inches from Donald's nose.

'The Woods' House in East London. Scene 1. Take 2!'

Donald takes a deep breath and starts again.

'The name is Woods. I am a white South African and as such could have been played by Robert Redford, but he said no, and so here I am playing myself. I have changed radically as a person in the last few pages. I once used to be a liberal. I allowed our maid to watch *Dynasty* while she was doing the ironing. But now, thanks to the terrible things that this government is doing to black people all around us, we have become progressives: now we do the ironing, while our maid watches *Dynasty*.

'Because I am paying income tax to this hated Vorster regime, I feel like a collaborator, but what can I do? My activism is restricted to writing anti-apartheid editorials in my own paper. Like so many white progressives, I was committed. Totally dedicated to evading responsibility.

'Until this page.' He steps forward with intent to share his Damascus road conversion. 'Yesterday, as far as I was concerned, "forced removals" were just a painful form of contraception, but not any more. Now we believe in

real power-sharing: we help the maid do the washing up, while we all watch
Dynasty!'

Sir Richard interrupts tensely.

'Oh darling, skip all the boring crap about your awakening from
complacent white liberal to relatively angry moderate wanting the best of
both worlds. Skip the meeting with Steve Biko and the cause of Black
Consciousness ...'

'But that's what it's all about ...'

Dickie shuts him up.

'Not commercial! Let's get a smidgen of sex and violence.'

Donald is flummoxed.

'Sex and violence?'

Mrs Margaret Thatcher enters enthusiastically.

'Oh goodie, that's obviously my cue.' She greets the dumbstruck Donald.
'Hello, my name is Margaret Thatcher and I'm a radical British Prime Minister
in my third term, because I am radically right. Like your PW Botha, I am often
labelled a dictator, which is absurd. Unlike your PW Botha I sometimes take
consultations. If a woman like Eva Perón, with no ideals, can get as far as she
did, just think how far I can get with the great ideals that I have. And who
are you? Are you someone important?'

Donald needs to put her in the picture. His introduction sounds like 007.

'The name is Woods. Donald Woods. My wife is called Wendywood and
our children are the Vienna Woods ...'

There is a pause. Maggie seems to have dozed off. Then her smile returns
automatically.

'Woods? Any relation to Sir Henry Woods of Promenade Concert fame?'

Donald is bashful.

'No, I'm just an ordinary person.' He adds under his breath, so that
Dickie can't hear, 'Sir doesn't really want to be upstaged by anyone famous.
He doesn't even allow us to drop names.'

Maggie looks at Donald with a bored smile.

'Can you?'

Donald thinks and shakes his head. He can't.

She is irritated.

'Are we in this scene together?'

She takes the script and reads: '"Donald is declared a banned person and
his family is subjected to a campaign of intimidation by the security police."
Ah yes, that's me.'

Dickie's voice brings us all back to the work at hand.

'Stand by for a take, please. Now remember, Maggie, this is the mid-seventies. The policeman you play doesn't have the total power they have today. We are only at the start of the present neo-fascist state ...'

'Sounds just like home!' breathes the Iron Lady.

'Mark it!'

The clapper obeys.

'Donald Woods is banned. Scene 43. Take 1!'

'Stand by for the narration of the scene. Marlene?'

Out of the darkness flows the sexy, deep voice of Marlene Dietrich.

'I'm wready, Wrichard, wready ...'

'Action!'

*   *   *

In shadow play behind a screen, we see the action as it is described by the great German legend.

Marlene speaks, low and inviting, as if she is singing and yet there is no song.

'It was a day like any other day. And yet it wasn't.

'It looked like a house like any other house, but no, it ain't.

'They should've looked like any other policeman, but they couldn't.

'They were John Vorster's policemen – and where have all the flowers gone?

'They bwroke down the door of the house and stampeded into the livingwroom, but it was the wong house!

'When will they ever learn?

'Eventually Donald Thingummy stood on the stoep of his house and called out ...'

Donald stands on the stoep of his house and calls out.

'Hello? Sergeant Swanepoel? Are you looking for me?'

Maggie Thatcher enters in the guise of that policeman, still in her blue suit, but wearing heavy police boots, a London policeman's helmet and a rubber pig snout over her nose. She carries a truncheon.

'Are you Donald Woods, editor of the famous *Daily Mirror*?'

'The *Daily Dispatch*,' Donald corrects her.

'Really?' Maggie loses her character for a moment. 'It says *Daily Mirror* in my script.'

'No,' insists Donald, who knows where he works. 'It's just the very ordinary *Daily Dispatch*, really.'

Maggie understands.

'Maybe they're trying to give you a bit more glamour. Oh, never mind, who cares.'

She gets back into the character of Sergeant Swanepoel.

'Donald Woods, you are hereby declared a banned person!'

Donald is shocked,

'But what about my golf?'

Maggie bulldozes her announcement with familiar edge, reading from her official form.

'You are now a banned person, which means you are restricted to your home and can't be in the room with more than one person at the same time.'

Donald is appalled.

'But I'm a white person!'

Maggie shrugs and smiles graciously.

'That's the law against you liberal bastards ...' She stops, having lost the character of Sergeant Swanepoel. She regains the guttural tones, '... you bleddie bastard!'

Donald is beside himself.

'But what about Natalie Woods?' The black cat is still snuggled in his arms. 'Can she be in the room with me?'

Mrs Thatcher peers at the cat.

'Is she a person, or is she a person?'

'She's a cat.'

Maggie now recognises the cat.

'Oh, a little kitty? How sweet.' She confides intimately. 'You know, I also had a black kitty like this in the days when I still rode a broomstick.' She suddenly hits the cat with her policeman's truncheon and, in the voice of the sergeant, roars forth. 'Blerrie kommunist poes!' Then she is racked by a coughing fit. When she recovers she is out of breath. 'Oh dear Lord, I find this Afrikaans accent so difficult!'

Donald shakes his head.

'But you don't sound Afrikaans. You sound more Cockney.'

Maggie pats him gently on the arm.

'I suppose it's because most of these scenes are set in east London ...'

Donald studies her face carefully.

'And that nose is not quite right for the part of Sergeant Swanepoel. Actually, the nose makes you look just like ...'

Maggie has dropped her act. She looks defeated and pulls off the pig's snout.

'Hendrik Verwoerd, yes. And he wasn't even South African. And another thing: there were also black policemen at the time, not just white Neanderthal

Boerboys.' She sighs and peers into the dark auditorium. 'Oh pish! Sir Richard doesn't seem to be bothered with authenticity.' She looks back at her script and reads slowly. '"Donald Woods, you have been placed under house arrest, because you are a liberal anti-government communist bastard and will be punished …"'

She takes a deep breath and replaces the pig's snout. Then in her best Afrikaans accent:

'"… you bleddie anti–South African bastard!"'

Donald backs away.

'I'm not anti–South African, Sergeant Swanepoel. I'm just anti-apartheid.'

Maggie's sergeant is confused.

'Hey?'

'I'm not against a non-racial South African future. I'm just against institutionalised discrimination.'

Maggie wags a finger at him.

'Then you're in the wrong place. Go to Australia!'

'Australia?'

'Oh yes,' agrees Mrs Thatcher as Swanepoel. 'In Australia they have a system of institutionalised discrimination applied to all South African citizens wishing to visit there.' She looks down at the script and lifts her truncheon. '"And don't talk back, you piece of liberal rubbish!"' She sighs. 'Oh God, who wrote this dialogue?'

Donald shrugs.

'History?'

Maggie becomes the policeman.

'Voertsek!'

She beats Donald mercilessly with the truncheon, and kicks him with her boots. He tries to escape.

'No wait …' he cries, but she traps him and beats him again. He appeals to the director.

'Sir Richard? I was never beaten by the police …'

Maggie stops her performance and leans towards him.

'Oh, hush dear, they'll pay you another thousand dollars.'

Donald thinks for a moment, then throws himself at her mercy.

'Beat me! Beat me!'

She does so with relish.

'Cut!'

Dickie's crisp order ends the scene. Maggie steps back, while Donald lies whimpering into the cat on the floor.

'Very nice, very nice ...' the director repeats.

Maggie flexes her arms.

'Very invigorating. Like aerobics. One should do it to music.'

She sits in her chair.

Donald crawls out of the limelight to nurse his wounds. He approaches the clapper boy, who has been sitting on a box reading a paper. Donald hopes for sympathy but gets none.

'Being banned like that would have caused most ordinary people to jettison their moral convictions, you know.'

The clapper boy doesn't take his eyes off the paper.

'You don't say.'

Donald nods in agreement with himself.

'Would the world have known about all this if it wasn't for me? I wonder ...'

The clapper boy turns his page and yawns.

'We are all very grateful.'

Donald obviously isn't getting anywhere here. He looks at the audience and comes towards them, hugging his cat and looking for sympathy.

'It was when my freedom was taken from me that I became aware of those around me who were so used to their freedom. I couldn't talk to them. They didn't hear me. Natalie Woods was my constant companion, as I scratched out my story on scraps of paper, hoping for that chance to escape and tell the world about my friendship with a very extraordinary man.'

Maggie Thatcher comes up to him, waving her script with irritation.

'I can't make head or tail of this script,' she hisses. 'Maybe you can help me? What does "Third World" mean?'

'Third World?'

Donald looks at where she is pointing.

'Third World, yes.' Maggie shrugs. 'Bergvliet, I suppose.' (Bergvliet is a middle-class Cape Town suburb.)

The clapper boy folds up his newspaper.

'Third World is what you drive through before you reach Sun City.'

He laughs at their bemusement. Then he addresses the audience.

'The South African government's definition of independence is the right of designated ethnic groups to their own place in the sun: the Cape Sun, the Venda Sun, the Mmabatho Sun, the Thaba'Nchu Sun, the Wild Coast Sun ...'

He has run out of hotels.

'I want to do the scene in the Bloemfontein Sun,' suggests Dickie out of the darkness. 'The National Party Conference. Stand by.'

The clapper boy jumps to attention.

'National Party Conference, September 1977. Scene 46. Take 1!'

*   *   *

Martial music introduces a familiar flurry of South African flags.

The background is that of a National Party rally, with echoes of Nuremberg.

But Maggie stops the scene.

'Excuse me, I'm frightfully sorry to butt in here, but Sir Richard, I'm very confused about this scene. Firstly, my dear, far be it for me to interfere, for as you know, that's not in my nature. But I really feel you're approaching this scene from the wrong angle. Now I know you're a very fine film director, Sir Richard, but I really wish you'd stick to films and leave the politics to me. Now, when I directed the Falklands War, which, as you know, was a great success ...'

Richard Attenborough cuts her short.

'Thank you, Maggie. You can direct the sequel in Northern Ireland. Now can we get on with this scene?'

But Maggie won't give up.

'But Sir Richard, I'm supposed to play this Welshman James Thomas Jones in this scene, but I can't find the character anywhere. It's just Broederbonders having a braaivleis celebration and Jimmy Kruger making a speech.'

Donald Woods comes to her rescue.

'But that's him. Jimmy Kruger, John Vorster's Minister of Justice.'

Maggie is now very confused.

'But where is James Thomas Jones?'

'That's who Jimmy Kruger was when he arrived in South Africa from Wales as a baby and was adopted by the Krugers.'

Maggie takes it all in. The clapper boy is fascinated.

'You mean ...' she stutters, 'you mean this Jimmy Kruger is just another British policeman for me to play?'

'No,' assures Donald, 'he's playing himself.'

Maggie shakes her head.

'But I thought Jimmy Kruger was dead.'

Donald takes an urn out of the coffin that the clapper boy has rolled into view.

'Yes,' he says. 'Just throw his ashes to the winds of change while laughing.'

Maggie holds the urn uncomfortably. Peers into it and shrugs.

'But what do I say?'

'It's all on the urn,' Donald replies, pointing to the wording.

Maggie reads. "'It leaves me stone cold.'" She is impressed. 'And on a stone-cold urn too? There must be a God.'

'Not when Steve Biko needed him.'

Donald's words make Maggie Thatcher look up sharply.

'Steve who?' she snaps.

The moment of tension is broken by the clapper boy, who jumps to attention and holds out his board.

'National Party Conference. Scene 46. Take 2.'

The clapper claps.

A spot falls on Maggie with her pig's snout on. The clapper boy replaces her policeman's helmet with a black hat familiar on the heads of Afrikaner politicians. She pins on a badge that says JIMMY KRUGER.

What we hear is on tape. Maggie mouths the words as they are spoken.

We are at the National Party Conference and Minister of Justice Jimmy Kruger is speaking in Afrikaans.

'Meneer die Voorsitter, die man is dood in die hospitaal. Hoekom? Want hy was op 'n voedingstaking. Hy is dood aan honger. Dit wys hoe demokraties ons in hierdie land is, dat ons prisoniers die reg gegun word om hulself van hongersnood te laat sterf. Steve Biko se dood laat my koud!'

Huge laughter, applause and martial music greet the words, and then Maggie goosesteps off stage.

Then there is silence.

After this the audience has no sound to add.

*   *   *

The only person left on stage is the clapper boy.

He slowly steps forward, pulling the coffin into place.

'Stephen Bantu Biko was part of the future of this country, and when he died in police custody, everyone thought that would be the end of it.

'But it was just the beginning.

'If Steve Biko was still alive today, the anger so brutally ended would have been moderate in comparison to the black anger of today.'

He looks around the audience. By now the auditorium lights have gently been brought up so that everyone is aware of one another.

'You white South Africans have done something terribly wrong.

'You carry the guilt of countless horrors, and that guilt will be the terrible birthright of every white baby born in South Africa for generations to come.'

You could hear a pin drop, or a gun being cocked in the audience.

The clapper boy lifts his board. He gets back to work.

'A black man died. Scene 52. There will be only one take.'

The board claps the entire scene into blackout. Then a single spot makes a circle in the centre.

A large golliwog doll is thrown into the light, where it falls with a clank of chains, which are bundled round its legs and wrists. It lies in the spot.

In the silence.

Then a song is heard throughout the space.

Frank Sinatra singing a famous Cole Porter number, 'I get a kick out of you.'

Into the light step the booted feet of Maggie Thatcher, still playing her part of the policeman. And as the song takes us through the descriptions of the punishments that love will demand, the heavy boots crash into the golliwog, kicking it over and over, stamping on it, grinding it into the ground.

As the song comes to an end, red confetti floats down from Maggie's outstretched hands and covers the mutilated doll like flecks of blood.

The spot slowly dims into black.

There is no applause.

*   *   *

When the lights return, the clapper boy is sweeping up the remnants of the confetti.

Margaret Thatcher is now portraying a local doctor in a white coat, peering at the chained dead golliwog on the ground.

The clapper boy introduces the scene.

'The local doctor is called. Scene 53. Take 1.

The Jewish doctor just shakes his head.

'This is outrageous, absolutely outrageous! I was just sitting down to my dinner at home, when I was called out to look at a prisoner who slipped on the soap, or fell down the stairs, or banged his head on the ceiling, and what do I find? Another kaffir just sleeping off a drunken binge. You've seen one, you've seen them all.

'But listen, don't involve me with your film. The Medical Council has exonerated me of all malpractice, just as all the police involved have been promoted and acquitted, so life goes on.

'It's ten years after. So who cares about one black dying in the back of a police van on his way to Pretoria? Meanwhile, I'm doing very well here, being a doctor and making money, and nobody remembers. Not unless you dig up old cows out of the mass graves with this fucking film of yours and give me a reputation.'

Donald has appeared, still horrified by the happenings.

'But you are a doctor!' he shouts. 'You have a reputation!'

The doctor is not impressed.

'Don't be such a klutz, cunt!' he spits. 'Can't you see the woods for the shekels? Leave me alone, for God's sake, and let me die honourably in my bed anonymously!'

But Donald won't give up.

'What did your say your name was, Doctor?'

'Doctor X,' comes the reply.

'Doctor Lange? Doctor Tucker?'

Donald Woods uses real names. The doctor runs off screaming as the director ends the scene.

'Cut cut cut! Let's try that scene with a different accent tomorrow.'

Donald goes closer to the golliwog, which is lying broken and grotesque in the centre of the stage.

The clapper boy wheels the coffin closer. He picks up the chained doll-corpse and lays it in the coffin.

Donald comes towards the audience, drained and frightened.

'Disregarding constant police surveillance, the bugging of our home and the constraints of my banning order, which expressly forbade it, I started writing my book. The manuscript, which I keep hidden, is a biography of Steve, intended to reveal, following a laughable sham official inquest that totally exonerated those responsible, how he met his death.'

He looks around fearfully.

'But I have been warned by friends that I must either destroy the manuscript or somehow get it, myself and my whole family out of South Africa. But how?'

He asks that of the clapper boy, who thinks for a moment, then smiles.

'Donald gets a call. Scene 67. Take 1.'

The clapper boy presents Donald with a ringing telephone.

Donald carefully picks it up. A deep, monumental voice fills the air.

'My name is Orson Welles,' the voice booms. 'I can't talk. I'm dead. Get out now ...'

Donald looks around wildly, then at the phone. He talks carefully and as softly as he can.

'But they watch the house all day and night. They tap this phone ...'

There is a pause, and then Orson Welles replies:

'Yes, well, the reason I'm saying all this in Latin is therefore obvious. Donaldicus?'

Donald tries to make sense of the word. Then nods.

'Affirmicus!'

Orson Welles takes a deep noisy breath.

'Fuckofficus!'

The call ends.

Donald turns to the audience, excited but sad.

'Fuckofficus! Oh my God, is it now time to say totsiens to my home, my heart and my beloved Natalie Woods, my faithful dumb feline friend?' He gives the lump of fur a kiss. 'I must disguise myself and try and get out of here. Let's see …' He waits for help, looking at the clapper boy, who just shrugs. Donald repeats his words pointedly. 'Let's. See!'

The clapper boy understands and presents him with a globe of the world. Donald twirls it and studies his options.

'I could go to Jan Smuts Airport and take a Boeing …' He changes his mind. 'Who important will notice? A boat from the harbour?' He thinks. 'Too complicated. Maybe if I just run across the border?'

He considers the possibility.

'Ah? What's this funny dried-up river? Die Mossiepielspruit? The Raging Sparrow Cock River! That will read well in the *Guardian*!' He is now motivated. 'I'll carefully disguise myself as someone nondescript.' Then he remembers. 'But what about my precious manuscript? It's too bulky to hide on my slim person.'

The clapper boy presents him with his manuscript, which is too bulky to hide on his slim person.

He also hands Donald his beloved black cat and indicates that maybe the manuscript and the cat have some connection. Donald discovers to his amazement that the cat has a huge anus, big enough to hold …?

He gasps with joy.

'Ah, Natalie Woods, truly this man's best friend. I will hide … I will jam … I will ram the manuscript up your little kattegat where no one will dare probe, and so smuggle it out of South Africa!'

He calls musically to his wife.

'Come Wendywood, pack your minimum. Bring your bobotie recipe and the phone number of your cousin in Surbiton, England. Bundle the little Vienna Woods into their anoraks and meet me across the border in Lesotho!' He is ready to flee. 'Farewell!'

He holds out the black cat for the clapper boy to take and hold.

'And now, Natalie Woods, close your eyes and think of Hollywoods!'

He jams the precious manuscript up the cat's arse.

The director ends the scene.

'Cut. Okay darling, someone sew up the kitty-cat. Let's do yet another take on the scene we can't seem to get right. Stand by narration, Richard Posthumous Burton!'

The clapper boy is ready.

'The escape. Scene 68. Take 62!'

* * *

Dramatic music accompanies Richard Burton's snarly narration of the escape scene. In strobe light we see Donald escaping, clambering, swimming, nearly drowning.

'And so Donald Thingimy escaped from South Africa disguised as a noble nobody. He got away from the dogs ...'

Donald gets away from the dogs.

'... the police in pursuit ...'

Donald hides from the police in pursuit, but is stopped by Burton's aside.

'... actually they were after a bank robber, but never mind ...'

Donald is about to complain to the director, when Elizabeth Taylor's fifth husband carries forth the flow of action.

'... and soon found himself on the bank of the mighty Mossiepielspruit. With a mighty leap he immersed himself in the raging waters and made for Lesotho on the opposite shore, and freedom, leaving behind the full might of the South African onslaught baying ... baying for his blood. Crocodiles attacked him ...'

Donald is attacked by crocodiles.

'... and when he reached the shore he was roared at by an impala ...'

Donald reaches the shore and ducks as an Impala jet flies over.

'... but he was safe.'

Donald gives the thumbs up.

'He was in Lesotho.'

Donald dons a Basotho hat, as a Jewish African Princess totters past, in heels, beehive and sunglasses.

'Well, not quite, doll,' she twitters. 'Go up the road and turn left. That's Lesotho. The right? That's the road to Bloem. Bye!'

Once she leaves, the action can get back to serious tension.

Richard Burton sets the scene.

'In the Lesotho Sun, he is reunited with his family.'

Donald waves wildly across the audience to where his family is waiting.

'Wendywood? My little Woodlettes? What a relief! Let me slip into something a little less obvious and a touch more Gucci, and then I'll get our United Nations Refugee-Citizens-of-the-World Passports and free airflights at the expense of the British government. Wendy,' he sobs, 'we're going Home!'

He waves until they are gone, then he confides in us.

'I'll be on talk shows on the BBC and Channel 4 and *Good Morning America* and I'll lecture at universities and I might even meet famous film stars and they can autograph my manuscript and Robert Redford can play me in the film, and Natalie Woods ...?'

He looks down and realises that the cat is truly dead. Natalie Woods drowned in the raging river! 'Oh, my poor late ex-kitty! We'll have you restuffed and sent to Walt Disney Studios.'

He is now ready to take on the world, calling out to all and sundry as he leaves.

'Anyone looking for a movie to make? Film script for sale? South African Police Kill Detainee. Sequels quite possible!'

As he exits, the director gushes his pleasure.

'Cut! Print! Lovely, darlings! I'd like to rehearse the next scene. Are any of the major stars here yet?'

The clapper boy attracts his attention.

'Mr Attenborough? Miss Joan Collins is here!' He is very excited and turns to the audience. 'Ladies and gentlemen, Miss Joan Collins!'

*   *   *

The famous theme music from *Dynasty* crashes like waves on the beach. As befits a legend, Joan Collins enters with shoulder pads erect, earrings dangling, eyelashes bristling and long red nails at the ready. Alexis Carrington has arrived at the Nico Malan Theatre.

The audience goes wild, paying homage to the superstar they welcome into their homes every week when she chews up logic and linoleum in the most popular soap opera since the days of *Dallas*.

Joan poses and peers into the darkness.

'I can't stay long, darling. There is still a slot between six and seven in the morning that I'm not seen on SATV.'

There is no reaction from Attenborough. Joan Collins peers out again.

'Sir Richard? What part are you offering me? I haven't had time to have the script read to me. Dickie?' She smirks and mutters. 'Maybe I shouldn't think so small.' And calls again. 'Dick!'

He answers.

'Now Joanie, you realise what risks I've taken to cast you in this major starring role? You do realise?'

Joan flutters exquisitely.

'I'm very grateful, darling.'

Richard rubs it in.

'It's a huge part.'

Joan is pleased.

'I'm always grateful for those.'

'It could make you a star.'

Richard has gone too far. She turns on the ice.

'I am a star, thank you very much!'

Dickie grovels and mews.

'No, Joanie, wait! I mean, an ethereal star! Ingrid Bergman played Joan of Arc, Charlton Heston played Moses, Jeffrey Hunter played Jesus Christ ...'

Joan is impatient.

'What's left for me?'

Dickie is patience personified.

'How do I describe your character in the script?'

Joan thinks for a moment.

'Wasn't it a cross between Princess Diana and the Virgin Mary?'

'So?'

Joan cackles.

'I want to play someone real, Dickie, someone like Alexis!'

Dickie plays his trump card.

'What if I tell you that this woman commands the attention of millions of people?'

Joan Collins shakes her head.

'I'm too pretty to play Margaret Thatcher.'

'That she has been nominated for countless Nobel Peace prizes?'

'Too tall for Mother Teresa!'

'That she was on the cover of *Time* magazine and *Huisgenoot*?'

Joan stamps her foot.

'I won't play Zola Budd!'

'That she wears Calvin Klein originals?'

Joan gasps. This puts a different complexion on it entirely.

'That changes everything!' she purrs. 'Can I keep them?'

'Of course,' Dickie purrs in return. 'And all the jewellery!'

'Earrings? Rings? Bracelets?'

'You keep everything!' Dickie assures his superstar, who is now trembling with anticipation.

'Does this character wear necklaces?' she asks breathlessly.

Dickie laughs.

'Does she wear necklaces? Chunky designer numbers that glow in the dark?'

Some members of the audience titter nervously. They understand the double meaning, with its reference to the necklace method of execution recently touted by Winnie Mandela. Joan is oblivious and convinced.

'I'll do the part,' she announces. 'I want locations at the seaside. I want four hairdressers. I want champagne, oysters and a script.'

The clapper boy hands her the script.

She glares at him.

'And I want a chair.'

He positions her star chair, with the name JOAN COLLINS emblazoned on the back.

She sits down grandly.

'Merci.'

Joan Collins now opens the script.

'What is my character called? "Winnie"? Nice English name.'

The audience know she will play Winnie Mandela and enjoy the fact that she doesn't. The fact that Joan Collins (as played here by me) is the wrong colour doesn't as yet seem to be an issue.

Joan peruses the text with an eye for detail.

'Scene 1: I enter as a social worker. Meet the man I will marry. He is tall. Hair parted in the middle. We have our first date, Scene 2, but it is a disaster, as everyone comes up to him to discuss their problems.'

She closes the script angrily.

'Shit, who is this man? Blake Carrington? The Pope?' She sits for a moment, then opens the script again. 'We get married. Not the Pope. He gets arrested. I have a baby. Baby? Baby!'

The clapper boy brings her a baby. It's a doll. A black baby doll. While Joan holds it in one arm, she reads on.

'He is sentenced to life imprisonment. I have another baby. Another baby? Oh no, *Dynasty* was a picnic in comparison to this. Oh well …' She turns to the clapper boy. 'Darling, will you give me another baby?'

He is ready and presents her with her second black baby doll.

Joan Collins looks from one black baby to the other.

'Dickie? Is there something about this character you haven't told me? Two black babies? A husband in jail?'

But there is no reply from the director. Joan cannot hold the script, as her arms are full of offspring. The clapper boy holds the text as she reads:

'"I didn't marry a man. I married a Struggle ..."'

She reads the next page.

'Scene 56. December 1976. Minister of Justice Jimmy Kruger banishes me to Brandfort. Very dramatic, darling ...' The clapper boy turns the page. 'Scene 70: Winnie visits Nelson on Robben Island?' She becomes wistful and her eyes focus on the distance as she imagines.

'I can just see it, sitting in the waiting room of the maximum security prison, being stared at by the Nazis in their uniforms. Me, dressed in a simple black Calvin Klein original, hair just slightly off-centre. And then the crash of steel doors and there he is! My Nelson! Behind thick plate glass. We touch and kiss, with glass between us. I see his lips mouth my name: Winnie, Winnie, Winnie ...'

We hear the name echoed off in the dark.

'Winnie!'

Then James Coburn enters, playing the part of Nelson. But he is not dressed like Nelson Mandela in prison garb. He is in full uniform as Admiral Lord Horatio Nelson. Someone made a mistake!

But James Coburn knows how to deliver a performance in one take.

'Winnie, your Nelson has arrived!' he swaggers. 'Shiver me timbers and swash my buckle. Walk my plank and haul my keel.' With an impersonation that borrows from Captain Hook and Captain Bligh, Horatio Nelson strides the stage like a colossus.

Joan Collins is furious.

'James Coburn? What the hell are you doing in *Cry Freemandela – The Movie*? And dressed like that?'

'Land ahoy!'

James as Horatio espies Joan, hands on hips and furious.

'Ha ha! What have we here? A pretty lass, a fulsome wench forsooth! Let me Braille over thee!' He runs his barnacled hands over her famous extremities. 'Ha, I'd know these cannonballs from anywhere! Joan Collins!'

She pulls away from his clawing grasp.

'Oh, go jump off your poopdeck, James!'

James Coburn is delighted at his find.

'Joan Collins. The American Open!'

'The British Open, if you don't mind!' She narrows her eyes at him and wants to curse. 'James ... bloody Coburn! This is a serious film and I'm a serious actress!' His lopsided smile makes her think again. 'Now ... again ... and I hope someone will discover me again! Someone like Spielberg or Femini ..." Coburn doesn't detect the misnomer. 'But I can't play this Winnie Whatsername with you mooning around me dressed like that! What are you going as?'

Coburn seems to dither until the clapper boy brings on his chair. The star points to his name.

'James Coburn!'

'No, fartface,' sniffs the Dynasty Doll, 'what character are you playing in this film?'

'James Coburn.'

The man knows where he stands.

'Just as I thought,' Joan sighs. 'You're in the wrong film.'

'No, I'm not,' drawls the veteran of countless hokum. 'I'm Lord Horatio Nelson. Kiss me Hardy!'

By now the majority of the audience have caught the joke and applaud wildly. But Joan will not take any pinches from this old rogue.

'Take your calloused claws off my siliconed posterior, you old has-been!' She disentangles her derriere from his probing hands. 'Ow! A pox on your box! You're not supposed to be Lord Nelson of Trafalgar!'

'I'm not?'

'No, darling, you're playing Nelson ...'

She hasn't read further than the first name. The clapper boy helps her out.

'Mandela.'

He hands her the script at the correct page.

James Coburn is now very perplexed and a bit hurt.

'You mean, I'm not Horatio Nelson?'

'No, James, you play ...' she reads from the open text '... "probably the most famous political prisoner in the world today, a man who has not been heard or seen for twenty-five years".'

The Hollywood legend nods.

'James Coburn.'

Joan carries on reading.

'... "the real leader of the South African people ..."' The penny drops for her too. 'South African? Good heavens.' She goes back to the information. '... "the Emperor of Azania ...?"'

James Coburn is pleased.

'Emperor?' Then he realises who that is. 'You mean, I play Pee Wee Whatsisname?'

Joan has once seen a picture of Mrs PW Botha.

'Not if I'm playing your wife!'

James Coburn has also seen the picture. He smiles ruefully.

'That's true. Okay, so what happens now?'

Joan studies the script for clues.

'Eh … it seems you did something naughty. You're in jail for life. You're also a banned person, which means you can't be heard.' She smiles at him. 'You can't be quoted by anyone. Not even me. So, darling, whatever you say is irrelevant.'

James Coburn looks deflated.

'Oh. So that's why my agent sent me up for the part.'

Joan whistles as she learns further information.

'It seems your picture may also not be seen!'

'You mean I don't exist?' For a Hollywood star this is worse than death.

Joan appeases him with a pat on his braided arm.

'Only as James Coburn.' She reads on. '"But Nelson Mandela exists in the minds of millions of people."' She thinks for a moment. 'Sir Richard said this film will bring about the immediate liberation of …' She looks at the script again to check. '… South Africa.'

James whistles his amazement.

'Well, I'll be blowed.'

She doesn't look up. 'Later darling.' Then she smiles with pleasure. 'Just think, we'll be filming in Cape Town!'

James Coburn has a moment of conscience.

'It's against my principles to go to South Africa,' he declares. 'Even as a character. Can't they change the setting of the film to somewhere more acceptable?' He thinks for a moment. 'Leningrad? Or Beirut?'

Joan tries to put him at ease.

'But everyone's making films in South Africa. Grace Jones's blond boy, Robert Vaughn, Anthony Hamilton, Oliver Reed …'

James nods gravely.

'Sure. He plays Rambo. Spends most of the time in the bars of Switzerland or Monte Carlo.'

'Oliver Reed as Rambo?' Joan isn't sure.

James is.

'Sure. Oliver Rambo.'

This rings a bell for Mrs Carrington-Colby-Dexter.

'Oliver Sambo!'

The clapper boy interjects politely.

'Oliver Tambo.'

Joan's had enough.

'Sir Richard?'

They both stare out into the darkness.

Margaret Thatcher's terrible voice fills the void.

'Sir Richard and I are embroiled in a script conference, Miss Collins. Why don't you and that old actor get on with rehearsing the Arrest Scene in the meantime?'

She then adds the kiss of death.

'Don't worry. Everything is under control.'

Joan and James wait for more, but there is no more.

'What is that Iron Lady doing up there?' whispers Joan.

The clapper boy laughs.

'Coup d'etat?'

They ignore him as usual.

'Come on, Coburn,' says Joan Collins. 'Let's take it from page 450. Before your arrest. You're a lawyer in Johannesburg and I come and see you one night at your office. You're deep in discussion with your associates, Oliver Tambo and Walter Sisulu, talking about the ANC …'

James Coburn interrupts her.

'Is that important? The ANC?'

Joan Collins laughs.

'My darling, if I'd known about the ANC, I wouldn't have had such a messy divorce.'

James Coburn thinks for a moment, then for another. Then another. And then laughs uproariously.

'Oh!!! Ante-nuptial contract!'

Joan calms him down.

'Okay! It's 4 a.m.! Suddenly there is a terrible banging on the door and Michael Caine as "Captain Groenewald" enters with the whole bloody South African Police Force …'

But no one enters.

They wait.

They look from left to right.

They are alone.

The clapper boy comes to the rescue.

'I'll stand in for them!' He beams at the audience. 'I've been looking forward to this moment ...'

He puts on the police helmet and calls.

'Action!'

*   *   *

Dramatic fight music erupts as the clapper boy revenges himself on the stars. He eventually beats James Coburn offstage, leaving a tearful Joan Collins preparing for her close-up.

'No! No! No ...' she sobs. 'Nelson, don't leave me ...' Her body is wracked with gasps as she cradles her head in her hands, carefully, so as not to smudge her make-up. Then, slowly, knowing the effect of the fluttering eyelashes, she softly speaks her aria:

'My husband has been dragged away and I am banished to the middle of nowhere, far away from hairdressers and delicatessens, where no fashion magazine or gossip columnist dare venture. But then, in the dead of night, with the clouds across the moon, I cross Table Bay in the south-easter wind and find you waiting for me ...'

She stands with arms outstretched, underscored by music from a romantic drama.

'... holding me while the violins play. And we walk, hand in hand on the beach, with the lights of Sea Point winking at us from the shore. And then we sit down for a candlelight dinner for two, Dom Perignon champagne, Beluga caviar and luscious oysters ...'

The clapper boy stops her. He is angry.

'No, Miss Collins, no! This is not a soap opera!'

She looks at him, alarmed. He doesn't want to frighten her, so he takes her hand and talks to her gently.

'This is a true story, an important story. You are portraying Winnie Nomzamo Mandela. Millions know her as Sis Winnie, but to me she's simply Mama. A lioness towering protectively over her cubs against the vicious human predators. She's being mercilessly skinned alive in public ...'

During this he pulls ethnic fabric round her, to cover her glittering finery, as well as the piece of cloth that folds into the famous turban.

'Please, Miss Collins, do it right ...'

While he dresses her, he sings a Xhosa song.

Joan stares ahead, allowing herself to be transformed. Eventually she stands there convincingly as Winnie Mandela, posed and dressed as in so many press pictures of the Mother of the Nation.

The clapper boy now holds up the script for Joan to read the lines.

"'But then I didn't marry a man. I married a Struggle ...'"

The clapper boy moves away with the script and a light falls on Joan, suggesting prison bars on the floor behind her.

'When my husband was transferred from Robben Island to Pollsmoor Prison in Cape Town in April 1982, everyone thought it was just to bring him closer to Groote Schuur Hospital, that there must be some truth in those rumours of his health after all.

'It was a shocking thing for us all. The enquiries that came were just unbearable.

'I didn't know about it. I was studying at home one day and sent one of the children to get me the newspaper and there I see the front page story. And I also heard it on television in the evening.

'Some time later I got a letter from the Prisons Department in the usual cold way, informing me that my husband had been transferred to Pollsmoor.

'My first trip there was an unforgettable experience. The drive to the prison through the plushest suburbs of Cape Town, the most beautiful scenery, with those original colonial buildings. An area I had never been to.

'I just prayed that he had also seen that scenery, the vineyards, the beauty of this country he was dying for. Because, having been confined to the Island for twenty years, obviously he had forgotten about the ordinary vegetation. How lovely the country is.

'But Nelson looked very very well.

'Incidentally, he hadn't seen one tree on his way to that prison. They were transported in an army truck which could take ten elephants. And they were put in some special cage, he said. There were three of them. They had to stand all the way. It is about an hour's drive to the prison.

'He said the last time he saw a blade of grass was on the Island, as he was leaving. Now he can only see the sky. The prison is in a valley. He must be in a part of the prison that is so enclosed that he doesn't even have a view of the mountains.

'Isn't it strange that there can still be a difference between nothing and nothing? That Island – which was nothing, which was death itself – suddenly became a paradise. There he had a cell with his name engraved on the door to give him that psychological feeling of eternity. There he had a little garden where he used to till the land with a fork and watch plants grow. And he was free to move around in the big yard.

'This now is the end of life.

'The irony of it all. Pollsmoor is a virtual palace when you compare the structure itself to the other place. And yet he is certainly worse off there than he was on Robben Island.

'But still, Nelson is that same man who left us those many years ago. And who will come back to us in that same spirit. Nelson exudes that. You don't have to ask. You don't have to be told, if you know him as well as we do. His spirit remains untouched.'

Out of the darkness round her, the clapper boy starts singing 'Nkosi Sikelel'iAfrika'.

'All his colleagues are just as untouched as he is. They are absolutely fantastic. Such total dedication, such total commitment. No erosion of the soul. They are all like that.

'They are totally liberated, of course. It is a government-in-exile. The fact that they are incarcerated is just a reality they have to put up with. They give each other the mutual inspiration and the unshakeable belief that they are fighting for a just cause. And the incoming new prisoners support them in the knowledge that the Struggle outside continues …'

As the last notes of the haunting anthem end, the light slowly fades into darkness around Winnie Mandela.

The shocked silence from the audience says it all.

*   *   *

In a flash of light we are back into the action.

Donald runs on, now with his book in his hand.

He gestures to people in the front row.

'Excuse me … aren't you? … Are you? … Are you in my story?' He checks in the book itself. Then explains himself. 'My struggle to become world famous continues …'

He carries on mouthing the same question to other people in the front rows, as the clapper raises his board.

'Donald tries to sell his book around the pool in Hollywood. Scene 83. Take 1!'

The familiar music from *Some Like it Hot* establishes the atmosphere of Tinseltown.

'Hello? Excuse me, but my name is Donald Woods and I'm here in Hollywood to sell my story about a wonderful, inspiring man and you must read it, because it will make a good film and it will tell the world about this young man who I wish I'd known for longer …'

The clapper boy impersonates a producer, cigar in hand.

'Sorry, not commercial, have a nice day!'

Donald is left standing.

'Have a nice day ...'

Sir Richard Attenborough interrupts the scene from his vantage, deep in the darkness of the auditorium.

'Cut! No, darling, too apologetic, too dull. Stand by. Take 2!'

The sound of Marilyn Monroe singing her breathy sigh fills the air. Donald is now panicked into overreacting. He rushes from one side of the audience to the other, desperate.

'Good afternoon, the name is Woods ... I'm a banned political ... no, what about: I knew a young man who was the forty-sixth person to die in police detention, on 12 September 1977 ...'

Sir Richard is fed up.

'No darling, too heavy! Too political! Try something the public will understand!'

The clapper boy runs in and claps his board like a pistol shot.

'Beverly Hills. Scene 83. Take 3!'

Marilyn Monroe sings at an ever-increasing speed and ends up sounding like Mickey Mouse. The sense of hysteria envelops Donald, who is feverishly trying to deliver what his director wants.

The clapper boy hands him a fancy phone.

Suddenly the music stops. Donald is smooth and American in his approach.

'Hi, Donald here. Donnie-baby! Have I got a property for you. Hot, man, hot! Paul Hogan will love it! "Crocodile Woods"! Great cameos for Sidney Poitier, Harry Belafonte. Even walk-ons for Michael Jackson and Bill Cosby.'

He listens, then laughs loudly.

'Jesse Jackson? Great idea! With some luck we can shoot it in the White House. The Black House! Whatever ...'

He listens and laughs in agreement.

'Songs? Great songs! Dance? Rhythm. Great beat! Paul Simon? He can write the music ...'

Donald suddenly changes his tune.

'He can't write the music! Little sanctions buster!'

He is oily, seductive and repulsive.

'It's a winner, man! Like *The Great Escape*, but also *Raiders of the Lost Ark*. Africa and Martyrdom! A cross between *The Gods Must be Crazy* and *Gandhi*!'

Sir Richard Attenborough appears now as Gandhi.

'Gandhi? Gandhi? Gandhi! Please come back Mahatma, all is forgiven! Gandhi? Did someone use my talisman in vain?'

He shuffles over to a startled Donald Woods and takes his book.

'But what have we here? I must peruse this magnum opus. It looks like it's just up my Via Appia.'

He holds the book admiringly.

'A weighty tome. Did your fingers do the walking? Or did you swim the mighty Sparrowcock River and escape the wrath of the vicious evil South African Police Force, the horrible South African Security Forces, the vile South African crocodiles, the yukky South African tsetse fly and the totally repulsive South African Receiver of Revenue, to bring me this story to make into a great award-winning film? We will force that fascist regime in Pretoria onto their knees, if only to beg to have their names mentioned in the film!'

The clapper boy applauds all this.

'Sir Richard, your film will end apartheid overnight and freedom will be ours tomorrow!'

Dickie looks the black youth up and down with a casting-director's eye.

'Dear boy, you tell jokes? You are worthy of better things than clapping.' He puts his arm round him protectively. 'My dear boy of interesting hue. We're in the middle of casting the crowd scenes for the film. We need dead bodies and prisoners. And you will be perfect for the parts. Come with me and audition for a starring part. My name is Sir Richard, but you can call me Cute Old ...'

'Dick?'

The clapper boy is willing to go all the way to become a star.

'Bang on, old sausage,' laughs the crafty old Brit. 'You really have attracted my attention. I'm planning to make a film about Mother Teresa of Calcutta, and maybe you'd be perfect for the part.'

He waves to the left and the right, emulating Gandhi in all movements and gestures. When he turns to exit, we see his bottom peeping out from under his short cloth!

*   *   *

Donald looks around, but he is alone. He listens, but there is silence.

Just him and the audience.

I then used real words uttered by Donald Woods.

'If I were allowed to speak to every person in this country, I would speak of my friend, Steve Biko, who died naked on the floor of a prison cell, after suffering torture and torment at the hands of men who represent an especially horrible form of evil – the evil of racism, which inflicts hatred and rejection upon its victims for being born with a dark skin.

'I would tell you of how the society that bred such a system then exonerated his killers, condoned the laughter with which their superiors greeted the news of his death, and voted the man chiefly responsible for it back into office with an increased majority.

'I would tell you of how Steve Biko's death, although especially tragic for me, was by no means the first of its kind in this country. Nor the last. And that it was but the most publicised, most heightened dramatisation of the ultimate effect of unbridled apartheid.

'Steve Biko's death could be regarded as a symbol of the sufferings of all blacks under the apartheid system. His death was physical. Most of the deaths caused by apartheid are spiritual. There are countless deaths of morale and hope and self-esteem.

'For many of his fellow blacks, Steve Biko ended such deaths of morale. He shattered many of the psychological bonds that used to shackle young blacks here in South Africa, and in terms of their self-esteem particularly, he was a breaker of chains. Perhaps that, more than any other, was the reason why the system killed him.

'If I could speak to every person in this country, I would say: Help finish the work of Steve Biko. Help smash the remaining links of the chains he broke. And let the sound of his voice and his words echo around the world, so that chains may be broken wherever they hold in bondage the bodies and minds of men.'

For a moment he stands motionless, then realises that he has found the soul of the story. He turns to share it with the director.

'Sir Richard! Sir Richard?'

Margaret Thatcher enters as the Queen, trailing a long red velvet cloak and wearing a big state crown. It is covered in fairy lights that twinkle as she walks.

'Please don't prostrate yourselves. As you can see, I am here incognito. The name is Margaret Regina and I am a legend in my third term. And who are you? Are you someone we should know?'

'I was a friend of Steve Biko,' is all Donald can say.

Queen Maggie is delighted.

'You too? Steve, dear Steve! He was such a close friend of our family and my government. Such a sweet man! Marvellous tennis player. Died so young. Like James Dean. We do miss him, don't we, Ronnie?' She refers to the immobile Ronald Reagan doll. 'Ronnie? Oh dear, I think he's still fast asleep, or his hearing aid's slipped up his arse again. Ronnie! This boy knew Steve Whatsit! Isn't it a small world?' She turns to Donald with a royal flutter. 'Any friend of Steve is a friend of mine. Please help me with my cloak ...' Donald becomes a servant to her demands. 'Thank you so much. The trappings of office can become such a strain. Let me introduce you to my hero.' She gestures towards Ronnie in his chair. 'Ronald Reagan, the leader of the free world. Say hello to this nonentity, Ronald.'

Donald introduces himself.

'Donald. I am the hero of this film now.'

Queen Maggie laughs.

'Not any more. You go and play on your lilo in the Persian Gulf. This story is not big enough for two heroes. Fuckofficus!'

Donald tries to stay in the centre, but she makes it impossible.

'But ... Sir Richard? I still had so much to do ... Sir Richard ...?'

But it is the end of the road for Donald. As funeral music fills the space, the clapper boy wheels on a small coffin and hands him the dead cat.

Donald buries Natalie Woods with pomp and ceremony. The clapper boy hands him his Oscar.

Donald leaves the stage.

Meanwhile Queen Maggie has Ronnie on her lap.

'The burden of responsibility rests heavily on my head.'

She sighs and takes off the crown, boffs her hair and then slips a hand up Ronnie's back to manipulate his eyes and mouth.

'Ronnie, I have wonderful news for you. You always said that you wanted to act in a film once again before you joined that studio in the sky? Well, I think we've got you the perfect part! You might win an Oscar!'

Ronnie rolls his eyes with glee.

'Ronnie? Can you hear me?'

Maggie overarticulates into his ear. Ronnie nods with glee.

'I've had a very productive conference with Sir Richard and I convinced him to retire gracefully onto his next project and leave the completion of this film to me.'

Ronnie nods his head with glee.

'Ronnie? Do you realise what this means?'

He nods with glee, then looks at her. Then shakes his head, also with glee.

'I've got you the lead in the film.'

Ronnie nods his head with glee.

'We will now have just the nice things. No police brutality. No political assassinations. No bannings or riots or torture.'

She cradles Ronnie to her bosom like a baby.

'It is now 1988. Nowadays prisoners don't slip on the soap, or fall down stairs, or try and escape from the seventeenth floor of buildings. Nowadays they don't even leave bruises or marks, and thanks to a State of Emergency, no one even knows when people vanish.'

She leans down and whispers confidentially in his ear.

'Ronnie, between you and me, we can solve all the problems of this sad and bleeding land.'

She puts Ronnie back in his chair, as Zulu chief Buthelezi enters. We see it is actually the clapper boy who makes a point of winking at the audience and showing them that it is, in fact, he.

Maggie pats her Ronnie.

'Let's have a happy ending.'

She turns and sees Buthelezi in all his Zulu finery.

'You're not exactly what I had in mind!'

Gatsha bows deeply, charm personified.

'My dear Mrs Thatcher. Please do not prostrate yourself. I am here incognito.'

'That's why I don't seem to recognise you,' sniffs the British Prime Minister.

'You do remember me?'

'Of course. Robert Mugabe.'

Buthelezi shakes his head.

'No.'

'Kenneth Kaunda!'

Gatsha smiles.

'Do I look like a monkey?'

Maggie is frustrated.

'Am I getting warmer?'

'My humble name is Dr Mangosutho Buthelezi, but you can call me Gatsha.'

Maggie immediately recognises him.

'Of course, Gatsha! You are so often on my mind. We in London talk about you all the time. How are things in Nigeria?'

'No.'

'Ghana?'

'No.'

'Am I getting hot or cold?'

'Cold.'

'Kenya?'

'Warmer ...'

'Oh, this is fun,' squeals the Iron lady. 'Mozambique?'

'Vary warm ...'

'Pietermaritzburg!'

'Hot as hell!'

She embraces him carefully.

'Of course, you are the Zulu Emperor. We had tea together at Number 10 and then posed for snaps for the *Telegraph* and then I signed your spear.' She fingers his spear suggestively. 'And what a fine spear you have.' She now decides to get down to business. 'My dear Imperial Brother, please help me. My friend and I, the leaders of the free world, want a happy ending to this sad and shocking story. Do you have any ideas?'

He has prepared an excellent idea.

'Make me State President of South Africa,' he suggests. 'That will be a happy ending.'

'That will be a bloody ending. We want a happy ending!'

Our first policeman reappears, dressed the same, still waiting to pass his audition.

'A happy ending?' he shouts. 'You want a happy ending?'

He shakes his head, unable to believe their naive stupidity.

'This is April 1988 in Cape Town, South Africa, and you want a happy ending?

'We have a State of Emergency!

'We're fighting a bloody war in Angola!

'There is civil war in the townships.

'Press censorship! No freedom of speech!

'The world doesn't like us and you want a happy ending?

'We have detention without trial, political prisoners, an official right-wing neo-Nazi opposition and an unofficial communist onslaught and you want a happy ending?'

He holds up his quirt menacingly. Maggie and Gatsha cower.

We wait.

The policeman suddenly relaxes and turns to the audience.

'Why not!'

His quirt is actually a magic wand!

Fantasy music gushes around them as the lights flicker and in silhouette we see Gatsha become the clapper boy again and Maggie being changed into PW Botha.

In a flash PW Botha appears. Maggie's cloak has been inverted: it is no longer red, but the banned ANC colours of yellow, black and green. PW wears the laurel crown. He is Emperor.

'Baie dankie, thank you very much,' he says, wagging his finger and licking his lips. 'Please do not prostrate yourselves. As you can see, I am here incognito.'

He goes up to the policeman, who stands transfixed by the magic. The magic wand is still shaking in his hand. PW fingers the wand with interest.

'That was a very nice thing you did. What else can you do with that magic thing?'

The clapper boy is familiar with his friend, the policeman.

'He tells jokes, Imperial Broeder.'

PW is impressed.

'Jokes? Ja-nee, we need jokes.'

The policeman knows this is his big audition. He clears his throat.

'Treurnicht and Terre'blanche jump out of a plane. Who hits the ground first?'

PW shrugs.

'Who cares.'

'That's a joke,' the policeman explains.

'That's wishful thinking,' PW replies.

The policeman wants to try again.

'What is your definition of one man one vote?'

PW wags a finger menacingly.

'Oppas boetie, that's no joke!'

The policeman is determined to finish his joke.

'No, no! Your version of democracy is: when all whites vote for one man!'

PW laughs.

'That is a joke! Baie geluk. I hereby appoint you Court Jester!'

The clapper boy nudges the policeman.

'See you in court!'

PW Botha lifts an Imperial finger.

'Just one thing. Remember. We have no political prisoners in South Africa.'

He turns to the audience slowly, preparing to make an Imperial decree.

'I'm sure you never thought that inside that Iron Maidenhead was this Boerewors Emperor just ready to pop out?'

He plays the gracious host.

'Enjoy your visit to the film studio? Well, we have all seen, during the last ninety minutes, that South Africa desperately needs heroes. Oh, we have official heroes: Naas Botha, Bles Bridges. But we have just seen how our banned and officially ignored heroes are being cruelly exploited by commercial concerns overseas, just because we have chosen to ignore these South Africans and cast them into the political wilderness.

'This will now cease.

'By Imperial decree I hereby appoint these people as Heroes of our whole nation!

'Firstly: there will in future be a Biko Day and a Mandela Day to be celebrated by all peoples in South Africa!

'Secondly: we will make our own films about our heroes. At present SABC-TV 2, 3 and 1 are preparing a seven-part series called: *Steve Biko: His Life in Politics*. This will be uncensored and, of course, quite unbiased.

'Thirdly: we hereby lift all restrictions on Mrs Winnie Mandela, so that she can happily and authentically portray herself in any film of her choice. We also unban the ANC and Donald Woods, so that they can put their mouths where their money is and compete with everyone else in the arena of politics.

'Fourthly: Johannesburg's John Vorster Square and Cape Town's Caledon Square are being demolished and in their places will be built multiracial schools where all our children will learn together how to live with one another in a future South Africa.

'And finally ...'

He steps forward and the lights heighten the significance of the moment.

'I'm on my way from here, through Cape Town, with a key in my hand.

'I will go to Pollsmoor Prison and I will free Nelson Mandela.

'Then I will invite Dr Mandela, his wife Winnie and their children to join us at our home in Rondebosch, where my wife Elize will prepare us a wonderful Sunday lunch that we will enjoy together.

'After the meal, Dr Mandela and I will sit together calmly and discuss matters of urgency and very likely solve most of the problems that stand between us and a peaceful future for all people in our beloved South Africa.'

After a stunned moment, the policeman steps forward apologetically.

'But Your Majesty, none of this can happen.'

PW looks at him, tongue darting across his lips.

'What about the State of Emergency?'

'Wat?'

'Die Noodtoestand!' translates the policeman.

'Die Noodtoestand!' echoes the clapper boy.

'Die Noodtoestand?' muses the President of South Africa. Then he decides.

'Fok die Noodtoestand!'

The policeman waves his magic wand.

'Freedom for all!'

The clapper boy does a dance.

'Vrystaat!'

PW Botha and the policeman stand together and say in unison, their fists held high in the clenched salute.

'Amandla!'

The blackout ends the show.

*   *   *

There is a curtain call. PW takes a bow with the policeman and the clapper boy. The policeman stops the applause.

'I have a joke. Why was Jesus born in Bethlehem and not Pretoria?'

They all think.

PW shakes his head.

'Why was Jesus born in Bethlehem and not Pretoria?'

'Because they couldn't find three wise men in Pretoria!' chortles the clapper boy.

'But they did find a virgin in Bethlehem,' giggles the policeman.

Blackout.

When the lights come up, including the auditorium lights, the Official National Anthem of South Africa, 'Die Stem', is played.

People are applauding, but there is no further curtain call.

Now they have to decide. Do they keep clapping? Do they stand in respect? Do they walk out?

On the first performance of *Cry Freemandela – The Movie* at the Market Theatre in late 1987, it should be noted that the entire audience stood to attention during the illegal rendering of 'Nkosi Sikelel'iAfrika'. When they heard 'Die Stem' at the end, they also all stood up, and made a dash for the exits!

Amandla!

11

HER DIPLOMATIC IMMUNITY

Cry Freemandela – The Movie was never recorded on video for distribution. My original proposal fell on deaf ears. The companies were not interested in anything that didn't feature Evita Bezuidenhout. She was my Elizabeth Taylor. Pieter-Dirk Uys as Joan Collins as Winnie Mandela did not fit the bill. Which brings me to a detailed explanation of where this creature, known as the most famous white woman in South Africa – and now Africa – comes from.

Back in 1978, Koos Viviers, assistant editor of the *Sunday Express* and a fan, offered me a weekly column. It certainly changed my life. Within a few weeks, I knew I was beaten. I couldn't fill a page! Yet there was so much to write about. Things were happening in politics that couldn't be believed. Not only the daily list of people who lost their lives as a result of Prime Minister John Vorster's iron fist round the flaccid penis of Afrikaner Nationalism. The crazy things. The stupid, mundane, typical things that politicians did and would then proudly call 'policy' or 'achievement'. The success of censorship lies not in external control. It is self-censorship that leads to the destruction of intention and inspiration. We do the regime's job for them. Instead of writing about the very essence of what appals and intrigues us, we pussyfoot around, even scared of using the word 'pussyfoot' in case it's seen as obscene.

The press knew what lay ahead. We were blowing out the candles to try to see better in the dark.

It wasn't just state displeasure, but also commercial unhappiness that forced self-censorship. Advertisers insisted on what they wanted to see on the page, and bad news wasn't on the list. Forget about truth. The government frowned in the direction of freedom of speech and lifted a finger to wag and warn.

PW Botha was still Minister of Defence, and his portfolio was protected by the Official Secrets Act. But when the rumour was outed that Information Secretary Eschel Rhoodie had allegedly flown a party of colleagues and friends – the bribed and the bizarre – in an aircraft to Antarctica for a braaivleis, I nearly died with laughter and gratitude.

But how could I put this into the column? It hadn't even made the front page. And was it true? Or just another urban legend that was part of the body of facts breathing its last gasp around us? Then a woman took over my life, and thanks to her I kept my job, got paid and my thin cat got fat.

When the future Evita Bezuidenhout appeared in the column for the first time, she didn't have a name. She was just the wife of a National Party MP. She gossiped and whispered about fresh scandals and more. She told the secrets that were better left alone. She was funny and visual, even though there was no picture of her.

The editor of the newspaper asked me who she represented. She was so familiar. I shrugged. 'Just a way of getting things across,' I said. He didn't believe me.

This nameless familiar woman appeared again in a column a few weeks later. And again six weeks after that. Whenever there was a stench emanating from the temples on the Boer Olympus, she would be at a party in Pretoria, and overheard to say what no one would mention.

The extraordinary interest shown by readers during the first year made me focus on the success of this woman. She obviously pressed many buttons, and it seemed everyone thought they knew who she was. Everyone except me.

After a year of using her as a mouthpiece once a month, someone said: 'This woman is the real Evita of Pretoria.'

Evita Perón, the wife of the Argentinian dictator, had just been reinvented as an all-singing, all-dancing, all-glorious death-scene superstar on the British stage. The double album of the musical became a favourite, and 'Don't Cry for Me Argentina' the anthem for many a drunken parade round the pool. Once I read a serious biography of this horrible, fascinating monster, a blueprint became obvious. If this other woman in print, this Evita of Pretoria, was to have a life, why not be inspired by the other Evita? Ambitious small-town girl, with big dreams, goes to Big City, becomes an actress, bad at acting but good at giving head and heart to up-and-coming politicians. Marries one and then dies?

Madame Perón exited the stage before she was forty. My lady was already older than that, and so was I.

*　　*　　*

I had yet to appear as Evita, although I'd already explored the outrage of wearing women's clothes on stage. After my dazzling walk across the Little Theatre stage as Marlene Dietrich in the mid-1960s, and playing the kabuki wife in *Seppuku*, I'd created a silly lunchtime concert called *Just Hilda* in 1974. I started as a cinema usherette selling programmes and harassing the audience as they came in.

The show was a collection of women: Millie, Hilda, Margaret, Hermien, Miemsie and Marlene. Tannie Hermien was the doyenne of Kultuur, later echoed in Elsabe Lategan in *No Space on Long Street*, and probably the closest seed to a later Evita, although she was blonde. She was inspired by Hermien Dommisse, actress, author and Boere superstar, who as self-appointed guardian of Afrikaner cultural morality made her voice heard in support of the censorship of my plays. A lot of her went into Mrs Bezuidenhout too. In the 1990s, Hermien became a close friend and, in spite of her seventies tunnel vision, turned out to be a woman with surprising insight and occasional brilliance. Skirmishes, it seems, tend to bring out the stupidest in the cleverest of people.

There was Miemsie, the Killarney movie star in search of her heart-throb tenor Gé Korsten, encouraged by his singing voice on tape while sidestepping cow pats in the veld, as well as a direct crib from Lily Tomlin and her telephone exchange lady, Ernestine – 'one ringie dingie, two ringie dingie ...' – which sent up clunky bureaucracy and ineffective office behaviour. I ended with a Marlene.

Just Hilda – Hilda being gay slang for 'hideous' – was tatty, cheap, camp and successful. I was learning that less is more. You do six women, don't give the first one all the tricks. Find only one aspect of her body language, her vocal colouring, a facial alphabet, which then leaves you enough of your limited range to invest each character with something unique.

*   *   *

In *Adapt or Dye*, Evita took to the stage in a pink dress, huge pink hat, white gloves, platform shoes, rings and eyelashes. A perfect drag queen cartoon of the familiar Afrikaans matron. She giggled and fluttered her eyelashes. She skirted along the edge of that not-to-be-crossed line. She sprayed her territory with her scent like a jaded Persian cat. She grabbed the attention of the press and the people.

'What's her surname?' a journalist asked.

I hadn't thought that far. On the Market Theatre canteen wall was a poster of *The Seagull*, featuring Aletta Bezuidenhout.

'Bezuidenhout,' I said. Now they believed me.

Around this time, the homelands were born. The Transkei was ripped prematurely from the body of the land, and Bophuthatswana appeared from an expensive Caesarean, its five barren pieces spread across the motherland like bits of a dismembered body.

'Ludicrous, absurd, crazy!' they all shouted.

'Wonderful!' I whispered, because it was real. It was policy. And a perfect job for a non-existent diva. Evita would become the South African Ambassador in her own homeland!

We were doing *Uyscreams with Hot Chocolate Sauce* at the Market. My sister Tessa and I had already done a sibling revue called *Uyscreams for the Wimpy Archipelago*. During the run at the Laager, we met Thoko Ntshinga, who was working the coffee bar in the theatre foyer between plays. She joined us in the 1980 sequel. It was a significant shock for the audiences, who didn't expect a sophisticated black comedian, singer, actress and activist with charm, cheek and submerged anger.

Thoko's husband Teazer was a banned person. He couldn't come and see his wife act. He was only allowed in a room with one person at a time. And yet in our audience would sit Dr Piet Koornhof and his entourage, the National Party Minister responsible for the state of Thoko's fractured family.

Dr Piet was a fan. During our Baxter run he invited us all to lunch at Parliament.

'En bring die oulike meidjie.'

I took my father instead.

In *Uyscreams* we combined the character of Madame Quazilesi, who appears in the final scene of *Die Van Aardes van Grootoor* to claim the farm, with the reality of the developing homeland fiasco. Evita had not yet appeared on stage. We had to find a name for a fictitious homeland that would sound as absurd as the real ones. Thoko inspired the combination of familiar sounds that resulted in 'Bapetikosweti'.

And so Evita Bezuidenhout became the South African Ambassador to the Independent Homeland Republic of Bapetikosweti, a homeland also fractured into pieces, with a lavish hotel and casino, and an entertainment centre where South African laws could be put on hold and tits flashed.

Constant questions demanded quick answers.

Does the Ambassador have a husband? Children? What movies did she make when she was with Killarney Studios, following in the Argentinian woman's footsteps?

What does Tannie Evita think of apartheid?

What did *I* think of apartheid!

Thanks to my friendship with Thoko, I had to think about it all the time. When we travelled down to Cape Town in the Kombi to perform *Uyscreams* at the Baxter Theatre, Tessa would sleep on the back seat, while Thoko sat next to me, knitting. Many cars tried to force us off the road: a black woman sitting next to a white driver!

We'd booked three rooms at the beautiful Lord Milner Hotel in

Matjiesfontein. When the white receptionist saw that the third person was black, suddenly only two rooms were available.

Tessa said: 'I'll share with Thoks.'

The receptionist then said there was a room round the back.

'For ... Thoks ...'

I said: 'I'll stay there. It's okay.'

It was a maid's room and not that terrible for a white boy to enjoy. We sorted it all out, thanks to Thoko's great sense of humour and tolerance. But it must have been appalling for her.

Incidents like this happened again and again during the eighties. Where could we have dinner in Joburg to celebrate her birthday? Which restaurant would allow blacks? Did they need to apply for a permit from Pretoria? And how do we get a banned person called Teazer into a party of more than one person?

The mercurial Nino Zanazi owned Nino's in Melville, our local Italian eating trough, and he just shrugged and said: 'Fuck the government. Bring your friends.' And we did.

It was fun and frivolous and fabulous, and, under all the fluff, tense and terrifying. But possible. Things like this happened in the eighties too. People just looked the other way, so we could get on with our lives, and, in doing so, took the chance of losing their few freedoms too.

The year of our Lord 1983: Evita had a job.

Her husband Hasie was the National Party MP for Laagerfontein. They had three children, twin sons and a daughter. And all had a glittering future as the family of the glamorous Ambassador, now a prominent member of PW Botha's 'Diplomatic Corpse'. Tannie Evita carried *Adapt or Dye* through the major centres of the land, changing outfits to suit new occasions. After an opening of Parliament she'd appear in what she'd just worn to the event, with big hat and matching accessories. A political death would see her in black, her veil hiding a tragic face. The marriage of Charles and Diana saw her festooned in Union Jacks and souvenirs.

Whenever something happened on the local political front, she was there. When PW went to Europe for the first time, she went along, and the powerful Sunday newspaper *Rapport* featured her on the front page in one of her chosen outfits – the one in which she would meet the Pope. Not a week passed without Tannie Evita appearing in the press, on television or the radio. She fitted in perfectly, never a square peg in the official round hole.

She never used bad language, or took the name of the Lord in vain. She was polite and sweet and charming and a total supporter of the National

Party, who started believing in her. She was the ideal image of a good, white, Christian South African. And she hated the idea of a man in a dress!

*   *   *

The title of the next show again came out of someone else's mouth.

I was in the raucous gay bar of the Skyline Hotel in Hillbrow with Dawie Malan. He was perched on the edge of the bar like a tinselled hobbit, his long crooked fingers curled round a cigarette with the elegance of a *Vogue* model, eye-shadow enhancing his piercing eagle-blue eyes. The best in the room were jostling for his attention.

I sat next to a fat queen who leant across and whispered:

'You should call your next show *Farce about Uys!*'

'What?' I snapped, irritated by his bad breath and the scaly touch of his hands.

'You know? Arse about face … *Farce about Uys?*'

An orchestra exploded in my head. *Brilliant!*

'Oh, fuck off!' I snarled, and moved to share it with Dawie. What a great title!

'*Farce about Uys.*'

It was set in the homeland embassy, 'Blanche-Noir', in the main reception room with the familiar kitsch Tretchikoff. The staircase is dominated by a large painting of the Ambassador. There are suitcases spread around, showing that someone's packing to leave.

A policeman arrives. Sersant … Uys!

This would be a farce around him. Sophie the maid is in attendance. Thoko was the obvious choice and made the part her own, not shy of making fun of her tribe's easy adaptation from warrior to worrier, but also crossing many politically incorrect boundaries of comedy.

'Madam is not here,' she says.

'Then who is?' the sersant growls, and adds, 'And don't be so cheeky, hey?'

Chris Galloway took over the part of Sersant Uys from Blaise Koch, who fell ill on the tour. Chris took over in a fraught two days!

Sersant Uys is investigating the Bezuidenhout family for corruption.

While this was rife in the politics of the land, it was seldom referred to. So we created our first minefield. Every aspect of government corruption was mentioned and mulled over, from arms deals to homeland scandals. Immorality and sexual deviation were also on the list, in the form of Evita's husband Hasie's dalliance with a local hotel maid, her son De Kock's obvious homosexuality, and her daughter Billie-Jeanne's dangerous liaison with the son of the President after hours at the Glitter Pit casino. Evita's other son, Izan, was involved with the military and its raids into the townships, the accompanying violence and possibly even murder. The Bezuidenhouts were in deep shit. And even Evita, the Mother of the Nation, was suspected of money-laundering and 'even worse'.

The play was about the whole family, but only one member, De Kock, appears. The gay son impersonates his mother, father, brother and sister for the benefit of the snooping policeman, ably assisted by Sophie. We never see the real Evita. It is De Kock in drag as his mother. Those classic elements of farce added to the hilarity, and Sersant Uys's clunky racism was expertly foiled by the mercury-quick Sophie, who took each racist onslaught and tied it round the cop's thick neck like a hangman's noose.

After *Adapt or Dye*'s two-year season around the country, now boosted by a record-breaking video, *Farce about Uys* sold out in every centre before it even opened. It took a year to tour the circuit, and then it went onto video, specially designed and filmed in a Johannesburg studio. Today it survives as a monument to the madness and monstrosity of the state of South Africa in the 1980s. And Sophie's cheekiness is now seen as a prophecy of the future, where her generation would lead, as there would be no more Sersant Uyses to follow!

The next step was a feature film.

*   *   *

Clustered round the braaivleis, wine in hand, Dawie, Nico de Klerk and I would fantasise about the possibility of Evita in a movie or in a TV series set in her embassy, where the news of the day would be featured against the background of the homeland idiocy. My own idiocy took over here. I was approached by an Afrikaans film producer, known for his bland and kitsch Afrikaner-Baroque films that all made enough money on government subsidy for him to invest in huge hotels and blocks of flats on the Natal coast. His father had been head of the security police and was now running his company.

Albie Venter was a charming man. His past was my past. He was no worse a South African than the rest of us. He liked what we did and laughed in the right places. He wanted to make a film with Evita. He saw the commercial possibilities. How much would my fee be?

Instead of thinking about it, I blurted out: 'Let's go into this 50/50.'

He smiled and said yes.

The movie cost me every cent I'd made since the dawn of *Adapt or Dye*.

Instead of taking the money and delivering my performance and text, my 'integrity' forbade me to work for the enemy; rather work *with* them on equal terms. Be in charge, have control. All rubbish. Even though we qualified for that skewed government subsidy within days of release, the money was held back for months owing to 'bookkeeping reasons'. Which meant I had to liquidise all my assets and ended up owing, in today's terms, about a million rand.

I'd walked into the oldest trap in the book with legs wide open and eyes wide shut.

Many years later I met an old Broeder who seemed keen to tell me how anti-apartheid he had been in those bad days. By now Albie had died, and his company had dissolved with the old South Africa.

'No one was going to be responsible for banning you or your work,' the old enemy wheezed. 'No one wanted to turn you into an international martyr. They knew your ego would do the work for them. Get you to commit your investments and then bankrupt you.' And then he added, with watery eyes, 'I tried to warn you, but they were watching me all the time.'

I thanked him for his part in the Struggle.

They'd succeeded not only in wiping out this enemy. They also took all the 35-mm prints of the film and, within six months of the release date, pulped them. Thank heavens my 'ego' had arranged for one copy to be sent to my agent in London, in the hope that the film could go to that year's Cannes Film Festival. Of course it didn't, but today that single copy has allowed the film to still be with us. And today, *Skating on Thin Uys* seems to have kept its tongue firmly in the nation's cheek.

The Afrikaans was subtitled in English. In 1985 this was seen as insane wastage and insulting to the Kultuur and Taal.

'How would they understand the Afrikaans at the Cannes Film Festival?' I asked.

Today the subtitles make the film accessible to the majority of our people, who don't speak Afrikaans.

Skating was a combination of inspiration and bad mistakes.

The choice of director was a compromise, as I'd wanted Dawie Malan. It was logical that he branch into films, especially directing a story he had done so much to develop. But, come the crunch, Dawie had never directed a film before. As if, among the rank amateurs who were making films in South Africa during that barren period, this should have mattered. On the contrary, it would have been the ultimate achievement.

I handled the issue badly. Dawie was insulted and upset, and the appointed director spent more time teasing his hair and plucking his eyebrows than reading the text. Again, my timid gratitude didn't allow me to fight for the film's essence. To talk, to argue, to demand, to be difficult and impossible until the material was properly served. Most of the subversive comedy fell by the wayside, and the few moments that remain are the highlights of the film.

Evita goes to Pretoria to demand the reincorporation of the homeland into South Africa, so that Pretoria can get the oil that has just been discovered in the scorched earth. At the Union Buildings – and they allowed us to film there, which shows what clout a Broeder on the board has! – she tells the relevant Minister, who looks like future President FW de Klerk, that the President of Bapetikosweti will agree to all South Africa's demands. But only if his black son can marry Evita's white daughter. At that moment the heavy portraits of past Afrikaner Prime Ministers crash to the floor one by one, as if by divine intervention. Only the portrait of the Prime Minister of the moment, PW Botha, remains in place, swinging ominously by one nail.

In another scene Evita is received by President Makoeloeli in his residence. She stands in front of the huge curtains in his reception room. The curtains and her dress merge; they are made of the same material!

While Sersant Uys waits for her at the Union Buildings, polishing the pride of his life, the white 1967 Cadillac De Ville convertible, a family plus their nanny pass by. The husband and wife are elegant blacks. The black baby is fussed over by a white nanny!

Then comes the intrigue of organising a summit meeting between the Presidents of the homeland and the motherland. Evita disguises herself as PW Botha. We did the switch in one take: Evita sits and stares at a portrait of PW. She practises the jutting lip and piercing glare. She adds a stocking to the top of her bouffant and pulls it down, creating a bald-head effect. She takes off her lipstick, adds the slightly tinted glasses, pulls off the earrings – and there is the State President of South Africa. She wags her finger at the image of PW Botha wagging back at her:

'South Africa is …' She echoes the words of the sketch from *Adapt or Dye*. The summit takes place.

PW (Evita) sits opposite the old black man, formerly her gardener, now President of the homeland, while Mrs Bezuidenhout (De Kock in drag as his mother) sits between them!

*   *   *

The film starts with a short documentary, based on the 'Know Your Public Service' shorts that constantly bombarded us in the cinemas. Its function was to establish Evita's history. The coup was getting real politicians of the day to comment on camera.

Dr Connie Mulder had been the Minister of the Interior who was instrumental in banning all my plays in the 1970s. He was a casualty of the Information Scandal, chased into the political wilderness, where he formed a party in opposition to the governing National Party. He was now the leader of the Conservative Party, and any enemy of PW Botha was his best friend. He shook my hand warmly and hinted that he had always secretly been on my side.

'You just moved too fast, man, too fast.'

Dr Piet Koornhof, then Minister of Cooperation and Development, was in charge of the homelands and, an old regular in the audiences of my shows, arrived for his film shoot with a big smile. To our delight, he fluffed the pronunciation of Bapetikosweti, making it sound like Babiskatwotti. He also hinted that he was firmly against apartheid. Helen Suzman didn't have to convince or audition. As the only member of the official white Opposition in Parliament, she was brazenly anti-apartheid and said so loudly. She delighted in slagging off Mrs Bezuidenhout's husband as sly and dishonest, outing Dr Hasie Bezuidenhout as a crooked politician. Even former Miss World Anneline Kriel, whose marriage to the Bophuthatswana Sun City hotel boss Sol Kerzner had just collapsed, cheekily took the part of Moon Levine, the blonde hotel magnate in charge of Bapetikosweti's Lunaville complex!

The film's climax was supposed to be the wedding of Billie-Jeanne and Leroy Makoeloeli – the white Afrikaner girl marrying the son of a black President. This is where the Broederbond put down its booted foot. No one would buy tickets to see that! In the meantime, the Immorality Act and Mixed Marriages Act were repealed, which was good news for the majority of South Africans, but bad news for the topicality in the film.

I reacted to President Botha's repealing of the laws by spreading the story that he had done it all on purpose to spite Evita Bezuidenhout and wreck her film's impact. Some press reports supported this and added to the delicious confusion. None of this had any significance to the majority of South Africans, who as blacks were not allowed in the white cinemas. Our release plans for the film showed no consideration for a potential black audience. I don't think there was one; my insistence on extra prints being made for screenings in black areas was an expensive gesture.

And so the ending was adapted: Sophie the maid comes to the rescue. She disguises herself as Billie-Jeanne for the wedding and afterwards exposes herself as 'a member of the Bezuidenhout family', thus meeting the demands of the black President. And none of the decent, good Christian Afrikaners in the cinema needed to vomit in the aisles. Looking at it today, it is a better ending than the original one, which, in democratic terms, is very normal now.

There were premieres all over the country. Evita would arrive on the red carpet like Liz Taylor. But the press had decided that the honeymoon with this emerging farce to be reckoned with was over. The reviews were terrible, some dismissive, most insulting. And after a great opening week, the film stagnated. I see now how all the short cuts and compromises killed it. If we'd shot it clandestinely as we'd originally intended, *Skating on Thin Uys* could have been a minor subversive cult classic today. Now it's just a quirky flashback to the quicksand of where we were.

When all was said and done, the practical demands had to be met. I had to find close to R800 000 to repay the banks! Conjuring up some inspiration from my first invitation to appear in London with *Adapt or Dye*, I went back on the South African circuit. PW Botha fatefully crossed his Rubicon and flooded me with dangerous new material and a title. I started a national tour with *Beyond the Rubicon*. I earned the money and paid off the bank. It took hundreds of performances.

Evita still had her slot in this new show, but now the party was over. She appeared in a fur coat, demure and sombre, and darkly set out a monologue about the future of whites in a black country. The laughs were there, but the edge cut far deeper than before. The experience of the film and the journey I had travelled with my major clown had pushed me into another paragraph. I wasn't satisfied with Evita the social butterfly and occasional political assassin. Maybe I wanted more? Maybe there was no more. Once the season was over, I took the advice to look closely at my dependence on Mrs Bezuidenhout and decided to put her away for two years. I took a journey on the SA *Bothatanic* and watched *Cry Freemandela – The Movie*.

12

CATCHING
SERIOUS DEMOCRACY

O nly as the decade of the 1980s shuddered to a close did Evita resurface in my chorus line, this time on television. Bill Faure had by now become the top television producer in the country. We'd become friends back in the late 1960s when we both attended the London Film School. It had been exciting watching Bill's rise to the top, not that he had any competition from the bungling idiots who called themselves creative people in the still-fledgling South African television industry. Bill could not sit and read a script. He would pace the kitchen floor and one would tell him the story. He would then watch it unfold on his monitors in the studio on the day and be the traffic cop. It resulted in terrifying, but exciting, nail-biting television.

We decided to punt a television chat-show series, in which Evita would interview controversial guests. It would be called *Evita's Indaba*. M-Net, the new pay channel, was keen to become involved. It is ironic that during the filming of *Skating on Thin Uys*, M-Net, vying for the contract to become the only independent station outside the SABC, presented their proposal to a Cabinet committee. The young Afrikaners involved with this bid asked Evita to present their proposal! Risky, but appealing. They came and filmed her in all her glory, the Cabinet watched her and, hey presto, awarded M-Net the contract. So they owed her one.

The *Indaba* series hit many speed wobbles and potholes.

There was no lack of personalities, but PW Botha was still captain of the stricken ship of state, and white politicians from most parties were not keen to be exposed on television by Evita. And remember, she was a he! So Evita interviewed old friends, like Afrikaner opera star Mimi Coertse and *Sunday Times* editor Tertius Myburgh, and, in a major coup, she convinced Archbishop Desmond Tutu to join her and Anneline Kriel in a delightful, spirited programme, where he teaches her how to toyi-toyi. The Arch later told me how important that programme had been to help break down the anti-Tutu propaganda that had encased his reputation in the lies attributed to him by the Botha regime. Maybe that's why the series was shelved after the Tutu interview was aired. It was said that 'someone' from PW Botha's office phoned the station, which then, in spite of their supposed editorial independence, pulled the plug on Tannie's show.

Using the interviews we'd already recorded but not screened, we produced a TV special, in which Evita approaches her homeland TV company to convince them to take over the series. John Kani, fresh from his triumphs in New York with *The Island* and *Sizwe Bansi is Dead* plus a Tony Award, played the sinister head of productions for BAP-TV. Another special followed, celebrating Christmas with various guests, but it had lost its freshness. As the eighties came to an end, Evita presented a retrospective on the decade. At least this treasure chest of political hiccups allowed us to piss into some National Party picnic hampers!

The local press viewed the work, sighed and moved on. They sounded bored with Evita. The public enjoyed the nonsense. But M-Net was still a minority luxury, and too few black South Africans were able to afford the subscription.

By now PW Botha had left power to make way for FW de Klerk.

I went back to the one-man show format, and, with the promise of extreme changes in the air, presented *A Kiss on Your Koeksister* at the Market Theatre. When we eventually recorded it for television – M-Net wanted it, paid for it, but then refused it – Bill Faure again directed the proceedings. But it was an unhappy experience. He was constantly ill and died soon afterwards. His death was cruel and untimely, and the industry in South Africa has never replaced his mad and vibrant energy.

*　　*　　*

Mrs Evita Bezuidenhout, the South African Ambassador to Bapetikosweti and Calvinist Mother of the Nation, was by now very famous. Not just a character on the stage, she had broken through the fourth wall of the theatre and become a real personality. A suggestion that I write a cookbook from her point of view, with anecdotes and opinions, started a process of exploration that eventually led me to write the biography of Evita Bezuidenhout.

A Part Hate A Part Love took some years to shape and flesh out, but once the excitement of research took hold of me, it became unstoppable. I wrote the story in the first person, as the 'third-rate comedian Pieter-Dirk Uys', who was known for his impersonation of this important South African icon. Her suspicion of me kept me on a string until, eventually, through the naive trust of her secretary Bokkie Bam, I was allowed to interview the Ambassador.

Establishing her as a real person, as opposed to the character I played, gave this Evita dimensions that I'd never needed to explore theatrically. Starting the story during the Anglo-Boer War with the birth of her mother, Ossewania Kakebenia Poggenpoel, I followed the lives of the Poggenpoel family through the tribulations of growing up in Bethlehem, moving to Johannesburg, and Evangelie's marriage to Hasie Bezuidenhout.

For Evita was not yet her name!

I researched the period of her childhood in the 1940s, and her teenage Hollywood ambitions in the 1950s brought back memories of my own dreams as an Afrikaans kid. Miss Poggenpoel's early film career in the mid-1950s had to parallel real productions. My parents had appeared in the first Afrikaans film musical during that time, called *Kom Saam Vanaand*, and I asked the director of that film, Pierre de Wet, if he might have 'discovered' the talented girl from Bethlehem. He went even further and confirmed the fact on television, with a straight face. Life imitates kitsch!

The geography of Johannesburg had to be precise. Cars had to have the correct names and the right colour. I studied politicians, reading their autobiographies and noting their 'official' achievements. The reality of their destructive policies then had to be offset against newspaper files of the time, so that the full picture could be considered. Even if Evita just passed through their lives on one page, the truth of the tale was paramount.

I drew up a huge wall chart of the ninety years of the twentieth century, noting when everyone was born, when they reached adulthood, got married, had children, started their jobs, created their legends and became what they were at the time of writing, which started in 1988 and ended in 1990.

Hasie Bezuidenhout's history was pivotal. He had three terrible sisters, who would be a trio of scheming Bette Davises to Evita's timid Debbie Reynolds. The birth of official apartheid in the 1950s at the hands of Dr Hendrik Verwoerd paralleled the rise of Eva Pohl, the Killarney film star, formerly known as Evangelie Poggenpoel. The two lines of reality and fantasy had to be joined, knitted and webbed. The political fortunes of Dr Bezuidenhout, and his wife's rise to fame, had to mesh with the details of our history. After reading the lives of Hendrik Verwoerd, JG Strijdom and BJ Vorster, I realised how the idiosyncrasies of power lent themselves to the drama of this soap opera, and the funniest and most absurd details in the hysterical story were the real historical facts.

When British Prime Minister Harold Macmillan visited South Africa in 1960 before his famous 'Wind of Change' speech in Cape Town, he stayed at the residence Groote Schuur with the Verwoerds. They gave the Macmillans the main bedroom with its en suite bathroom and stayed in the guest room. Both Verwoerds ended up locked in their lavatory off the passage and had to get out via a small window! Delicious fall-about comedy.

When the white dove of peace was thrown into the air by Verwoerd to symbolise the birth of the new Republic in 1961, it refused to fly and someone had to kick it up the arse to get it off the ground! Who could make that up?

The most fascinating part of the exercise was creating a relationship between me as author and Evita as subject. Her disapproval of this unwanted investigation into her life gave her a dual personality. There was the official diplomat who could sell anything with her smile, and then the manipulative boeremeisie from nowhere, who was still fighting for her survival.

The book was accepted by a major publisher, which produced a disastrously amateurish first edition. The cover looked like a rental video, and there were so many mistakes in the text, including the careless merging of entire chapters, that for the first time my reaction was adult enough to refuse to accept the version as final. The publishers convinced me, of course, that a delay would mean missing the Christmas rush, and promised to print an addendum apology with all the necessary corrections. They could have filled a second volume! I pathetically agreed and so put the first nail into the book's coffin.

A Part Hate A Part Love was published in 1990, which brought another handful of nails to the funeral. It was too soon. They say satire is tragedy plus time. I had not allowed enough time to pass. Nelson Mandela was going to be released, yes, and everyone knew the apartheid merry-go-round was over, but it was still too early in the day to have the necessary distance as a reader for this satirical history of apartheid. While the edition sold well, the feedback was confused and sometimes angry. The tensions and fears that were building up in the period before democracy in 1994 did not allow much space for humour.

I spent much time in bookshops and CNAs sitting at small tables with piles of books, signing and selling and getting comments from customers. I was amazed to see how many young South Africans were buying the book for their parents.

'It's for my dad!' the schoolgirl giggled.

'A Christmas present?' I asked.

'Yes. It will make him crazy. He hates what you do! And loves Evita!' She pulled a face. Her sense of anarchy was catching.

'Then why buy him this?' I laughed. 'What about a nice safe Robert Ludlum?'

'No,' she said forcefully, 'when our parents get angry at what you do, then we can talk to them. It helps.'

I sent the book to some contacts in local TV and film, waiting for a reaction. Wouldn't this make a delicious series, using humour to tide us over the rapids of reconciliation? There was no reply. The initial interest from the publisher's London office for a UK edition also faded. Looking at the sloppy product in hand, I am not surprised.

In 1995 I republished the book in paperback, after the edit for the Dutch translation *Een Leven Apart* streamlined the story. By adding a postscript about Mandela's release and the 1994 election, I brought the saga up to date. An independent maverick Afrikaans publisher produced a handsome edition, but the mainstream distributors showed no interest, and I still have a few hundred copies for sale at the Perron bookshop.

Professor Kader Asmal, the Minister of Education in the late 1990s, read the book and said it would be the ideal textbook for today's schools, to help learners come to terms with the brutalised past through the perspective of humour.

* * *

After the book was published, Evita sued me for libel!

Quite rightly, the original publishers were nervous about the use of real politicians' names and true political events intertwined with the passions and perils of this fictitious Miss Poggenpoel. It was a risky book. People could sue. In consultation with Lauren Jacobson, who'd been advising me weekly since that censorship trial in 1985, we concocted a plan of attack. And the day the book appeared, the newspapers played along by running a sensational story: 'Evita Bezuidenhout is suing Pieter-Dirk Uys for libel! His book – published today – is a collection of lies and distortions, insinuations and fabrications.'

It was couched in real legal terms, and not only amused the potential readers, but, it seems, deterred other potential suitors. Years later, I was told that when PW Botha read about the book, he approached his lawyers, who meekly said: 'We can sue, Mr Botha, but you will have to stand in the queue behind Evita Bezuidenhout.'

Sadly, nothing came of this tantalising possibility.

The 27th of April 1994 came and went. The first democratic election was free and fair, and millions of South Africans queued up to vote for the first time, and some voted many times. I was performing *One Man One Volt* at the time. Pieter Cilliers, firebrand producer with M-Net, came up with an idea: a new Evita talk show, where she interviews the democratically elected politicians. Already, a few months after the election, the whole alphabet of our politics had changed from A to Z. The former enemies were now the leaders. The jailbirds were the new birds of paradise. What frightened us yesterday had to inspire us tomorrow.

I sent letters to a choice of six politicians, inviting them to share in a celebration of our democracy and freedom of speech, and suggested that we now laugh and use humour to heal. They all agreed!

The first series of *Funigalore* was introduced with a title sequence in which Evita plays Scrabble with Minister Pik Botha, the letters each time spelling out the name of that episode's guest. Pik Botha and Evita were by now linked by media gossip as lovers! She was, after all, his most beautiful and famous Ambassador. It was whispered that he'd sent her faxes late at night, after possibly too much wine, giving the rumour much tongue in cheek.

After thirty years as the NP's Minister of Foreign Affairs, Roelof F Botha was now Minister of Mineral and Energy Affairs in this new Government of National Unity. We met at a magnificent old Victorian mansion outside Pretoria, me hidden behind Evita's fine façade, and he in his dress suit and aura. It was there that, through the juggle of letters, we discovered that the name Botha could also spell Thabo, although in those years Mr Mbeki was just one of a crowd of civil servants. It came into good use after 2003!

The series was a great stirrer of the pot of political confusions.

For the first time, the South African public could see their new leaders as real people, and look beyond the successful state propaganda that had turned them into monsters, from Joe Slovo, leader of the Communist Party, to Mac Maharaj, former 'terrorist', now Minister of Transport. Frene Ginwala, the Speaker of Parliament, Jay Naidoo, Minister without Portfolio, and Terror Lekota, Premier of the Free State, all took part in this entertainment that was bending over blackwards. The swearwords of a white past were now the passwords to a democratic future.

All the guests captivated with their passion and patriotism. The so-called dangerous terrorists were inspiring and compassionate. They treated Evita with affection and trust. She giggled and flirted and skated on very thin ice. She looked good. They looked good. The country looked good. And M-Net saw that *Funigalore* looked good. The former Broeders still in charge relaxed their knuckle-white grip on the can-it button.

We prepared a second season, this time with my old fan, Dr Piet Koornhof, now in retirement with a non-white partner, as part of the introduction. In a scene reminiscent of *Les Liaisons Dangereux*, everyone was dressed in eighteenth-century drag, dancing a seductive court quadrille, with Evita camping Dr Piet across her elaborate fan, on which appeared the name of the guest in that specific episode. To see the former Boere-Goebbels to PW Botha's Adolf play silly buggers with a man in a dress is still something that boggles my mind. Pik Botha was rewarded with his own programme, and when, during the first take, he kissed Evita on the lips warmly and called her 'My skat', I realised that she was in fact very real. I was the one-dimensional cartoon!

The highlight of the entire *Funigalore* series was Evita's interview with Nelson Mandela. The most famous man in the world and probably the busiest, and yet he found time in his schedule to talk to a woman who doesn't exist. Sitting in the office of the presidential mansion Tuynhuis next to Parliament in Cape Town, waiting for Mandela, was an experience that will always be ingrained in my memory.

Firstly, the process of getting into that chair. Arriving at the venue early enough to do a calm transition into the lady. But more than anything else, planning the interview. What does any interviewer ask Nelson Mandela? His private life was off-limits, as his marriage was in the process of dissolving in the public eye. His politics is blandly biased towards the ANC, and his generous refusal to take credit for the peaceful transition to democracy is not very interesting. And, on top of it, there you sit in a frock! Imagine Tony Blair in conversation with Dame Edna Everage, or George W Bush in conversation with ... well, maybe just in conversation!

President Nelson Mandela entered the room, filling it with his charisma and warmth, welcoming everyone. He turned and espied Evita. He beamed that perfect smile.

'Evita, my dear, ah, you look so beautiful!'

He kissed her on the cheek. He sat down and was miked. I leant towards him, careful not to pull my microphone cable out of its carefully plotted passage under the dress, past the stuffed bra and between the birdseed tits, lying on top of my chest hairs.

'President Mandela, thank you so much for giving us this time. I know how busy you must be.'

He became serious very quickly. His mouth turned down at the edges and his eyebrows levelled into a ledge above his calm gaze.

'No no, Pieter. I want to be on Evita's show, because I have important things to say. And no one watches the news.'

He was going to use the interview for his 'New Year's Message to the Nation', as this was being broadcast nationwide on New Year's Eve. He leant towards the cameras and gave a very serious message of support to the

South African Police. Outside, in the real world of 1995, three former armies were being joined together as one. The hated enemies of the police were now their colleagues. Many members of the force were dying daily. Their President stressed their importance and his support for their needs, with Evita Bezuidenhout at his side!

It was genius statesmanship. Nelson Mandela was right as always. On the news, policemen die, so no policemen watched the news for relaxation. But on a silly drag queen's chat show, things could be said with more honesty than a recited statement from a mere official. The interview had its sticky moments of toffee, when Mandela needed to be the man of the people and recite some of the slogans that would hold the ship of state more or less together. But when Evita bubbled along and told him how once, while he was still imprisoned, she'd seen him in Sea Point, he relaxed. I'd read this in a book on Mandela's prison years, that on occasion his warder would take him out for a drive, and buy him an ice-cream.

'Yes, President Mandela, I was in Sea Point. It was a Sunday. I suddenly saw a black man sitting in a car. Alone. And eating an ice-cream?'

Mandela nodded gleefully.

'Yes, yes …'

'And I knew it was you.'

'Oh yes?' His eyebrows shot up in question.

'And for a moment I thought, maybe I should go to you and say: Come with me, Mr Mandela. Let's run away and rescue you. But I was too scared.'

'Oh … that's a shame …'

He laughed and looked around at the crew, who just melted with delight.

When it was over – a thirty-minute interview in one take with only two cameras – I found myself alone with him for a moment, unattended by the film crew or his staff.

'President Mandela, you've never seen me without my hair?' I nudged.

He looked startled and then realised that the man within Evita was talking.

'No, Pieter … no.'

'Do you want to see?' I asked.

'Yes, I do,' he nodded enthusiastically.

I whipped off Evita's wig.

Nelson Mandela gave a horrified cry.

'No, no, put it back!'

We laughed and hugged. It was like being reborn.

Recently it happened again.

Evita was summoned by him – 'Please bring Evita to entertain my guests?'

– Ja Baas! – and after her fifteen-minute presentation to an audience of millionaires, including Oprah Winfrey, raising money for AIDS orphans, Zelda la Grange called me away from my dinner. She is Mandela's guardian angel, constantly at his side and keeping the press at bay like a blonde police dog.

'Madiba wants to see you.'

I wove my way through the tables of guests. Nelson Mandela was speaking to a famous person. Zelda leant towards him.

'Madiba? Pieter is here.'

The old man with white hair turned to me.

'Ah Pieter ...' He started to rise with difficulty. It is now hard for him to move very quickly.

'No! Please don't get up ...' I stammered.

'No, no ...' he insisted. And then put his hand into his full plate of food. A moment of realisation, and then he giggled. He looked at me with twinkly eyes.

'I put my hand in my plate of food ...' He winked. 'I'll do what I did in prison. Eat with my tongue.' And like an old farm cat, he licked the food off his hand.

As he sat back, he pulled me closer to him with his other hand. He whispered to me with careful enunciation.

'Pieter. I ... like ... very much ... what you are doing.'

When the 2004 general election came along, with the tenth anniversary of the democracy, Pieter Cilliers approached M-Net with the idea of taking six of the original twelve guests from the 1994 *Funigalore* series, and after showing them what they'd said ten years previously, interviewing them again, and re-releasing the series as part of the celebration. The M-Net comrades showed no interest. They pronounced the series dated and dead.

*   *   *

I met a young television director called Roger Smith, and through various people we presented a concept to e.tv, a new, supposedly more 'free' television station. It would be called *Evita: Live and Dangerous*. Once a week we would assault the nation with a live programme, structured with a few pre-recorded sections that had been prepared during the previous week. The guest of the day would be live and usually political. Each episode would also feature a new local comedian.

That was the most exciting part for me. I was lonely. Where was the competition? What I needed now was an energetic nineteen-year-old firebrand who would dismiss me as an old fart and infuriate me enough to pull my finger out and reinvent my onslaught on the nation's fears. There had to be someone out there? I knew there were bright, young and angry talents trying to make an impact in Cape Town, most of them coloured and black performers from the Cape Flats. And so we invited them to join the show. I was told to audition them. We didn't. We met and chatted with the comedians, and they understood the importance of doing the right thing: You're live! Be honest, be sharp, be professional. And be on time!

Our first guest was not on time! For the first episode, we were supposed to have Winnie Mandela live in all her glory, but she didn't pitch, and Evita ended up interviewing the empty chair – and then quickly sitting in the chair to give what she thought Winnie's answer would be. It was ad lib improv TV at its most terrifying, and the smell of adrenaline nearly set the fire alarms off. Winnie never responded to the experience.

It was the programme on AIDS that best demonstrated the importance of live television. Supreme Court Judge Edwin Cameron was the guest. He also was HIV-positive. By nature, Evita was nervous of him, because she doesn't think the virus is something a decent Christian Afrikaner should have to deal with, but he disarmed her and convinced her to be open-minded. The programme created an uproar. As we were 'live', we encouraged viewers to phone in. Some reacted with disgust and anger, underlining the denials and fears that were still numbing the nation to the reality of the need to confront the virus as a life sentence, not a death sentence. The filmed insert of Evita's visit to Nazareth House to play with little AIDS orphans was moving and memorable.

But the reality of power soon made itself felt and heard. Producers jostled for control of the show's content. Lawyers demanded changes and watched the live transmission with suspicion. The media were perplexed and uninterested. The programme didn't seem to deliver its promised danger. E.tv hadn't marketed with imagination, and so *Evita: Live and Dangerous* came and went after twelve weeks, leaving only small skid marks on the underpants of live television.

*   *   *

During the Election Trek of 1999, which I cover in detail in my previous memoir *Elections & Erections*, Evita had been the conscience of the politicians and the concubine of the people. Four years later, when the 2004 election was announced, it was logical to use Evita once again for voter education.

Now the whole premise was different. In 1999 we had said farewell, not goodbye, to Nelson Mandela as President, and hello, if not welcome, to Thabo

Mbeki as the new Madiba. No one expected him to follow in our first democratically elected leader's huge footsteps. Besides, Thabo's reputation for being a hard worker and behind-the-scenes manipulator was well known, and people felt comfortable with his commitment to the job of vice-captain.

The election of 2004 would hand Mbeki his second term in a very different atmosphere. The honeymoon was over. His perplexing blind support of Robert Mugabe in Zimbabwe and confused reactions to the HIV/AIDS pandemic had been exposed countless times. Even his most admirable diplomatic triumphs with the newly created African Union and NEPAD paled in comparison to the fact that over 600 people were dying in his country every day because of his government's carelessness. It all stemmed from his casual denials of the seriousness of the pandemic. Although I didn't realise it yet, Thabo Mbeki was taking the place of former apartheid leader PW Botha as my major target.

From the point of view of voter education, apathy was a greater threat than ever. People were bored by the politics of the day; they were uninterested and not angry enough, in spite of the lack of delivery. The unexciting projected programmes, so desperately needed by our young developing democracy, didn't appeal to the media, hungry for sensation and sexed-up solutions. The system of proportional representation still meant the party list was the issue and individual politicians did not have to deliver opinions or show passion in order to get into power.

And AIDS was now the sinister joker in the pack.

How many citizens registered on the voters' roll had died of this disease, unheralded and uncatalogued? Would the list be adjusted, or would the dead also be allowed to cast their ballots? Would the thousands too sick to travel to the voting booths just be ignored, or would they be catered for with special votes? Would women who were members of the ANC, but who had lost their children and husbands to AIDS and government paralysis, vote for the politicians who were responsible for their losses?

'Put the erection back into the election!' was the cry, and Evita started the ball rolling with a koek-and-koffie meeting at the newly refurbished Metropole Hotel in Long Street, Cape Town. Before the last weekend on which people could register to vote – millions were outstanding – we put out the feelers and invitations. To their credit, every major political party attended Tannie's party. Tony Leon of the Democratic Alliance swept in confidently, surrounded by his security guards. Patricia de Lille of the newly formed Independent Democrats arrived, with no security guards at all! The New National Party, already in an unholy alliance with their former nemesis, the ANC, was represented by a clever blonde. The ANC sent a white comrade. Even Cassie Aucamp, leader and seemingly only member of the ultra-right-wing Nasionale Front, flew all the way from Pretoria to be seen on this televised reality show! We had hired a camera crew to film the proceedings, and a good thing too. The SABC cameraman arrived late and pissed!

Tannie Evita, wearing a suit festooned with proteas and looking live and dangerous, opened the proceedings. She focused on the need for all to register before the end of the weekend. She celebrated the fact that everyone could now vote in South Africa and make their choices for the future. She was funny and adorably naive. I knew people would listen. It wasn't a lecture. It was a performance. She gave each politician three minutes to put across their specific point of view, threatening to hit them with a large protea if they overstepped the mark. They each had something positive to contribute, and graciously acknowledged one another. Tony Leon and Patricia de Lille smiled through gnashed teeth and will probably never be seen again in such close proximity. The ANC's Cameron Dugmore didn't smile at all, and made feeble comments about his rivals. But the others, all on their best behaviour with a nervous eye on Tannie's poised protea, were surprisingly bright and funny.

The message was clear and crucial. Our footage went to all the television stations and was featured on news bulletins throughout the weekend. It obviously couldn't match up to Evita Bezuidenhout's legendary address to the members of Parliament before the 1999 election. But by now the people were expecting Tannie Evita to be out there, keeping an eye on the fairness of the fight and the fragility of the vote.

Sylvia Vollenhoven was again in charge of the SABC's election coverage, and she organised five slots for Evita on *Morning Live*, short live interviews with different political parties. By now the ANC had decided not to play along and didn't respond, but the smaller parties came to the party and bravely faced the acid sweetness of Mrs B.

At the same time, thanks to a grant from George Soros's Open Society Foundation, Roger Smith and I prepared a selection of short information bytes disguised as 'commercials' about voting. I did some of my well-known characters in the humorous ones, but the majority were serious and original. We used children who were not yet old enough to vote from three Cape schools: Mitchell's Plain's Rocklands High, Simonstown HS and St Cyprian's, the girls' school where I was still regarded as head boy! Each child stood in front of the camera and answered three questions from me:

'What does democracy mean to you?'

'Why should everyone vote on election day?'

'Why are you proudly South African?'

The answers were electrifying, and, with the exception of one young man who was so nervous his stutter defeated him, all were usable. The hope was that people who weren't going to bother to vote would see these inspiring calls to action from tomorrow's potential voters and would change their minds. Whatever the form of voter education, be it from us, the Independent Electoral Commission, the media or the people themselves, the third democratic election was free and fair. The fear of mass apathy proved unfounded, and Thabo Mbeki was sworn in as President for his second term on 27 April 2004, the tenth anniversary of the democracy. He did not appoint Evita Bezuidenhout to his team of new ambassadors.

Meanwhile, in Darling, Evita Bezuidenhout continued to present her dual entertainments: *Tannie Evita Praat Kaktus* and *Tannie Evita's Cooksisters* at Evita se Perron every Saturday and Sunday at 2 p.m. *Kaktus* started in 1996 when the Perron was created and has reinvented itself weekly, based on the news of the day and focusing mainly on a revisionist history of the Afrikaner.

Cooksisters is about her use of cooking as a means of reconciliation, and explores what life and politics look like from the kitchen. Because that's where she went – from Ambassador to cook! With wonderful irony, she confronts leading diplomats and politicians with the line: 'In the old South Africa I was Ambassador and you were in the kitchen; now it's visa versa!' It has never failed to crack even the most steely of smiles.

13

BRING ON THE BLONDES

Evita always had a younger sister. In *Skating on Thin Uys* she featured briefly in the documentary about the Ambassador's life. Filmed in Paraguay with a black cat called Adolf on her lap, she snarled a few curses at the camera and, like a cracked Dietrich, dismissed Evita with one word. 'Bitch!'

But before that dangerous blonde took control of the dark side of my drag, another blonde was reigning supreme. Nowell Fine, the Jewish African Princess, the kugel, was created before Mrs Bezuidenhout even saw the light of print in the column. In the 1970s, kugels were a noisy, glamorous and wealthy cog in the wheel of white supremacy. The fact that most of them were super-rich didn't necessarily mean they were all on the wagon of exploitation, to make enough money and then pack up and leave the country. As the line went at the time: When the Jews start leaving, it's time to go; when the Portuguese start leaving, it's too late already!

Kugels have a specific sound, a nasal whine that cracks plate glass. They have big hair and long nails, they wear false eyelashes and genuine designer clothes. They need maids and gardeners, husbands and nannies for their children. They are appalled by the injustices of apartheid, but seldom bother to check the details of their own prejudices, and probably vote for the National Party anyway, because 'better the devil you know than the devil you don't'.

Among the whites who were passionately committed to the struggle against apartheid, some of the most effective were Jewish. In Parliament, Helen Suzman single-handedly held up the torch for freedom and justice; in the world outside, there were many others, including Joe Slovo.

When I discovered my Jewish heritage, I was pleased to confirm what I had suspected. I have always loved Jewish humour, Jewish food, and the extraordinary bonds of family and friendship that keep Jewish communities strong and vibrant. Being a Jewish Afrikaner also meant that I belonged to both chosen people! So, adding a familiar Jewish character to my chorus line was not a choice, but a necessity.

Nowell Fine was the first of my female clowns, probably because she was the easiest to conjure up. As an extreme example of woman-as-drag-queen, all Nowell needed was wild blonde hair, huge sunglasses, earrings, make-up and attitude. The mere sound of her voice and the inane stupidity of her charm was enough to make audiences laugh. So in 1981 she appeared in *Adapt or Dye* for the first time, organising a garden-party meeting of her local underground anti-apartheid branch of women, while having a clandestine affair with her garden boy, Nimrod.

'And if you don't do exactly as I say, Nimrod, I'll just pick up the phone and call the police. You'll be in jail before you can whisper Free Mandela!' She sighs with relief. 'Thank God for the System!'

In *Total Onslaught*, Nowell was building Dora her maid a house in the black township – 'So that after the revolution me and my husband can move into our house in Soweto. Not only will we have a Jacuzzi, a pool and a patio, but also a nice spare room. For our maid!'

Beyond the Rubicon developed her relationship with Dora.

'Dora? Are the kids ready for supper? Kids? Are you ready for supper? Okay kids, get in the car!' She smiles at the audience. 'Aren't I a lucky mother. Thanks to Dora's driver's licence, all I have to make for supper are four reservations!'

Dora represented so much in every white South African's daily life: the faithful maid in the kitchen, the sensible sounding board in the lounge, the helping companion at the supermarket and the saving grace at the dinner party. Liberals loved their maids. They were their best friends.

'I don't care if the police shoot blacks in the streets, as long as they leave my maid and garden boy alone.'

Already from early days there would be complaints from Jewish women about my über-kugel.

'I don't know why you do that character, because I don't know anyone who speaks like that, I swear to God.'

Some comments pointed out my emerging 'anti-Semitism'.

I said: 'I'm a Jew. Let me shit on my own doorstep!'

And so every new show took Nowell Fine a step further towards her legendary status, eventually resulting in a full evening's entertainment called *Going Down Gorgeous* in 1998. More a play than a revue, here I could present the entire life of this blonde butterfly from 1976 to 2004. The seven scenes were set at different stages in the history of her society, developing along the apartheid highway, with places on the way to stop and shout.

The story ends in what was then the future. The new century has dawned. Nowell has been to Australia to spend time with her grandchildren, with faithful Dora in tow. She returns to her beloved Cape Town. Dora had already returned from Perth and is now in Parliament. Nowell goes to live in the V&A compound on the Cape Town Waterfront, now protected by tall walls and top security. Dora comes to tea. They celebrate a life together, first as maid and madam and now as friends. But the edge of a future darkness on the verandah does not go unnoticed.

The trouble is that now, in this new century, the kugel is a rare and unprotected species in South Africa. It's when I perform her in Australia (Sydney, Perth, Melbourne), or in the USA (San Diego, Atlanta, Seattle), or in Canada (Vancouver, Toronto), that the reaction from the audience matches the roars of recognition Nowell received in South Africa in the seventies and eighties. The kugels have all left, and the few who stayed behind, protected by their high walls and heavy security, don't venture out at night to come and see themselves in a local revue.

Kugels have now re-emerged in the form of black divas – beautiful, glamorous, loud and opinionated women who set store by hair and nails, sunglasses and cars. The same mould, a different mauve. The last century ended with the Nowell Fine saga being filmed for South African TV, inspired by the successful stage presentation.

Going Down Gorgeous was structured here as a twelve-part television series – a story in parts, a development in stages, an all-in-one soap opera that followed the life of a familiar blonde in our lives. Each episode would focus on a specific period and often a well-known incident. The series was soaked in Nowell's unique brand of designer democracy and closet prejudices.

'There are two things I can't stand about South Africa: apartheid and the blacks.'

Right from the start the project was doomed.

My producer and director were a high-flying husband and wife team who were great hosts, and looked gorgeous and sexy after hours of preparation, but didn't have a clue what the project needed to work as drama. I think they saw a successful drag act that could attract future contracts from the corporation. Besides, the package had been tried and tested. It would take a genius to fuck it up.

I had two! She failed to sell the project to the TV bosses as a series. They presented it as a variety show! He attempted to read the script, which he did like a copy of *MAD* magazine, and saw no subtleties, which, believe it or not, were there and essential.

My guardian angels had already put a way out in my path, which I stupidly refused.

I needed urgent eye treatment at the end of a season in London before shooting commenced for the series. The retina of my left eye had become detached, and thanks to the rapid response of a Harley Street specialist, I was operated on and recuperating within days. I had a feeling this was a sign. I could have pulled out then, as the text was strong enough for many excellent actresses to play the part with conviction. Maybe more conviction than me! But the producing team insisted that the sale and success of the series depended on my participation as Nowell Fine, and stupidly the inflated ego purred, and that, as they say, was that.

Going Down Gorgeous died a slow and hideous death by indifference. Some of the reviews were so appalling that they have pride of place in my folder. Robert Kirby, an old behemoth from early satirical days and an occasional irritant in my life, had a field day in his column in the *Mail & Guardian*. I enjoy his brilliant acid mind, which vomits out its weekly bile. He also loathes everything I do, and it's refreshing to be shat on by such a splendid old bitch. His slating of the series was written with such an ironic twist that it actually read like a rave review! I pointed that out to him, but he didn't see the joke.

I saw the joke. It was short and sweet and not funny.

The writing was on my wall. Reinvent! Burn the blueprints! Yesterday's goose doesn't lay tomorrow's golden egg.

It's a new century, new country, new generation, new rules and new needs. Keep the blonde wig. Just find a new graveyard!

Enter Bambi Kellermann.

* * *

When Nelson Mandela stood at the Union Buildings on 11 May 1994 and swore to uphold the new Constitution of the democratic Republic of South Africa, I knew I had to find a real job. Apartheid was officially dead and no longer an issue, even though racism would take years to weaken. To attack a white Christian President because of his racist dishonesty was something of the past. Mandela made it very clear: there would be no retributions, no Nuremberg Trials, no punishment for the crime of apartheid. Reconciliation was the key to the rusty, swollen door of the future. That and the oil of truth. Would anyone tell the truth? Did anybody still know what the truth was?

As Archbishop Desmond Tutu prepared his unique Truth and Reconciliation Commission to confront the still-bloody wounds of our devastated country, I took a sabbatical from politicians. This was my victory too. I'd voted for this new government and they stood for everything I had dreamt of all my life: equality, justice, hope, fairness and freedom. Nelson Mandela was the man who'd freed me from the jail of my fears and frustrations. I would not pick up the sharp pen of satire and stab the new leaders. It would be bad manners. A honeymoon was needed, not just by them, but also by me.

Evita's sister had already taken shape in my imagination as a clown of the new era. Because she had married a Nazi as a young girl, her background was filled with familiar symbols and secrets. The Nazi past and Germany's long struggle to come to terms with it, compared now to South Africa's similar exercise in legalised racism and its, some said, hasty need to confront the pain, was a perfect page on which to scrawl a performance.

'I want to thank the German People for being such an inspiration to us Afrikaners,' Mrs Evita Bezuidenhout haltingly announced in her Pretoria German during the show *Negerküsse*, which toured Germany for four months in 1992. 'You set us Afrikaners a very high political standard. It would have taken us Afrikaners a long long time before we had killed six million blacks!'

It was appalling and magnificent. Older members of the audience walked out in horror, while everyone under the age of thirty crowded round me and insisted that they were too young to take the blame. One woman, slightly older than me, cornered me, her eyes flashing and her thin lips dry and cracked. 'Go back to your apartheid and leave our Adolf alone,' she hissed in German. The liberated youth jeered her and applauded me, and I'll remember the moment forever.

Bambi had her personal Adolf through her marriage to Joachim von Kellermann. And so I had to create a life for her, the details of which would separate her from the other blondes in my chorus line.

Bambi was born Baby Poggenpoel in Bethlehem in the Orange Free State, younger sister to the fatter Evangelie. Their mother, Ossewania Poggenpoel, was the organist in the local Dutch Reformed Church, supposedly the youngest in the land. There she pumped away at her organ, as well as those of the young Boers in her church choir. Two of them were rumoured to have fathered the Poggenpoel sisters – the bass-singer with the blue eyes siring the future Mrs Bezuidenhout, while the small, thin tenor with an eleven-inch penis was the father of the future Madame Kellermann.

The sisters never got on with one another, the older girl always restless and unhappy with her ungainly body and spotty looks, while the slim, pretty young blonde giggled and flirted and always got the biggest toffee from the Father Christmas down Hoofstraat in front of the OK Bazaars. Father Christmas, in real life the butcher, was later banned from his December job for fiddling with the girlies.

In 1956, Baby and Evangelie left South Africa with their mutual friend, the young Mimi Coertse, to go to Vienna, where Mimi had been offered a glorious career as a soprano. She became a world star, and, to this day, Mimi will happily play along with the fantasy.

'O ja,' she recently twinkled on television, 'that Evangelie ... I mean Evita ... she knew which side her bread was buttered. About Baby? I don't remember much ...'

That's because Baby visited the town of Graz to take part in a hair-dressing competition. She didn't win anything and returned to Vienna, just in time to see her older sister leave for South Africa. Evangelie hated Vienna, because there were too many foreigners. She had eaten too many cream cakes and her wide bum had become like the hump on Quasimodo's back. She went back to Pretoria, married Dr Hasie Bezuidenhout and became the legend we know her as. But Baby stayed in Vienna, trying her attractively appalling German on every sexy young man, and eventually was known as the best piemel-sauger on Maria Theresa Allee.

She was introduced to the proprietor of a sleazy nightclub called Der Blaue Engel and, after blowing his mind so expertly that his wife in the kitchen and his mistress in the bar wouldn't realise, got a job. First as waitress, then as an exotic dancer.

'It was my generic Afrikaner sense of rhythm,' Madame Kellermann told Larry King in 2001 on his CNN chat show.

At the club she met an old German cabaret star who'd fallen on hard times. The legendary Zarah Leander befriended the Afrikaans girl who didn't have a clue that the older woman had been one of the great film stars in Adolf Hitler's Third Reich. Zarah would sing in her deep, rich, masculine voice, belied by a soft femininity and Garbo-like glamour. Baby Poggenpoel was smitten, and happily changed her name to Bambi, as suggested by Tante Zarah.

As fairy stories go, hers was not that unusual. One night Zarah Leander introduced her young protégée to an old friend. Joachim von Kellermann was over fifty, with silver-grey hair, and still wore a monocle when he wanted attention. The excited chorus girls called him Pappi. Bambi called him Oom, until he suggested she call him General. The other girls said he reminded them of the famous German film star Curt Jurgens. He said Bambi reminded him of Elke Sommer. She didn't know who either of them were.

And so they got married and he took her back to Germany. To Munich. To introduce her to his old friends. In a beer hall.

'A beer hall in München. That's when I realised I had married a Nazi.'

'You mean you didn't know, or suspect anything?' asked Larry King.

'Darling, in those years I didn't even know what a Nazi was. Remember, I was just an Afrikaner ...'

But in Germany the von Kellermanns had problems. Bambi had to get a job to earn money to protect him from Simon Wiesenthal and his Nazi-hunters. So they moved to Hamburg in the dead of night during a raging snowstorm, where she got a job on the Reeperbahn as a stripper.

'You stripped naked?' asked Larry.

'Isn't that what happens when you strip?' she purred. 'It brought us the money we needed. My husband hidden by day, and me stripping by night. We seldom saw one another.'

'And then came Amsterdam,' Larry King sighed.

Bambi glanced at the camera.

'Can we talk about that on this programme?'

'No,' he laughed.

She had sex with a donkey on stage in a club hidden in the Red Light District. She still had a photo of the two of them and wanted to show it on the CNN interview.

'And so you spent a life on the run?'

'Yes, Larry. We hid here and hid there, until we eventually found a safe haven. In London. We lived in London ...'

He checked his notes.

'From 1969 to 1975?'

'Yes. It was very nice in London. Sehr gemütlich. The weather was terrible, but no one recognised my Nazi husband. Thank God the British are so bad-mannered, they never look you in the face.'

Eventually Bambi and her General ended up in Paraguay, where he became Minister of War in the government of President Alfredo Stroessner. And then he died.

'Your husband died.'

'Yes.'

'1988?'

'Yes.'

'They say it was murder.'

'Strychnine poisoning. Don't blame me, Larry. I was in Uruguay with a girlfriend.'

'Lesbian?'

'No, Larry, not all girlfriends are ...'

In 1994 Bambi returned to South Africa from Paraguay. Her husband's ashes were in the urn she held in her hand as she came through customs with nothing to declare other than her happiness to be home.

'Apartheid chased me away; democracy brings me back!' she said fleetingly to a waiting journalist. The news was out. Evita's sister had reappeared from the cracks of a murky past.

Evita denied it through her secretary Bokkie Bam.

'Mevrou wants it known that her sister Baby died in 1956!'

But no one believed her.

And so Bambi Kellermann knocked on my door and came for an audition.

*　　*　　*

I had just met pianist/performer Godfrey Johnson, who had been working with Lynne Maree and Chris van Niekerk in their unique Weimar-type cabaret venue Eauver the Top on the Kalk Bay Main Road, facing the sea. A small, saucer-like stage, an old battered upright piano. A magical space. Godfrey and I started working on a vehicle for Bambi.

To introduce her to the fans of her sister, we decided to do a two-part cabaret. The first half was Bambi in concert, and in the second, Evita arrives to take her to the hospital. Bambi drinks too much and collapses just before interval. A perfect double act for *The Poggenpoel Sisters*.

I had Godfrey's remarkable talent at the keyboard, and his exciting singing voice. He wore a wig and a man's dress-suit – actually my pa's wedding suit. Together we forged through her life in song.

There were boereliedjies from the *FAK Sangbundel* that she sang with tongue in cheek. She sang the famous 'Yes Sir!', a song she learnt from Zarah Leander. One night an old musician came to us after the show in tears. He had been the great Zarah's pianist once, and here he was, hearing about her through the mouth of this clone diva called Bambi.

The fifty-minute first half electrified with its danger. Talk of Afrikaners and apartheid, Nazis and Jews. Hints of cunts and cocks and drugs and death. Marlene Dietrich mixed with Hildegard Knef with a dash of *La Cage aux Folles*. This was no campy *Priscilla, Queen of the Desert*!

After interval, Evita arrived. Fifteen minutes of frenzied make-up, new eyelashes, rebrushed wigs, different shoes, bigger tits, even another under-garment. Plus shorter red nails and the legendary Bezuidenhout flair. She waltzed in to happy applause, scooped up her sister's discarded top hat and lone shoe, and proceeded to apologise. The apology went further than one for a vomiting blonde. It was now time to say sorry for apartheid.

The next forty minutes electrified with horror. Talk of Afrikaners and apartheid, Bothas and Bothas. Hints of blacks and whites and democracy and life.

We took *The Poggenpoel Sisters* to the Grahamstown Festival, performing in a smoke-filled room that could have been from any old 1940s European movie. We performed at the Market Theatre to standing room only. It was the magic of the moment. The rhythm of our daily lives was changing by the day, by the hour.

The design for the new South African Y-front flag was shown on the eight o'clock news on TV. Nico de Klerk made a copy and brought it to the theatre, so that after interval Evita could walk onto the stage and show the people their new flag for the first time.

Godfrey and I started work on the next opus immediately.

The character of Bambi was already making waves and friends. Whereas Evita had become so famous and, in many ways, so passé, like a Queen Mother, Bambi was dangerous, with blood under her long fingernails. She took no prisoners, only her husband's ashes, which she kept on the piano as part of her bitter celebration of widowhood.

Going back to the bible of Boer folksongs, we studied the *FAK Sangbundel* in detail. I'd already made the shocking realisation, on hearing recordings of Nazi rallies, that many of the supposedly innocent songs we used to sing round the campfire as sweet white boerekinders were Nazi songs translated into Afrikaans.

That would be our focus.

Bambi Sings the FAK Songs was a title with an echo. She starts by recounting her meeting with Kurt Weill and Bertolt Brecht in a seedy East German hotel in the late fifties. After a night of drinking, singing and certain other activities, Bambi ended up with an untidy sheaf of music on which the great Kurt Weill seems to have arranged her beloved boeresongs in his style. So we had Kurt Weill orchestrations of innocent Afrikaans songs. Instantly the tits came out! Immediately the sweet 'Wat Maak Oom Kallie Daar?', for instance, became a hymn of disgust at the dominee's paedophilia.

We were in deep shit with the traditionalists, so the obvious thing to do was to take the show to the newly established Afrikaans arts festival in Oudtshoorn, the KKNK. The five performances were overbooked, mainly by young Afrikaners fascinated by this new blonde monster on the block. This was not the usual torch-song mea culpa. It was the steamy kotch from two crippled cultures: German and Afrikaner. One had broken down walls; the other had abolished laws. Both needed to reclaim dreams.

*   *   *

After two years of full-time cabaret with Bambi and Godfrey, the new ANC government had enjoyed twenty months of satirical respite from Pieter-Dirk Uys. Happily, they just couldn't resist becoming real politicians. A new show about the baby democracy was inevitable. *You ANC Nothing Yet* simply came about because, as I say in the show, 'Politicians are like monkeys. The higher they climb up the pole of ambition, the more of their arses we can see.'

The new piece took me all over South Africa: Joburg, Cape Town and the festivals. And overseas to London's Tricycle Theatre and the Brooklyn Academy of Arts BAM season in New York. But Bambi kept on practising her scales and her bumps-and-grinds in the backroom of my mind.

Suddenly, one day, while driving to the small Cape town of McGregor, which is to the east, I ended up in Darling, which is on the West Coast. Had a schnitzel, bought a house, moved from Cape Town, saw a deserted railway station, took it over as a venue and put Evita in it over weekends in her show *Tannie Evita Praat Kaktus*. Evita se Perron became a legend and could soon pay its own bills.

Bambi had been busy as well.

The media were starting to enjoy the fun of setting the two sisters against each other.

'My sister Evita hates me so much that, I can assure you, she and I will never appear together in the same place at the same time,' Bambi told Dali Tambo on his show *People of the South*. But this was television. It was possible to show them together. So, thanks to clever planning, the viewers saw an agitated Evita sitting on the left edge of the settee, with a confident Bambi on the right. Together at last. And in the middle sat a nonplussed Dali, who had obviously met his match. Or was it matches?

Bambi's new cabaret, *Concentration Camp*, was difficult to sell.

We made it clear that 'it takes a lot of concentration to be camp', and that seemed to take the edge off horrified expectations. But the material was firmly anchored in the blood and ashes of the sufferings of the past. Not only the camps of Nazi Germany and the Anglo-Boer War, but anywhere where people were herded together, with fear their only shelter and despair their only hope.

Again Godfrey conjured up some magnificent echoes of Kurt Weill, who by now had become one of the primary influences in my recipe for Bambi. Godfrey sang his own songs while Bambi changed slinky costumes off-stage. There was a substantial tribute to Marlene Dietrich as well, whom Bambi regarded as a mentor.

I have always loved Marlene, ever since I saw her perform at the Alhambra

Theatre in Cape Town in the mid-sixties. Bambi was my Dietrich doll, as Evita had already become my Sophia Barbie. At the Perron, Godfrey and I had structured a play with music called *Noël and Marlene*. We used an afternoon in their lives in New York in the fifties. While Coward was in his apartment rehearsing for his second visit to Las Vegas, Marlene, already on the skids as a has-been, though still a famous grandmother, pops in with some strudel. He inspires her to think of doing a cabaret too. They joke and tease, they bitch and parry. What eventually becomes her famous stage show emerges in stops and starts, encouraged by Noël. She even sings songs by Weill and Coward himself, something the real Marlene never did during her life.

While Godfrey was only in his twenties, he could look like Coward and certainly sing like him. I would play Marlene, not as Bambi playing Marlene, but in the back of my blonde wig, the comparison helped me a great deal.

When Marlene turned a posthumous 100 years old, we did a special day in tribute to her at Evita se Perron. The kitchen served her recipes, we played her records, and Bambi Kellermann presented her tribute to Marlene Dietrich.

*   *   *

The twentieth-century blues of Noël Coward made way for the Y2K of the new millennium. It was a heady, crazy, on-off feeling of being there for something special, as the world turned from a nineteen to a twenty. Yet the only memory of that magic was a small kitten that appeared bedraggled and hungry from the Perron's dirtbins. We called her Two-Kay!

Something else crawled out of the dirtbins of Africa. A virus with no cure had hitched enough free rides through the flaccid borders of the new Mandela Magicland to settle in South Africa, claiming women, men and children as its prey. AIDS, which had been a reality somewhere else, suddenly crashed onto our shores like a tsunami and took us all with it.

While I had already been trying to find my way into the maze of denials and fears surrounding the pandemic, knowing that this was my greatest target yet, I still didn't have the courage to confront the issue as part of my life too. It was still so easy to believe it couldn't happen to me. And even some close friends were dying of 'flu'.

Bambi Kellermann hijacked the issue from me with ease.

She would be the mouthpiece of reason. She would talk the talk and name the names. She would out the virus within her. For Bambi would develop full-blown AIDS. And, because she had the money and the knowledge, she could be treated and live life more carefully.

Evita is a more difficult reflective surface to use. She, like so many white

Christian Afrikaners, wants nothing to do with these issues at all. I had tried to weave the most famous white woman into the new struggle at various AIDS fundraisers. In a Durban effort, she crossed the stage in a magnificent ball gown to announce that she was obviously at the wrong place. Things like that couldn't happen to her.

'But then my son De Kock said: "Mama, you must go and tell the people that this virus is the most democratic thing in South Africa. HIV takes no sides. It can happen to blacks and whites, old and young, man and woman. And even Afrikaners!"'

The audience would laugh and Evita would smile, but, thanks to her lack of irony, she didn't see the joke.

'"Tell the people they must practise safe sex."' Evita would draw a deep breath and blurt out. 'So, skatties, put your love in a plastic bag!'

She had yet to find the courage to articulate the word 'condom'.

Bambi, on the other hand, says: 'Fucking kills! Get fucked in the arse, get fucked in the cunt, get a mouth full of come, and, without condoms, you're in kak!'

This was a new revolution. As my instinct developed, allowing me to confront the reality of the problem and see how my limited repertoire of tricks could be used to combat the lack of knowledge about AIDS, various projects emerged. The show *For Fact's Sake* moved shakily towards *Foreign Aids*.

Roger Smith and I went back to the drawing board to see how we could create punchy videos to help people change their fear into common sense. The first attempt was a corporate video called *Having Sex with Pieter-Dirk Uys*.

We approached the major corporations in South Africa and offered to make them a short film that incorporated what they were doing for their employees, balancing it with humour in my style. We had thirteen replies. And so we prepared a thirty-minute 'generic' comedy show, complete with my familiar characters as well as new ones, all reflecting denials and fears around the virus. Bambi was the star in her commercial for condoms.

There were four windows in the structure for each corporate's information to be edited in, so that each video was specific to each client.

We travelled round the country and filmed with the staff of Woolworths, I&J, Edgars, Gold Fields, Anglo American and others, often dazzled by the amount of good work that had been done for the protection of the work-force. The Minister of Health only had to phone up three of the companies and ask for their input, and she'd have the most comprehensive plan to fight the fear and scourge of AIDS. But of course, Comrade Minister Manto

Tshabalala-Msimang would not stoop so low as to confront her portfolio with any sense of care or compassion.

Standard Bank had made hundreds of copies of their *Having Sex* video and allowed the workers to take them home. This was ideal, to have families sharing the experience and talking about it. I knew that many would be unhappy, and some would be shocked and angry. I suspect that many were delighted. But no matter what the effect, that door had been opened, and once people talked, the fear factor would diminish. Not disappear, but to be in control of that fear meant being brave enough to confront it and give it a name.

'It's only a virus,' Bambi would say. 'It's not a bomb on a train in Madrid. It's not a tidal wave. It's not a bullet from a gun. It's just a virus ...'

Bambi's impact was so remarkable that we planned a second video. Called *Survival Aids*, it was a spoof of the popular quiz show *The Weakest Link*, which had just started on TV. We auditioned and cast twelve actors, people who would represent a wide cross-section of South Africans: the street kid, the schoolgirl, the housewife, the businessman, the student, the addict, the gay, the rugger-bugger. Easily recognised stereotypes who, through their fears and denials, had to put across the message of tolerance and calm to a very diverse and suspicious audience. Bambi Kellermann took the part of the quiz mistress. Inspired by the icy, sardonic British bitch who'd become a household spit throughout the BBC-watching world, Madame Kellermann would sit on her high stool and demolish with a hiss and a smile.

Our version was no weak link. The questions were all about AIDS and denials around HIV. The fears and the urban legends. The mystery and the secret had to be exposed, and here again, humour was the great weapon of mass distraction. If the contestants failed the round, they would be disqualified, not as the weakest link, but the biggest poep.

The first reaction from colleagues in the industry was a sniff and a shrug. Poep was too silly for something so serious. But the video hadn't been made for the sophisticated fans of Pedro Almodóvar or Spike Milligan! Roger and I planned that this video would be given away free. Originally we'd hoped to find a distributor to make it available to the public at a minimal cost. The question I get all the time is from parents who ask: 'Can't you make a video for us to take home and put into the machine for the kids? We won't watch it, but when we come into the lounge, we can ask: What have you looked at? And then maybe we can talk about it ...?'

We approached some major supermarket empires, but the subject was too raw for their clientele. We asked the petrol companies to make it available at their many garage shops, but again the talk of condoms and sex was not compatible with company policy. We didn't move from square one. Eventually we sent out an SOS to various interested parties that had already expressed support for our work. The Eric Sampson Foundation, Mark Shuttleworth, Pick 'n Pay, Shoprite, Foschini, Affrox, Iscor, Deloitte, MTN and Vodacom responded, as did mega-producer Cameron Mackintosh. They gave us enough financial support to film and package the video and send copies to as many places as we could before the Christmas season paralysed the land: schools, reformatories, clinics, hospices and colleges. Eventually we even had calls from desperate parents in disadvantaged townships. 'I have a video machine. I saw your video at the clinic. Please send me a copy and I can show twenty kids every hour over the holidays. We can reach a few thousand!'

Other reactions were predictably cold, accusing us of encouraging the use of condoms to promote unbridled promiscuity. The constant echo of the word 'abstain' made us realise where such a measure could work: in First World societies where sex is still the result of choice. In our Third World, that luxury no longer existed. Sex happened, often without consent.

Then the banks who'd already had *Sex with Pieter-Dirk Uys*, many times it seemed, requested a follow-up. To focus on the need for corporate HIV-testing, we prepared *It's Just a Small Prick*. Again we bracketed prominent corporate information about testing and knowing one's status and getting on with life with sketches and characters who'd underline the importance of it all with humour.

Bambi featured with flair in all three projects. And because she was the sister of someone everyone knew, when a Sunday newspaper wrote that Evita's sister had The Virus, my sister Tessa phoned me from London.

'I'm getting e-mails from people, darling. They are sorry I've got AIDS!'

Bambi gave me the needed backbone and punch for the new structure of *For Fact's Sake*, which became *Foreign Aids*.

'I often think of those days in Paraguay,' she says, carefully applying deep red varnish to her long nails. 'Beautiful weather, especially in spring and autumn. I remember one Saturday afternoon we were sitting on our patio. Oh, darling, we had a villa! You would die for it. Up on the hills that surround the city. Like Beverly Hills, except better. Of course in Paraguay we had old Nazis; while in Beverly Hills they have neo-cons!'

She laughs and sips her vodka martini.

'I shouldn't drink vodka with my antiretrovirals, but I can't help it. I was introduced to vodka by a sweet old nun in Stuttgart in 1966. She said:

"Bambi liebchen, always remember! Before you are forced to eat aeroplane food or give a blow job, first gargle with vodka!"'

She lights another cigarette.

'Remember, my husband was Minister of War. He knew many controversial people. And on this Saturday we were having strudel, schnitzel, schnapps und viel Spass. And Martin Bormann was with us for the weekend. He'd just come through from Philadelphia, where he'd had a facelift; now he looked like Gregory Peck. And Dr Joseph Mengele popped in with his three Persian kittens on the way to the cat show.

'And Martin Bormann suddenly said something very strange. He said: "How is it possible that during the 1930s, when there were so many decent and good British and American politicians and statesmen, who knew already in the 1930s that we Nazis were killing Jews – why did they do so little to stop us?"

'I, of course, had no answer to that. Until Adolph Eichmann came out of the guest cottage. My God, what a party pooper he was! No sense of humour at all. He said: "What a stupid question. Of course there were decent and good British and American statesmen and politicians who knew that a future with a few less irritating, successful, pushy orthodox Jews could only be good for their businesses. So maybe that's why they took their time before they came into the Third Reich to punish us Nazis. Conveniently six million dead Jews later."'

She takes a deep drag of her cigarette. The smoke whirls into her eye, making it water. Or is she crying?

'Like today. Africa is dying of AIDS and everyone knows. No one can say one day: "I didn't know what was happening."

'So why is so little happening? Or are there still too many decent and good politicians and statesmen who know that a future with a few million less starving, demanding, needy, arrogant blacks can only be good for First World globalisation?

'So maybe that's why we create this War on Terror to keep the front pages of the newspapers busy, and when it's too late, we can look around at Africa and say: "My God! What has happened to all those people?"

'And then we can donate billions of dollars and feel better. And give a televised Live Aids concert and wheel Simon and Garfunkel out to sing "Bridge over Troubled Water ..."'

She looks into the distance. Her eyes are still watering from the smoke, even though she's put the cigarette out earlier. That's when I realised what to do with Bambi Kellermann and her unmentionable disease and unwelcome words.

I'd put them all in a new show called *Foreign Aids* and tour the world.

14

TOURING AN ANGRY WORLD

M y world tour had started back in 1986.
Through Patricia Macnaughton, my London agent and a good friend,
I came into contact with Nicolas Kent. Patricia was the chair of the Tricycle
Theatre board and Nick the artistic director. The Tricycle is an exciting fringe
theatre on Kilburn High Street, that part of North London where Tessa and
I lived for our first years in the UK back in the sixties. We'd go and eat at
the Parthenon Restaurant. The takeaway in its place is no longer called that,
and the theatre is now next door.

Nick invited me to bring my one-man show to his theatre for the late-night
slot in September 1986. The offer came at just the right time. I had completed the disjointed experience of filming *Skating on Thin Uys*, and an offer
of interest in my work from an English theatre was essential and healing.
There was no money, but there was hope. It was also a political risk for Nick
to invite me. I was not a black, disadvantaged, suffering political animal. I was
a white Afrikaner who was reputedly anti-apartheid.

Was that anti–South African enough for the humourless liberals of London?

It seemed not. They picketed the theatre for the first few nights, handing
out pamphlets which spelt my name wrong and claimed I was a supporter
of genocide against little black children. I went out one night before the show
and asked a young white woman handing out the pamphlets what she was
doing. She shrugged. Didn't know, but handed me a pamphlet. I invited her
in to see the show. She never came back again.

The late-night slot wasn't easy. Thanks to my spartan stage settings –
the four cardboard boxes, minimal props and a few costumes, with me
remaining on stage throughout the performance – I could fit in with any
other production's scenery. I was late night to a busy show that had a large
cast, and all the dressing rooms were full. So I'd stand outside the side door
to the auditorium in the cold with my boxes, waiting for them to end before
I could scamper onto the stage and set up my show. It was the first of
many ridiculous compromises all over the world over the next fifteen years,
fitting in with other people, not wanting to be a nuisance, being timid and
polite and catching colds and coughs and flu. And once being bitten by, I
think, a bat!

The response to the UK version of *Adapt or Dye* in 1986 was cautious. The politics overpowered opinions of the performance. The repertoire of characters was taken for granted and I don't think the material was anti enough for many Brits. But the South Africans who came were warm and passionate in their embrace. Most of them were exiles. Many of them were black. A few of them carried the scars of torture and abuse. All of them missed home so much it hurt like cancer.

That short season did interest a producer from the Edinburgh Festival. The next year I made my first visit to that beautiful Scottish city, which is particularly insane when it's filled with constantly auditioning mad comedians, and the rush of adrenaline filled the air like tear gas. My venue was usually the Assembly Rooms. It was challenging and chilling to be in competition with so many brilliant and savage young comedians from all over the world. The festival had become the meat market of ambition. Everyone gave award-winning turns just in case the talent agent from Hollywood or the local television station was in the house.

I seemed to be the only performer doing 'stand-up comedy' with various characters as mouthpieces. As yet I had not discovered my own voice. In South Africa the occasional opinion ventured in a show would be shot down by critics as unnecessary and embarrassing. And of course I believed them.

'We don't want to hear what he has to say,' they trumpeted. 'We want entertainment!'

But at the Edinburgh Festival I saw the power of anger and affront, the effect of opinion and contempt so cleverly disguised as comedy and stand-up clowning.

I had already been performed at the Edinburgh Festival a decade earlier, when Roberta Durrant directed a production of *Paradise Is Closing Down*, co-produced by William Burdett-Coutts, who eventually invited me back to the Assembly Rooms, which he was then running. In 1979 I was there as playwright and mouse in the corner. But, with the growing experience of each festival, I allowed myself to take chances, to be less obvious in my fashionable attacks on white South Africa, and to reflect the similar blemishes of racism and intolerance that were all too obvious around me.

Wim Visser, Dutch producer and soon-to-become firm friend, flew over from Amsterdam to see me perform at the Traverse Theatre. Patricia had placed me in this wonderful main festival venue where my work could be appreciated alongside weird and dangerous work from Eastern Europe, the German underground and the professional British fringe. That led to an intensive four-week tour of the Netherlands. I stayed in Amsterdam and travelled out to various picturesque towns of Holland to perform in English in magnificent theatres, town halls and auditoriums.

The Dutch loved the material, especially the 'tijpetjes', the characters. Even in those days of anti-apartheid passions, there was still a deep affection for the strangeness of the Afrikaans language, this poor cousin of Dutch that had been demeaned by evil politics into the guttural sound of suffering. Even though my whiteness glowed like neon, the exiles were the first to support my work, and soon, with their raised fist of approval, Evita Bezuidenhout became a favourite Tante for Dutch audiences as well. The Nederlandse production of *Adapt or Dye* was filmed sensitively for Dutch television and broadcast nationwide, ensuring me a substantial audience in that country to this day.

The Dutch know what's going on in the world, especially in Europe, because all roads to anywhere go through Amsterdam. Every newspaper from any world centre is available next to the nearest coffee shop. It made structuring a satire all the more challenging, and daily research was imperative. In the United Kingdom, on the other hand, parochialism ruled: Europe happened to start across the water and the rest of the world came to London as tourists. My local material for the Edinburgh shows often had to be adapted and simplified to make sense to an audience that only knew their own familiar references. There I learnt how to cut my foreign foot to fit the local shoe.

Even when President PW Botha suddenly retired in the middle of my 1989 season, there were very few in the audience who seemed to know what he had done, or even who he was. I had recorded an hour-long TV special, directed by Penny Cherns, who'd been responsible for the London production of *Panorama*. *Bite the Ballot* went onto Channel 4 one night at 11.30. The midnight slot always seems to have had my name on it. Probably because the planners didn't think anyone would understand the material, or didn't think the material was suitable for anyone under the age of twenty, or some other reason.

When we'd packaged the show some months before, PW Botha was still playing Caligula, alive and well and wasting the land. The day he left the palace, frenzied efforts were made to bring *Bite the Ballot* up to date. We couldn't change the material, so they added a message at the beginning, suggesting that when PW Botha heard about this programme, he tried to have it cancelled by resigning.

My last visit to Edinburgh was at the end of apartheid. 1993's show was called *An Audience with an African Queen*, in which Evita Bezuidenhout takes questions from the punters after a first act of characters and quirks that put the South African political picture in context. But now there was too much explaining, too many footnotes, too much confusion. Lizz Meiring came with me as Bokkie Bam, Evita's squeaky secretary. The show had played as *An Audience with Evita Bezuidenhout* throughout South Africa during the changes that shook the foundations of the country in 1990/91. Then we toured Holland, with great success. People allowed themselves to go and have fun. They asked outrageous questions, and, of course, the humourless and hypocritical Mrs Bezuidenhout gave them more than they bargained for.

But not in Edinburgh. We were performing in an annex venue of the Assembly Rooms, a beautiful Spiegeltent that dated back to the previous century and where tarts had danced and morals had been muted. It stood elegantly on the gentle green grass of a local park, within earshot of the Moscow Circus! The hoots, screams and roars from that tent almost overpowered our little effort, and even though Evita commented that the noise reminded her of her maid's rooms on Friday nights, the piece didn't make much of an impression.

The politics of change in the world outside were more interesting.

Mikhail Gorbachev had emerged from Moscow and straddled the barbed-wire gulags of the Soviet empire, slowly unravelling the mess and immobilising the tension of the Cold War, while new South African führer FW de Klerk very simply ended the terror of apartheid. The sinister Berlin Wall crumbled into a heap of dirt and dust. The world laughed and sang and danced. Fuck the stage! The world had become the stage!

I will never forget that moment. We were in Johannesburg with *Rearranging the Deckchairs*, performing at the Market, and Chris and I watched the joins in the Iron Curtain buckle and bend on television.

'We should be there,' I screamed with excitement. 'This will never happen again!'

But our show had to go on, and so the Berlin Wall came down without us.

The inauguration of Nelson Mandela on 11 May 1994 also happened behind my back. I was touring Holland and watched the magical moment on television in my hotel room, in floods of tears and awash with South African wine. Was it even more moving being outside South Africa at that moment? There stood the tall, elegant man with the golden smile, who had come out of twenty-seven years of hell to help us find a hint of heaven.

My big tour of Germany took place before the birth of our democracy, but when Mandela was already free and conquering the world. Wearing the

'Mandela for President' election badge raised a delighted reaction from everyone I met, from Bavaria to the Reeperbahn in Hamburg. I had been part of a small South African/German cultural exchange the year before, visiting a few choice cities with a German/English version of *Adapt or Dye*, which was well received by audiences. Granted, most of them had South African connections, and I even met some brandy-soaked exiles from the Cape Flats who took credit for starting The Space Theatre. I smiled and congratulated them.

One of the producers, a former rock band manager, suggested that we follow this up with an intensive tour. The Uys ego purred at the idea, and so I arrived in Düsseldorf with a show called *Negerküsse* to start my seventy-performance, forty-city tour of Germany. And Austria. And Switzerland. And Hell!

Negerküsse was a famous politically incorrect German chocolate delicacy, with a dark exterior and a soft white centre. Like our Sweetie Pies in South Africa. Nigger kisses? Hello? Very up my street.

And so, with *A Kiss on Your Koeksister* as the basis for the show, I opened with most of the material in English, but, growing in confidence as we travelled, soon the majority of the show was in my Ausländer-Deutsch.

The show celebrated the end of apartheid and the coming South African democracy. Now Germans could visit our country without feeling guilty as they had during the many lavish visits during the worst years of our own Reich. The National Party bazaar – in this case, bizarre – was my theme, with costumes and props on a large trellis table festooned with flags and all the colourful propaganda associated with such jingoistic events. And because it was a German/South African connection, we framed the stage in an ornate arch with the simple words: 'Ferien Macht Frei' – Holidays make you free. But everyone icily read the original words that were once engraved on the German conscience like a festering tattoo, 'Arbeit Macht Frei', on a similar archway under which the inmates of Auschwitz would stumble, never to return.

It set the unsubtle tone of the material, which was full of odious but effective comparisons with Nazism, with our shared emerging democracies, with familiar national hypocrisy and social amnesia dominating the humour. What humour! A German joke is no laughing matter! The majority of the audiences in the smaller venues had come because they had photographed a nice giraffe in the Kruger National Park on a holiday and thought they'd have a nice time with this Afrikaans comedian. They had a horrible time. I had a horrible time.

Things changed radically when the audiences were under thirty. Some of the cities hosted me in university venues, and that was exciting and challenging. The material worked. The politically incorrect references and exposure of racism and bigotry found a welcome reaction from young Germans who were now confronting their new national geography and a million instant fellow citizens.

Like all tours, the bad experiences stay faint in memory, while the good ones are now tinged with sentiment. It is easy to forget the times I ended up in broken-down dressing rooms, once even on a smelly stairwell, preparing the show while practising the German pronunciation of a corrupt local politician's name. The memory of toffee-nosed conservatives walking out noisily is fainter now. Lonely, boring Sundays in deserted German cities with rubbish on television and no one to talk to? It still happens in other deserted Australian, Canadian, American, Dutch, Irish and Danish cities. Sometimes the discovery of a museum or art gallery brightened up the silent day as I waited, like a vampire, for the night in order to do The Show.

Some German cities had a beat of the past that couldn't be ignored. I performed in Köln on the chilling anniversary of Kristallnacht, when the Nazis torched synagogues and ashed and trashed the Jewish-German heritage. Berlin was electrifying under heavy snow. The Kurfürstendamm, its sombre memorial Gedächtniskirche looming like a destroyed spaceship against the muddy sky, was a sepia snap from the 1920s. I could feel my mother's childhood and smell the energy of that Berlin.

My producer's organisational abilities were ludicrous. I should've sensed it from the start. Besides booking the show into highly inappropriate places, he sent us back and forth on the Autobahn on a daily rush from city to city. From north to south, then east to west. He must have had geographical dyslexia. Stuttgart Monday. Hanover Tuesday. Köln Wednesday. Magdeburg Thursday. Husum near Denmark on Friday, and Bern in Switzerland on Saturday!

I had a few chances to walk out, and the temptation was huge. But the show was booked out to people who had shown interest. I was a professional, albeit an unhappy and lonely one, and I had work to do. So listening to the good German and Jew within me, I obeyed orders and, oi, did I march!

Sophia Loren phoned me at my hotel in Munich. I had sent her my schedule and she had just received the Christmas card I had made of our picture together, taken backstage at the Hollywood performance of my show that she and her son Edoardo had attended.

She was thrilled with the picture.

'We both look so beautiful,' she laughed.

My battered pioneering spirit soared.

When the seventy performances ended in Munich at a vibrant venue filled nightly with a sophisticated cabaret audience who had seen the best in the world and still found time to be surprised by the journey I took them on, my producer dropped his grenade. He could not pay me any money! There was nothing left after expenses and paying himself 45 per cent of the takings.

'Kein geld.'

I can still taste the dryness in my mouth, feel the dull knot of vomit in my gut.

'Don't cry!' was my first thought.

'Kill him!' only came later.

What could I do? Sue him? Sure, but that would have to happen in his own district of Düsseldorf, and we all know there's no future in that kind of panicked overreaction.

I limped back to South Africa, shocked and sobered. It was my own fault once again. Trusting, grateful, sweet, polite and no-trouble Pieter-Dirk Uys had signed the contract, while his literary agent was just across the Channel, a phone call and a fax away! Patricia Macnaughton would have given the whole package a sardonic sniff and torn it up.

I now think of this German Tournee as my karma. I remember it as a singular experience of a lifetime. I will never forget it, or do it again. The four months in Germany brushed up against my roots. Berlin. Charlottenburg. Dachau. Salzburg. Vienna. I want to go back one day and stay in Berlin for a time, at least so I can learn the language well enough to stand up on a local stage and hear Bambi Kellermann say: 'I am an Afrikaner! Ek is 'n Afrikaner! Ich bin ein Afrikaner!'

*   *   *

My tour of the centres outside South Africa became an annual thrill. Every year I'd go somewhere else for a time, doing a show that had been tested and tried in South Africa, but adapted to that particular society I was out to catch in my net of theatrical tricks. It became clear to me that I couldn't write a show for the UK, Canada or Australia in South Africa. I could structure one, so that the framework was clear and logical, but only on that foreign soil could I smell the special perfume of their problems and discover their secrets stuffed into cupboards of denial. I needed these for the show. I had to take South Africa to them, not bring them all those thousands of miles to South Africa. If I did that, most of the audience would want to see the lions and elephants. But when their rotten local government was sweetly exposed by Mrs Bezuidenhout, it had huge impact.

I also understood the importance of remaining universal in my material and not too specific. The world was still very fractured, and individual national disasters still had a unique flavour. Today it is different. Through the 'War on Terror', everyone is united by fear. Today the world is like South Africa was in the 1980s. Maybe apartheid was twenty years ahead of them after all.

A six-week tour of Canada in 1987 allowed me a week's holiday in New York, on that day in October when the Stock Exchange collapsed. During the first tour of Germany, I spent an Easter weekend in Lubyana, Serbia, just a few hundred kilometres from a bloody civil war. It felt as if I was in the eighteenth century. The show I gave there, in a large room on the roof of the massive opera house, was attended by a majority of black students from the local Serbian university!

I could share with them: 'What's your problem here? Your civil war is still hundreds of kilometres away! Mine is in my own backyard!'

After racing through Germany with *Negerküsse*, our insane schedule diverted us through Austria to perform in Graz, Salzburg and Vienna. That required a total rewrite of the material, because Germany was no longer the issue. Austria was. Then, three days later, the show became a Swiss obituary as it performed in Zurich's Rote Fabrik.

There something went snap. I was in a small hotel in a small street in this gorgeous frigid city, sprinkled with snow and Christmas lights. No one to talk to. No one to share anything with. I went out and bought a packet of cigarettes and a lighter. I returned to my small room and locked myself in my small bathroom. I sat on the loo and slowly, sexily smoked three whole cigarettes. I hadn't smoked since I gave it up in 1974. It was wonderful! Better than sex. I threw the rest of the packet away and kept the lighter as a reminder of my lack of fibre! Zurich felt better after that.

While apartheid was the issue, I was a problem. White was not black. Black was right. White was not supposed to be there. The cultural boycott had been in force for most of the 1980s and I'd often come across strict upholders of that boycott. I couldn't agree with it, no matter how righteous the passion of punishing Pretoria was.

'Do you have the answer to our question?' I would ask.

'The answer is: get rid of apartheid and free Mandela!' they would recite.

'Why don't you share that with us in South Africa?'

'It will be banned!' they sniffed.

'Yes, but let the apartheid government stop you from saying it. Your cultural boycott is doing their work for them. And believe me, no Afrikaner politician is going to change his politics so that you relax your boycott and send us your incomprehensible plays!'

The economic boycott of apartheid South Africa was constantly trumpeted by politicians, but it was hot air and hypocrisy. Trade went on as usual in secret through third parties. The sports boycott was painful for National Party supporters and probably did more than anything to weaken their Afrikaner pigheadedness. But the cultural boycott left a vacuum that has not been filled to this day. As always, American culture stands back for no conscience. So while British and European culture was carefully denied access to South Africa for all those years, the greasy, garish influx of American snap-crap-and-pop seeped through the starving society. Now in our young democracy we speak American, think American and eat American. The odd attacks on Eurocentric culture are empty political punches from those who often have no understanding of what the argument is about. The anger against those former colonial cultures is sharpened through an attack on cultures that don't even have a creative echo among the Rainbow Nation. We don't comprehend the accents of the United Kingdom. We don't relish the sounds of European languages. The cultural boycott boomeranged and we are all poorer for it.

'And if you're supporting a cultural boycott, why do you allow me here?' I would ask.

'You're anti–South African!' they'd say.

'No, I'm a white South African here in your society! Shouldn't I be banned from coming here?'

'No, you're anti-apartheid!' they flailed and fussed.

'Yes, but I'm proudly South African. I'm anti-stupidity! Legalised racism is stupid! To withhold culture as a weapon to fight that is also stupid!'

They stopped asking me to the parties.

*   *   *

America took over from London's West End as the mecca of my theatrical ambition.

By the end of the century I had managed to perform at the BAM Festival in New York with *You ANC Nothing Yet*. I visited San Diego, where Evita received her Living Legacy Award and rewarded the judges with a show at the Globe Theatre. I popped into Los Angeles for a performance where Sophia saw me become Evita on stage, and spent a four-week season in San

Francisco with *One Man One Volt* at the Mason Street Theatre. There I could feast my eyes on Alcatraz, the prison island in the Bay, so familiar to someone who had avoided looking at Robben Island for most of his life.

I sent a postcard to Winnie Mandela from Alcatraz.

'Dear Winnie, wished you were here. Love, Evita Bezuidenhout.'

I heard later how much she laughed.

It took a familiar battle to establish my style of work in America as more than just a weird foreign noise on the horizon. That bloody sword was the HI-virus.

15

THE MIƎƎION

AIDS is succeeding in South Africa where apartheid failed. More than 600 people are reported to die every day because of government carelessness.

The official denials from a President who doesn't seem to care, and a Minister of Health who couldn't care less, have condemned millions of our people to an untimely death and a wasted life. There is more money than can be counted in South Africa to fight the pandemic. Most of it stays safely in the clutches of those who enrich themselves. Very little filters down to the people who need it.

There is no point in discussing what is going wrong with the daily confrontations with the disease by South African politicians and international society. There is, very simply, no political leadership. Thabo Mbeki will not acknowledge the fact that South Africa suffers a 9/11-type loss of life every few days. There is nothing we can do other than bribe those in charge of the issues to change their minds. Not even Bill Gates seems to have that much money.

Using humour as a weapon once again seems to help in some ways. Whereas the first virus of apartheid was with us for over forty years, presumably without a cure, the cure was there all the time. It was called democracy, but we were too frightened to look in that direction. Apartheid was visible in its colour and sign-postings. HIV is a silent, secret, invisible terrorist. It comes when we come. And there is the real problem. Sex.

All religions are very particular about sex. The official morality that guides 'decent' societies avoids the words that describe the minefield. 'Sexual intercourse' used to mean something specific, but now has become a vague comic punch line since Bill Clinton got away with using it to deny it had happened between him and Miss Lewinsky.

So what would work to normalise the problem? All that is needed is talk. Talk! But no one is talking. Politicians are reciting and procrastinating. Doctors are repeating and nit-picking. Councillors are long-winded and boring. Statistics deaden any feeling of personal involvement. And fear is all-embracing and deafens and blinds us to the simple fact: it's just a virus!

Foreign Aids is probably the most important theatre I have created. It's more than just a one-man satire. It's not just a string of characters and a potpourri of issues like most of the other pieces in my repertoire. It has taken audiences away from their usual reactions of applause and laughter, and forced them into areas of emotion that amaze and frighten.

The story of HIV/AIDS is not new. In the First World it ploughed a deep and tragic path, especially in the gay community, during the 1980s. Every American star wore the red ribbon at every opportunity. The world adopted the symbol as a demonstration of care. Then, as medical research produced combinations of drugs and treatments, HIV became a treatable disease and the First World could live with AIDS. They had the money, the structures and the motivation.

The degradation of the African continent into a wasteland because of the virus has been documented to death, passionately dissected and financed on every level of media, business, state and church. But people are still dying as if nothing has happened.

Of course, every politician will eventually address the issue if he or she has any common sense. To fight for the future of children infected with AIDS is not a choice, it is a commitment. The focus remains on those living with HIV and those suffering from AIDS.

But what about those *not* living with HIV or AIDS? The majority of people in every society? How many times do I hear them mutter that their loved ones are suffering from TB, dying of cancer, enfeebled by Alzheimer's, stricken by strokes and paralysis. 'What is so special about the AIDS sufferers?' they ask, with an edge of prejudice.

Nothing is more special about them or their lonely lot. It's just that the route of the illness is so avoided, ignored, denied. If the virus happened in the lung, the ear or the foot, there would be no problem talking about it. But, like the ancient scourge of syphilis in the pre-penicillin era, HIV/AIDS demands discussion of sex in all its dripping, slimy, slippery, pulsating, erect and throbbing detail.

Nobody wants to go there. But theatre must venture where no man dares to tread. And I had to go there with tinsel in my dress and a neon spring in my step.

How does one entertain about death?

First, remove the fear. It then becomes an entertainment about life threatened, not death inevitable. When it became obvious a year into the new century that I was denying the obvious target in my work and life, I tried to find a way of confronting my own fear of AIDS by taking sex as the subject for a new show.

The title was the only thing worth salvaging. The rest was a collection of schoolboy smut, wanking gags, penis jokes and feeble cribs from other comedians. In other words: a general mess. *For Fact's Sake* stumbled through a few months of weekend performances at the Perron. None of the material warranted an audience, and yet the people there had a good time.

That's the magic of the place. It's like showing off in the lounge. There is no threat, because who cares! Here is a small pink, blue and green iron 'Baghdad Café' in the middle of nowhere, with nothing to commend it other than the hint of marvellous madness.

People love mad. Mad is good. When my friends heard I'd moved to Darling from Cape Town, they said: 'Shit! You're mad.'

I was glad. That meant it was the right thing to do.

For Fact's Sake helped me overcome my Calvinistic reluctance to confront issues of sex openly. We in the Dutch Reformed Church were trained to ignore the basic bodily function of reproduction, and, as a result, most of us made fatal errors early in our lives. We married too young. We went into relationships with no experience. We didn't respect nakedness or understand lust. We didn't know how to control ourselves.

I had created the commercial casing for the show, but there was no heart. The condom was there without the penis. As usual, the solution was far from the stage. When I realised that the only way to conquer my own denial was to face it, visiting schools with the AIDS awareness entertainment was the only way. Slowly but surely, it became a work in progress. I started to learn from the reactions to my actions, and understand the terrible responsibility of walking casually into the lives of hundreds of thousands of schoolchildren, armed with the word 'fuck' and a rubber penis, hoping to change their fear in order for them to focus on that fear. To swop confusion for care.

Now, after visiting five hundred schools and talking to one million schoolchildren of all ages, I can only take a deep breath and plunge back into the deep end. It's a never-ending commitment. As soon as the final-year students go, the small ones have got bigger, and within a year or two, I'm back on familiar ground with a new generation of the future.

Nothing changes when it comes to information about sex. Nothing helps when that knowledge is paralysed by fear. But the theatre is still the ultimate hothouse for developing small rare plants. The Perron allows me to experiment. And gives me the right to fail.

If there is one lesson I have learnt and treasure in my independence, it is the realisation that failure is often more important than success. Yes, it's great to win. It's wonderful to earn. It's even better to spend and celebrate. But when something that has taken your life's blood, your full attention, your all, fails? Does that mean you discard it as a flop? Is it a waste of time, an embarrassment? No. You pick up the pieces that work and start again. The second time round, the process is smoother, quicker, more careful and takes you closer to the success that eluded you before. I've learnt to be wary of success. It can become the ultimate prison, trapping you into repetition and disappointment. Of course people want the same. That's what success means. More of what they loved. But you can never give the same, because then you lose the element of surprise. It will inevitably be less rather than more. Then people say: 'Not as good as last time!' That's when you hope you were nice to people on the way up, because now you'll meet them on the way down. And, brother, you'll need all the help you can get!

I look back on my career of many years and even more projects, and it is the few that didn't make it as 'successes' that stick in the mind like flaming torches.

Failure doesn't mean it doesn't work, or that it is wrong. Failure means that your square peg is just not round enough to fit into the triangular hole! It needs more work and extra care. It needs a clear perspective. It needs time.

The failure of *For Fact's Sake* as theatre entertainment led to the success of *Foreign Aids*. And once I had visited enough schools to realise that the kids out there are the most important focus for the future, I had the backbone to the piece.

Statistics confuse and contradict. Numbers shock and alienate. Percentages horrify and numb. But one child's fight for life is enough to attract the attention and compassion of a billion people. One small person's need and one small creature's enjoyment of an embrace is enough to unleash a torrent of love and care that could solve the problems of the world in one deep breath. That, of course, will never happen, because life is not a musical. But *Foreign Aids* came close.

During the various seasons of the one-man, six-woman show – in London, Brighton, Sydney, New York, the Netherlands, Dublin and throughout South Africa – over a million rand was collected for the women and children associated with the self-help charity Wola Nani. Based in the black township of Khayelitsha on the Cape Flats, it assists women with AIDS and their HIV-positive children to deal with their illness as a part of life. To survive and be strong. It raises money by selling the now-legendary beaded brooches with the red AIDS ribbon on a colourful background. After I'd been introduced to Wola Nani by Noepsie Mkhwanazi when she was head girl of St Cyprian's School in Cape Town, the charity became the focus of *Foreign Aids*. The show informed and challenged people's sketchy details about the AIDS issue in South Africa, but it was afterwards that the miracle took place.

Standing in the foyer at a table covered with the colourful ribbons, I watched virtually every member of every audience open their purses and pour money into the plastic bag that acted as the piggy bank. People could take a ribbon as a memento. If they wanted to donate something, it could be anything they liked, from one dollar, pound or euro, to ten, twenty, fifty. Three hundred thousand rand was collected during twenty-four performances in Boston during January 2005 alone. Some cynics sniffed that the show played on guilt. I disagree. The show brought out compassion and care.

It is easy to send a cheque to a foreign place to help foreign people solve a foreign problem. Distance makes the heart go softer. Charity agencies throughout history have benefited and developed thanks to the generosity of such donations. But today the administrative costs of running such huge bureaucracies inevitably cut into the accumulated monies. Unfortunately, with many charities, less and less gets to where it should go, where it is most needed. But Wola Nani goes straight to the people who need it.

Members of the audience would say:

'What can we do? Can we write a cheque?'

'Yes, of course you can! But where do you go for your holidays?'

They were planning to fly off to Tuscany. 'It's an annual thing.'

'Why don't you come to Cape Town. Go to Sylvia Hayes at Wola Nani. She will introduce you to a family. A mother, hopefully a father, definitely children. Not all have AIDS, but very few have been to a movie. Take them to a film, buy them a hamburger, show them pictures of your world, your life, your grandchildren. Talk to them. But, more important, listen to what they have to say. And open a bank account for them and send them twenty dollars, ten pounds, twelve euro per month. That's your weekly hairdresser's tip. Not everyone steals from everyone in South Africa. That money can accumulate, and soon the child you support will have a thousand dollars saved. That's times six in today's exchange rate. It could mean life or death. Antiretrovirals. Further education.'

I suggested the concept of Care Tourism to the SA Tourism politburo, whereby people visiting South Africa who care can be professionally assisted to find the people who need help, and be confident that everything would be above board and controlled. There was no reaction other than an off-the-record rebuttal that 'South Africa doesn't need the world to come and help us. We do it ourselves.' Too much of that 'helping ourselves' could be regarded as stealing.

The most common question outside South Africa is about President Thabo Mbeki's 'weird' reaction to the virus.

'What's his problem? Why isn't he helping the people?'

I don't know. There are theories and urban legends, none of which are helpful, because none of us know. I have overstepped the line twice. Firstly through an open letter to 'Whoever Can Take it Further', suggesting that the President and Minister of Health be summonsed to appear in front of the International Court of Justice in The Hague on charges of genocide!

It caused an uproar. Party apparatchiks were furious. Political commentators ran for cover. There were some inspiring confidential messages of support, but far too many letters of agreement from white racists who still regarded Mandela and Tutu as enemies.

I hate the word genocide. It has shocking echoes of what happened in Auschwitz, Cambodia, Bosnia, Rwanda and Sudan. Is the comparison warranted or justified? When I use the word, I want to be proved wrong. I will spend the rest of my life apologising. But no one says anything. In fact, President Mbeki has managed to take the issue of HIV/AIDS off the agenda.

His success is dazzling. World leaders invite him to world events, and, like Bono and Richard Gere, he accepts and flies off into the sunset, leaving the confusions and mess behind. When he was in the USA in late 2003, in an interview with the *Washington Post*, he stated that he didn't know anyone who had HIV or, for that matter, anyone who had died of AIDS. The disbelief, anger and shock from within South Africa was intense. We all suspected that members of his inner circle had died of AIDS, disguised by the phrase 'natural causes'.

Over five days I carefully, angrily, nervously composed an open letter that went to the major newspapers in South Africa. It was copied to the President. I don't do things behind his back.

Friday 26 September 2003

To the Editor

When the President of South Africa speaks, he represents a democracy where 5 million citizens have HIV, where more than 600 people die each day from AIDS-related diseases, where 250 babies are born every 24 hours with the virus. Yet our President Thabo Mbeki says to the US-based *Washington Post*:

'I don't know anyone with HIV … Personally, I don't know anyone who has died of AIDS.'

He lies and so condemns his nation to death.

It is time to replace this man with a leader who cares about his people.

Not only does Thabo Mbeki spend most of his time outside South Africa speaking at international political jamborees, but he has now shown himself to be totally out of touch with his own country.

We are a young democracy, in which this man is but a chosen leader, not a royal dynasty.

The African National Congress deserves to celebrate the 2004 tenth-year anniversary of our young democracy.

The ANC is a former liberation movement, now a successful political party, committed to the issues of human rights and freedom. But this party of liberation will soon be remembered by history only as an accomplice to the genocidal Mbekivellian policies of their present leader.

Replace this failed leader with a comrade of compassion. There are many politicians in the ruling party and on the fringes of power. Men and women of compassion and care, of focus and commitment. They are needed now. Replace this failed civil servant in denial with a citizen who can heal and help, a leader who confronts the problems of our people and embraces our needs and aspirations.

No more Thabo Mbeki.

We need leadership to inspire confidence and optimism in our time of national fear and need. We need to inspire an impatient world to invest in us and believe in our future. With 40 per cent of our workforce HIV-positive, no one will invest in South Africa. And yet our President knows no one with HIV?

While everyone in our country has buried, nurtured, cared for, said farewell to, wept for and remembered a loved one who has died of this virus that has no cure, our elected President is confused and innocent of the pain and the tears.

Like when Steve Biko died, the then apartheid Minister of Justice Jimmy Kruger famously said:

'It leave me cold.'

South Africa leaves Thabo Mbeki cold.

There is not time for party politics here. Replace this man now, with a committed leader, and let him, or her, lead and help us to live.

Pieter-Dirk Uys
Darling

The reaction was far more intense than expected.

A week after my letter was printed in the Johannesburg *Sunday Times* of 5 October, Essop Pahad, Minister in the President's Office, wrote:

HIV/AIDS is a subject that engages the attention of the nation as nothing before.

The report of the national task team charged with preparing an operational plan on public-sector antiretroviral therapy is now with the Department of Health, and is to be discussed by Cabinet in the coming days.

Against this serious background, the antics of Pieter-Dirk Uys on HIV/AIDS – curiously afforded serious treatment in the *Sunday Times* via his letter 'Liar Liar' (October 5) – are a complicating irritant of minor scale.

But some damage is undoubtedly being done to South Africa's campaign against the scourge in terms of influencing public opinion, particularly the young, against government-led efforts, and particularly against the President personally.

These government-led efforts are widely acknowledged as the biggest and most comprehensive campaign against HIV/AIDS in Africa, which would presumably be news to Uys. Only last week, UN Secretary-General Kofi Annan praised South Africa for tripling its HIV/AIDS budget since the last UN summit on this issue.

House clowns in any democracy have some, mainly amusement, value. British society down the years would not have been what it is without the lampooning of *Private Eye* or *Spitting Image*. Uys's satire had some useful influence for enlightenment in the days when there was a total absence of democracy in South Africa, and his lampooning had something to do with helping to change attitudes away from apartheid and repression.

But his recent statements on the government's programme against HIV/AIDS can, if taken too seriously, hinder and confuse the national will to do something about the pandemic.

There is a need for all South Africans to remain resolute in the face of a grave challenge, which government and all sectors are dealing with responsibly. We should not be swayed by sideshows and contrived controversies.

Uys himself undermines what most of us took as a sincere and well-meant effort to spread awareness of the dangers of HIV infection, especially in schools. Something seems to go wrong, and he confuses satire and serious policy pronouncements. Or is this the problem of editors who choose to air some of his bizarre views in presumably serious columns?

In his latest assault on the President, Uys latches on to third-rate conclusions drawn from what President Mbeki said to the *Washington Post* about whether he knew people in his own family, or among his close associates who had died of AIDS, or were infected with HIV.

Evita's mother, Ouma Ossewania Kakebenia Poggenpoel

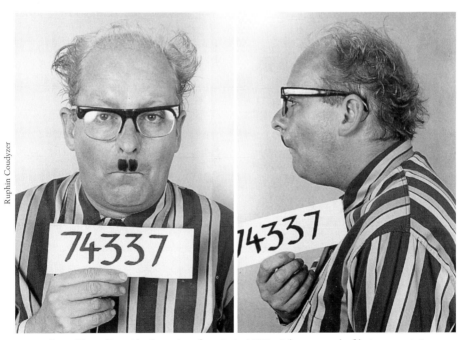

Oom Hasie Bezuidenhout in a futuristic ANC trial – accused of being a racist!

Izan Bezuidenh
member of the AWB   ,ner' twin
and twin son of Evita   .r of Bapetikosweti

Evita with her grandchildren – Winnie-Jeanne,
Nelson Ignatius and La Toya Ossewania

Ruphin Coudyzer

L[...] [...] kugel, African princess
leads [...] [...]ber-blonde, created in the 1970s
will eventually and still going strong

Anton Geldenhuys

Bambi Kellermann, Evita's sister who married a Nazi
and now runs a classy brothel in a Boland town!

Lionel Friedberg

With Sophia Loren in Hollywood

Benny Gool

Nelson Mandela shares an election platform with
the most famous white woman in South Africa, 1994

Evita's koek-and-koffie meeting before the 2004 election, with Tony Leon, leader of the official opposition, and Carol Johnson of the NNP

At the premiere of Evita's performance as Ester Viljoen in *Selle ou Storie* in Johannesburg in September 2004, an old flame pays tribute: Pik gives her a peck

The chorus line: Jan van Riebeeck; DF Malan; Hendrik Verwoerd; BJ Vorster; PW Botha; Pik Botha; Piet Koornhof; Chris Heunis; Hendrik Schoeman; oom in charge of Immorality Act; press photographer; Riaan Eksteen, head of the SABC; Jani Allen; AWB member; Koevoet security; security policeman; a white South African; Vause Raw; Ferdi Hartzenberg; Alan Hendrickse; a nuclear scientist at Koeberg; Wit Wolf; Mrs Pieterson; Cape Flats fairy; township terrorist; Nowell Fine; a kugel; Scarlett O'Hoera; Evita Bezuidenhout; Hasie Bezuidenhout

FW de Klerk; Nelson Mandela; Mandela's warder; Winnie Mandela; Desmond Tutu; Mangosuthu Buthelezi; Jay Naidoo; Frene Ginwala; Kader Asmal; Manto Tshabalala-Msimang; Margaret Thatcher; Queen Elizabeth II; Barbara Woodhouse; Richard Attenborough; Boy George; Joan Collins; Dr Ruth; Bill Clinton; Madeleine Albright; Boris Yeltsin; white SA voter; Ouma Kappie Kommando; housewife without a maid; civil servant post-1994; Felatia; Billie-Jeanne Bezuidenhout; De Kock Bezuidenhout; Izan Bezuidenhout; Ouma Ossewania Poggenpoel; Bambi Kellermann

PDU in front of the Duchess Theatre, London WC2, where *Elections and Erections* transferred from a sold-out season at the Soho Theatre in May 2004

Ruphin Coudyzer

As PW Botha with 'Thabo Mbeki' in *The End Is Naai*

President Mbeki gave an honest answer. He was speaking about a limited circle of family or close friends.

The government can endure the barbs flung by Uys. We even enjoy him at times. He was aptly described in one paper which ran his letter, as a 'comedian'. Indeed.

Surely the media should not dignify his twaddle by publishing it in serious columns. Unless of course we are wrong to assume that these are indeed serious columns!

An avalanche of letters hit the press. Cartoonists had a field day. The recent deaths of flu, whooping cough, lumbago and slipped discs by close associates of the President were exhumed and re-examined. Talk-radio stations were jammed with calls, and the issue became a public debate: is it unpatriotic to criticise the President, or the ANC government?

I went to London, taking *Foreign Aids* on tour, and ended up on a phone link with a late-night South African radio programme, sparring with party spokesmen and presidential advisors.

'Pieter, we are on the same side, my brother. You also did your bit for the Struggle. How can you suggest these things?'

'Smuts,' I replied, 'if I invited the President to join me in an HIV test, would he consider it?'

The gloves came off. Calls from other members of the ANC underlined the reality: there would no longer be argument or discussion.

'You're a racist!' they declared.

'You're unpatriotic!' they announced.

'You lie!' they screamed.

But by now we'd all lost the plot. The reason behind the original letter had been to underline the terrible fact that 600 people were dying every day because of this official denial. It ended up in pointless name-calling on an expensive satellite link between Pretoria and London in the middle of the night.

Mrs Evita Bezuidenhout came to the rescue. Her letter was published prominently by most South African newspapers. The *Sunday Times* of 12 October placed it on its leader page.

To the Editor

Nee, sies!

It is time for me to say something in defence of our President.

As the former South African Ambassador to the Independent Black Homeland of Bapetikosweti and confidante of the perpetrators of apartheid, I am ashamed to see in our newspapers how an Afrikaner is using his freedom of speech to insult and criticise Thabo Mbeki.

Pieter-Dirk Uys has always been a minor irritant to South African politicians. Unfortunately former President PW Botha wasn't brutal enough to end Uys's malicious agenda with imprisonment and/or death, and the present government is trapped by a democratic Constitution that enshrines tolerance and free speech.

Uys has insulted me for years through unhelpful criticism, so-called comedy and tasteless impersonation. I sincerely hope that the ANC will do everything in its power to counter his mischievous opportunism by focusing on real life and not on unwarranted satire.

I believe the President when he says he doesn't know anyone with HIV, or who has died of AIDS. Nor do I.

The ANC must rise above Uys's attention-seeking comments. They mustn't let a third-rate comedian turn them into fourth-rate politicians by overreacting with phrases similar to those once used by Botha's regime.

Evita Bezuidenhout
Laagerfontein, Mpumalanga

16

A LIFE SENTENCE

When President Mbeki accused Desmond Tutu of being a liar in his weekly letter on the ANC web page in 2004, the country gasped in disbelief. Our Archbishop Tutu? The icon who owns the moral high ground? Who could be so stupid, so tactless? So wrong? This remarkable giant of a man is not scared to be regarded as politically incorrect by his own comrades. He will stand up and say very loudly, as he had done: What is our relationship with that madman in Harare all about? Why is there so much official denial around HIV/AIDS? When are we going to help the apartheid victims we promised to assist?

Tutu also questioned the path black economic empowerment was taking, by which the same few rich comrades were being further enriched under the guise of empowering the formerly disadvantaged. Mbeki exploded in print, snidely suggesting that the Archbishop stay out of politics, which he seemed to not understand, not being a member of the party.

The Arch's reaction was vintage Tutu. He thanked the President for calling him a liar and promised to pray for him and his government, as he had done for the previous apartheid regime!

The unseemly spat was quickly covered over by a flurry of party statements and contradictions. But Mbeki kept scratching at the scab, making veiled comments about old men in politics. Could this nagging attack on Tutu be the result of an old gripe? Evita Bezuidenhout's explanation is perhaps too simplistic: 'The Truth and Reconciliation Commission refused to give the then Deputy President, Thabo Mbeki, amnesty for "actions committed during the struggle against apartheid". But we don't know what they were!'

In real political terms, this issue has been deleted. But my heart bleeds for my President. I know what anger can do. I have been there, vomiting out my fury onto the computer screen and sending letters to editors with terrible words like 'genocide' encased in opinion and protected by freedom of speech. That's why I have a small sign on my computer. I want to send a copy of it to President Mbeki.

'DON'T PRESS SEND WHEN PISSED!!!!'

*　　*　　*

Statements that are posted in a weekly presidential column on a political party website do not reach the people who are sick. The majority of the ANC supporters don't have access to computers. They don't switch on their Internet and read their leader's important policy pronouncements. So who is Mbeki aiming at here? His people or his peers? The First World leaders? The Bush and Blair duo? Kofi Annan? Is it still important for the President of South Africa to impress his former fellow students from his Sussex University days?

Back in the townships, being HIV-positive becomes a death sentence just by admitting to it. Access to clinics is free, but who will go? To be seen there, even with an eye infection, would be to feed the neighbourhood gossip mill. Many times I have asked local government officials where the young people can go for advice. Their rehearsed answer is usually the same: the clinic, the hospice. But they don't.

If anything will succeed, it is home care.

Already there are excellent structures to educate people to help each other. But candidates are taken out of their communities and trained far away in the cities. They stay there and find work. Strangers are then sent back to communities in small towns and rural areas to care for the sick and the frightened. That means Zulus could end up in Xhosa areas. This is about as successful as putting Palestinian home-carers into Jewish settlements!

Home-care centres should be in the townships. People from that township should be trained there and kept within their communities. They should then each be allowed to choose two more adults and two more children whom they personally train. Then it becomes a case of talking across the back fence. Familiarity and friendships allow for detailed conversations.

The woman whose husband works on the mines is terrified.

Who can she talk to? Her husband has come back and he demands sex from her. She knows he has women in Gauteng. So she asks him to wear a condom. He beats her up.

'I wear condoms with my girlfriends in Joburg,' he yells. 'You are my wife! I don't wear condoms with my wife!'

She goes to the priest. He condemns her from the pulpit. Condoms are frowned on by the Church.

But if she can talk to someone familiar to her, who has been trained to listen and advise, surely this is a step in the right direction? Does everything have to be so complicated? If the money is there, which it is? Well, up there somewhere. If the expertise is there, which it is? Well, over there somewhere. If the training is as good as it is, if there is so much available information, then why is there so little knowledge?

All the young South Africans at school know about condoms, although not all of them have actually seen one.

A thousand boys sit in the hall, transfixed by the small silver square in my hand.

'You know what this is?'

'Condom!' Their voices unite in a masculine growl.

'In this silver packet? Are you sure it isn't a chocolate?'

They roar with laughter, in anticipation.

'No! Condom!'

I wait for them to settle down. Silence. You could hear a pin drop. Or a zip open.

'Right, gentlemen. These condoms are made for us. Condoms go on cocks.' Sophisticated young men gasp like little boys. 'Stiff cocks.' Some giggle like schoolgirls. 'Now, to practise safe sex, we boys have to go into our rooms. And practise!'

A moment is needed for this to sink in, and the laughter ripples across the mass of men-in-the-making. 'Go into your room, lock the door, switch on the light, draw the curtains, drop your pants. Take out your piepie. Get it up and stiff. Think of someone sexy: Halle Berry. Paris Hilton. Colin Farrell. And when it's up and ready, you practise! Put the condom on in the light so you know what to do in the dark.'

I could be alone it is so quiet, so pregnant with pause.

'First, open it carefully.' I demonstrate as I talk. 'By pushing the condom to one side and tearing the other side open carefully. But see that your nail doesn't tear the latex. It's a fragile thing! Practise!'

Very often this is where I derail myself. The free condoms we get from government are sometimes very difficult to open. A disaster! What randy male is going to fiddle and fight with a small piece of silver wrapping with a throbbing erection pointing in the right direction?

'Remember, when you need to use this, you're as *jags* as a slang, and there's no time to mess about. Then, once you've carefully, expertly, opened the packaging, you must know what will come out of it!'

They know.

'Condom!'

'Ja,' I agree, 'but it feels like a snotty little bolletjie!' I slide it out. They grimace and shudder with laughter. 'See? Horrible! This you don't want to touch for the first time when your pants are round your ankles. You'll say "Ugh!" and let it drop. Now you must crawl around and try and find the condom in the grass, in the sand, on the carpet, in the sheets? No way!

That's when you just say: "What the hell! Fuck the condom! That virus can't happen to me!"

'That's your first mistake. It can. And it just needs one mistake to get it.'

The jokes are over. They all sit staring at the small latex parachute in my hand.

I also visit mature citizens with the information. Old people are getting infected as well. Grizzled grandfathers, sitting on their chairs in the township sun, have just collected their pension. The pretty teenage girl wants money. She gives the old man a great treat. He can just remain there with his pants open and she sits on his lap. In some retirement villages the sexy old gentlemen have smart cars and Viagra. They go out for their fun and bring the virus back and infect the pretty grannies with HIV.

Foreign Aids was recorded during its run at Pieter Toerien's Montecasino Theatre in September 2003. The SABC screened it on AIDS Day, 1 December, typically close to midnight. It should have been shown after the seven o'clock news when all the family could watch. It is now available through the rental shops of Nu-Metro. Now families can watch it together and be embarrassed, amused, shocked or disgusted. And talk. That's the first step in the right direction.

*   *   *

My most recent Afrikaans play was *Die Vleiroos* in 1991. Since then I have translated it as *The Marsh Rose* and written a film script of it for Sophia Loren. She didn't think it was right for her.

I am still under the spell of your beautiful story.

Only a pure and poetic soul could have built up a story like Marshrose.

It was a difficult reading, with too many flashbacks, but once you keep the main thread, you enter in a world of goodness, of purity, of fight against the many, too many crimes against the future of our world. These days after the Seattle and Davos events, your story takes more strength and credibility. Notwithstanding my positive approach to your work, as I look at it as an actress with my roots, with all the traditions I've been growing up, my emotional background, I must confess that I do not feel at home. The countryside, the family bonds, the social base – all that makes me a stranger and as a stranger, uncomfortable. I hope you will find a fine spirit who appreciates, as it deserves, the depth of feelings and the art of acting.

Do not give up! Please!

Thank you again and I congratulate you for your passionate and fine work.

Love to you and Tessa.

Your
Sophia.

Please call me if you need to talk further about it. Ciao.

I did call her. We spoke at length. I keep reminding her that the story is still here waiting for her. But now it was time for another play. There was no shortage of urgent inspiration.

Auditioning Angels is set in Johannesburg in a now disused wing of the largest hospital in the southern hemisphere. It had to be closed because of lack of money, all of which was swallowed up by the new luxurious cosmetic surgery wing and heliport. Here rich internationals could arrive by air for facelifts and be lifted to recuperate at expensive game farms.

A white child is raped by a black man who has AIDS. Because of the urban legend swirling around the country, he thought sex with a virgin would cure him. The child's family is gathered to hear the worst. The worst is not as bad as they imagine, but as a dysfunctional family, they have to confront their own ghosts.

Meanwhile, the precious antiretrovirals, still under ministerial embargo, are being stolen by a black nurse, who in turn gives the drugs to the small, sick, orphaned babies she rescues from the wards. At the end of the play, everyone leaves with a baby!

Auditioning Angels was commercially presented with no budget. As a result it couldn't be set in the right environment, as there was no money to fit out a state-of-the-art operating theatre. Lynne Maree worked on the script with me for weeks. She helped to streamline the dialogue and clarify the logic of the complex action. But she and the producer could not agree on her fee. Eventually Blaise Koch took over the direction of the play. I was very pleased to work with him again. Since the old Space days, we'd worked together occasionally, but this was the first big project we shared.

Blaise had just released his book. It tells of his fight against AIDS. He is openly HIV-positive and, as far as I was concerned, the perfect director to focus on the characters and not the chemicals.

We cast experienced, professional people, and joyfully Thoko Ntshinga headed the company as an elegant modern South African advertising executive, Majuba Xhaba, who is thrown headlong into the feud between members of the Nathan family, which is the core of the drama. We started with full houses on each opening night and then dwindled to a handful of interested and deeply moved people. The play was published privately, and was available from the first performance, making it part of the experience, and not, as so often, something that emerges as an afterthought a year later. That's like getting a road map after you've sold the car.

Life went on regardless of the play.

Every day, more e-mails came to evita@evita.co.za, asking for a visit to their schools.

Dear Mr Uys, or can we call you Evita?

Please come to our school. We are not in a city unfortunately, but in the rural Eastern Cape. But our learners heard from their cousins in Cape Town what you say and how you make them think and laugh. We need to do both.
    Please don't forget us.

JJ Hendricks
Principal

P.S. Don't forget your penis!

The loudly negative criticism of the words I use, of the stories I tell, of the adult attitudes with which I empower the kids, has now ceased to have any effect. The excited, positive reactions from youth and parents have been enthralling and encourage me to fill the car with petrol, get the cooldrink out of the fridge and drive up the road to visit each and every town with the message: 'You're on your own here. Be in charge!'

It is still free to all and will remain so as long as I have the energy to headline Evita Bezuidenhout to attract an audience and encourage them to buy a ticket.

The most theatrical reaction to my school visits happened recently in Johannesburg while I was performing at the Civic Theatre with *Selle ou Storie/Same Old Story*. I parked the car and headed for Rosebank Mall. The sidewalk cafés were full of people talking, reading newspapers, sipping cappuccinos, watching each other: a very normal heterosexual homosexual multiracial multinational crowd of South Africans doing what they do, calmly and with style.

Five fashionable young blacks came out of the mall. The young man saw me and I heard him say:

'Hey, there's Pieter-Dirk Uys.'

He whistled and waved his hands to get my attention.

'Hey, Pieter! Hello, Pieter-Dirk Uys!'

The coffee crowd looked up and some smiled. I joined the young fans.

'Hey man, Pieter-Dirk Uys! Hello!'

'Hello!' I said.

The young black man nodded in anticipation. Then he frowned.

'Do you remember me?'

He waited for my recognition and embrace.

Dear God! I've talked to a million kids! And, no, they don't all look alike! But shit, what do I say here?

I shrugged sheepishly.

'Help me?'

His eyes twinkled and they all laughed.

'Ja. You came to the Grahamstown township. Three years ago. I was in matric. You gave us your AIDS show. In the BB Zonani Hall!'

'Oh yes!' I remembered. 'The BB Zonani Hall? It was terribly hot in the BB Zonani Hall …!'

'Hey, Pieter man, you remember! It was very very hot. I was sitting on the floor right in the front. You looked at me three times and smiled at me! You must remember me!'

'Of course I remember you,' I said, because I think I did remember those shiny eyes and that excited smile, like all the other hundreds of thousands of shiny eyes and similar smiles. 'How are you?'

He gave a little dance among the fascinated mall-goers.

'Hey, Pieter man, look at me!' He threw out his hands in a wide stretch, yelling victoriously into the Johannesburg sky. 'I'm still alive!'

*   *   *

While a new show has emerged to celebrate the tenth anniversary of the rainbow democracy, called *The End Is Naai*, *Foreign Aids* keeps underlining the most important piece of information: that we are not just dying in South Africa. We are also living! The show now has a new ending, borrowed from *The End Is Naai*.

Having established President PW Botha at the start of the performance as he was in 1986, when our democracy was too good to share with just anyone, I end the evening with a snippet of useless information.

'Thabo Mbeki is my President, I shall not want. But PW Botha was also my President, and although they kept saying to me: don't hope – I did. But I never thought there would ever be any connection between the two of them. Until someone said to me: "Did you know that the name THABO can also spell the name BOTHA?"'

The PW glasses go on. That's all I need, because now I even look like the old fucker! Out comes a ventriloquist's dummy, a small version of the President of South Africa! Inspired by the many brilliant cartoons of Zapiro, Nico de Klerk took the tools of his trade and created a perfect likeness of Thabo Mbeki.

The eyes can look to the left, the top lip lifts to expose a skeletal smile, and the bottom jaw moves in rhythm to the words. Speaking upstage through my half-closed mouth while looking at the puppet, I have managed to present both politicians at the same time.

PW licks his lips and nods his head happily.

'Thabo! This is a great honour, being together with you! Also finding out that my name Botha is an anagram of your name Thabo? I didn't realise we have so much in common.'

Manipulated by my right hand, which is hidden up the back of the little white shirt, fingers curled round the three levers that work the eyes and mouth, Thabo looks to the left and then turns his head to glare balefully at PW.

PW clears his throat bashfully.

'Ja, well, actually … I just want to ask you one question. Very much off the record.'

Thabo doesn't answer, just looks ahead of him.

'Tell me, Thabo, how is it possible that you have been responsible for the deaths of more blacks than I was?'

The audience gasps. Thabo turns slowly and looks at PW. He then talks in Mbeki's familiar halting manner.

'We are … not responsible for their deaths, Botha. We … let them die by themselves.'

'You let them die by themselves?'

'Of course. Ignore them and … they will go away.'

PW Botha shakes his head and his tongue darts across his lips.

'But we tried that with you people for years and it never worked! You never went away! We even tried to chase you into the sea!'

'Yes, that was a terrible flop!' A movement of my finger on a lever makes his teeth appear in a grotesque smile.

Botha comes close to his ear.

'No. It's because the beaches were for whites only!'

The audience roars in recognition of the absurd reality of their past.

'But, Thabo, what is your secret weapon?'

There is a pause. I move the eyes and the head of the puppet.

'We have an invisible virus,' Thabo Mbeki says.

Botha sighs.

'And I just had a Whites Only sign!'

'We have an invisible virus that has no cure.'

Botha nods.

'HIV that leads to AIDS.'

Thabo agrees.

'Et cetera and so forth. But then ... we must confuse the people about the origins of the virus.'

'HIV that does not lead to AIDS!'

Thabo agrees.

'Et cetera and so forth. And then ... and then we do nothing.'

PW Botha looks at him, amazed.

'Then you do nothing?'

I manipulate a shake of Thabo's head.

'No. Nothing.'

Botha is confused. Lips get licked, a finger wants to wag.

'But I don't understand. I keep reading about your Minister of Health being on the verge of rolling out those antiretroviral drugs. That your government is poised to address the AIDS issue with vigour ...'

Thabo chuckles.

'Botha? It's called politics.'

Botha is impressed.

'I'd call it Mbekivellian politics! Magtig, Thabo, you're truly a genius. Without anyone realising what you're doing, you're actually using Structured Negligence to solve all your problems. "Ignore them and they will go away!" The poor will go away.'

Thabo pauses and then adds.

'The unemployed will go away.'

'The street children will go away?'

'And all those AIDS orphans will go away!'

'And all you will have left, out of 40 million, will be 20 million South Africans who can read and write, who can pay their taxes and also afford their own antiretrovirals! Thabo, hell, I wish I'd thought up something so clever.'

I turn Thabo's eyes. He looks at Botha.

'You didn't do too badly when you were in my shoes, Botha.'

PW nods, but is not convinced.

'Ja, ja, ja, our system was appealing to many people, but the name was wrong. Apartheid. Wrong name! If we'd called it Ethnic Cleansing, we would've got away with it!'

Thabo nods.

'So what name do you give your final solution?'

'I thought that was obvious, Botha,' Thabo retorts.

'Genocide?' Botha asks.

Thabo's head turns quickly.

'No!' he snaps angrily. His tongue, my tongue, gives an irritated click. 'No! We call it – democracy!'

I manipulate a terrible smile from him as the lights go to black.

17

NUTS AND BOLTS

What goes into making a show? It becomes simple when you accept
that in order to create a final product before the audience is invited,
you have to start somewhere fast. I begin with the title. A good, snappy,
funny title is important. Often I have a title and no show. Then I try the title
out on people casually. If they laugh at the title, then you've got them on the
way to your theatre!

The most difficult title to market was *Foreign Aids*, simply because no
one wants to spend fun time with a virus. But the other titles can stand alone:
*Adapt or Dye, Beyond the Rubicon, Farce about Uys, Skating on Thin Uys, A
Part Hate A Part Love, Dekaffirnated, You ANC Nothing Yet, The End Is Naai,
Elections & Erections.*

The structure of the show comes next. First I ask myself: What pisses
you off the most? What makes you angry? List the worst in the society
around you. List the guilty people. And then filter the whole unpalatable
mess through the prism of humour. Anger makes for dull entertainment.
And 'entertainer' is the job description in my passport.

Career? 'Entertainer'. 'Writer' is also something I put down with honesty
and pride. I never use the word 'artist', because I believe that should remain
in the eye of the beholder. The magical definition of 49 per cent anger vs 51
per cent entertainment has always been a good guide for me through the
thirty years of staying on top of my profession.

Being funny about things that aren't funny, being successful with issues
that no one wants to talk about, attracting a huge paying audience with stories
no one wants to hear: that's my show business! All encased in the syrup of
laughter and the cream of fun. Then you can slide many a bad oyster down
the open throat of your public. Always followed quickly with an antidote, a
hug and a farewell laugh.

People have survived terrible conditions with humour. Cancer patients can
laugh. Survivors of life's cruel disasters carry on with a brave smile. Within
minutes of Princess Diana's death, the jokes started coming. So laughter isn't
always because of the joke; often it's because of the pain. But it puts one in
charge of fear.

'My God, your CV is a recital in itself! So many plays and revues ... when do you sleep?'

I sleep like a log. Nothing keeps me awake, and, if it does, I get up and sort it out. The worst enemy of sleep is fear, and, yes, there have been moments of terrible angst and worry, horrible pain and loneliness. But night becomes light and there's always the next day, if you don't die in the dead of darkness. In the warmth of sunshine, stroking the cat in the kitchen, nothing looks so bad. Being called a 'terminal optimist' is also a compliment, when one ignores the sarcasm in the delivery. I have a glass in my study, filled with liquid exactly halfway. That's the philosophy of life: my glass is half full, never half empty.

Theatre is practical. There can be no bullshit. That's why there are no barriers of sex or age. Either you can or you can't. If you can't, get out of the way. If you can, prove yourself every time you show your face. Being responsible for everything is, they say, unique. I would say: essential. My training as a stage manager at the Little Theatre in the sixties was the best foundation I could have wished for. As an independent producer, I thank Mavis Taylor, Robert Mohr and Helen Rooza for their wisdom in pulling me down a few pegs and making me scrub the floors before I climbed the ladder to fame and fortune.

I still clean the stage. I saw Marlene do it in Cape Town. I slipped into a rehearsal on the invitation of Basil Rubin, one of the producers. I saw Dietrich in her jeans, cleaning the Alhambra stage to protect her costume. I do it all over the world, even though there is no full-length fox fur in my wardrobe! It doesn't go down well. Other people are paid to do that. Yes, they will do it for Shirley Bassey, but I can't expect them to do it for Evita. So I am her stage manager. I'm in charge of everything, and if someone offers to help, I'm happy but cautious. It just means watching what they do and correcting what they don't do. So much simpler doing it yourself.

Someone gave me a T-shirt saying 'I'm a Control Freak'. I suppose I am, although you don't have to be a freak to want things to go well. And when there's no time to redo an hour's work because of confusion and carelessness, the product suffers. So in my small world of twelve characters, one set, ten light cues, three sound cues, and the politicians of the world as my scriptwriters, I prefer to do things myself. Be in control? Yes.

In the major centres of performance, where unions control your bowel movements, if you touch a prop as a performer, the entire complement of workers goes on strike. At times I've been told to sit and stay, like a small dog. So I have to instruct those who have been paid to do my work to do my work. It's fun for a few hours. It's hell for a week. It's nonsense for a month.

It doesn't happen that often. I make it known from the start that there are three acts involving me as a 'one-person artist'. I call setting up the show Act I, performing the show Act II, and packing up afterwards Act III. And so, when I cross the line, there are gasps but no action.

No one wants to attempt producing, because it is so complex. Especially if you're producing *Phantom of the Opera* or *Cats* or *Turandot*. Yet, it all boils down to the same small question: 'Does it work?' If it works, don't fix it. If you need one light bulb, don't add twenty more for effect. Effect kills. Effects cost money.

I never had money for effects. So the only ones I could afford were those I could create in the imagination of the audience. Start with an earthquake, go through a climax and end with a tap dance. They see it all, if you believe it all! That happens once the caravan of mundane hammering and nailing and slogging and schlepping is over.

So I now have a title. It works. People laugh and ask when the show opens. That's good. I have structured the show, which is different from the previous one. I know it can work, if I lose some weight. I plan to start as Evita in a dress, then strip off the dress in view of the audience to become various males, before going back into females. I become blacks and whites without colour, just accent. Then end the show with a full make-up makeover to become Bambi Kellermann. And do the curtain call as me.

On paper it all works. In reality it will depend on courage, and that's the key. Do you have the guts to do it? Sometimes you end up on stage in underpants. You know you don't look great. You never looked that good, but at least then you had hair and a flat stomach. Now you look like a goblin's nephew from the sticks! That's fine as long as it's funny, and as long as the most famous white woman in South Africa looks like a goddess and has all the benefits of the magic of theatre: lights, angles, sound and colour. Exposing myself as a goblin on stage can be more fun than imagined, although it certainly doesn't fill the bed at night. Sometimes not even the theatre in the evening. But it keeps the rampant ego in check. Ego cancels out inspiration.

I've always been terrified of writer's block. But as time has gone by and this writer has never been blocked, I realise that Dawie Malan's logic was supreme: Relax and let it happen. Don't imagine what the cover looks like before you've written a page. Don't make Oscar speeches before you've learnt your lines. And remember, it's only entertainment! It's not cancer, it's not death, it's not horror or hell. It's heaven. For the audience. The hell you go through is never shown. Don't talk about the process! Don't show the seams of the perfect cloth!

Let me tell you about the nuts and bolts of producing a one-person piece.

You have the title, the text, the tap shoes. Now choose the venue with care. The size of theatre depends on your confidence in the material. I have the Perron to start things in. After making sure it works, I can move into a 600-seater theatre.

The set should be minimal, for the simple reason that the more complex the set, the more to pack up and move. If it can't fit on the back seat of your car, think again. A flag is a great centrepiece for a political show, and I travel the world with my huge Y-front flag. Beer crates are easy to find in every storeroom in every city all over the world. Plastic, firm, see-through and colourful, three of them make a great table and two a good stool! And you can leave them behind.

Costumes are more than just character clues. They have to have enough detail to fill in the blank spaces for the audience. They have to help tell the story. Revue doesn't have time to explain or share background information. What you see is what you've got. Avoid buttons. Keep your Velcro clean and crisp. And make sure the material used for costumes doesn't crease, so you can pack it in a suitcase. This goes for your props too. So avoid having too many high-heeled shoes!

Lighting can make or break a production. I grew up in awe of Mannie Manim's magnificent conjury with lights. At the Market Theatre, his genius lay in how to use a few spots to create the magic of light and shade. I've seen it at work and I love it. But I know my pieces need white light. Do not hide comedy in murk. I've also seen creative lighting technicians who, given the chance, will anchor you in an auditorium for hours while trying out an effect. Fuck the effect and cut to the car chase. Lights on and lights off!

If just on, even better. The best shows I've done have no lighting cues at all, which gives me the freedom to ad-lib structure and content, depending on the audience's reactions. Once there is a structured cue, you're trapped.

Sound is usually on disc, having been pre-recorded. Music is a great emotional wave. It can lift an audience like a surfer waiting to fly, but if it's uncontrolled it can detract from the passion of your energy. So if I can make sounds on stage that pass for orchestration and 'music', all the better.

A clear technical script with all the cues marked is essential for the sound and lighting people. I'm amazed how seldom this is done. Once technicians can follow the structure of the action with their cues clearly marked, it cuts down hours of preparation and list-making. Also try to structure the text so it's easy to cut a section without crippling the flow of the piece.

Publicity is all. If they don't know you're there with a new trick up your sleeve, they won't come and see you. So start early. Tantalise and tease. Foreplay is essential. Know who will publish and why they want the story. You don't want to be an item on the women's page for a theatre show. After the opening, yes, but be careful who needs your crucial information just to fill their empty space.

Pictures are the most important part of selling the product. One good image is worth a million words. Each production needs a new photo shoot. So plan ahead what you can do with the characters in your chorus line. A pose that can tell a funny story at the same time is priceless. A photographer you trust and who understands your changes of characters will help you individualise each face and expression. I have worked with the greatest theatre snappers in South Africa, starting with Brian Astbury at the Little Theatre and The Space, Ruphin Coudyzer at the Market in Johannesburg, and now depend on Pat Bromilow-Downing and Anton Geldenhuys to build up my portfolio of Uys's faces.

A concise press release about a new work, with an upbeat, exciting energy, can, when it's published, make the public think it's a rave review of the show. Use every chance you get to reinvent your product and pitch it with passion. It's very unlikely that you'll get a review that matches it anywhere.

When targeting the local media, don't spell their names wrong! Go and meet them so you can put a face to the voice and they can stick your poster up on the wall behind their desk. Listen to them, even though some of them haven't a clue. They hold the trump cards here: they will place your story. Today, every production has a public relations person/organisation/team – which is necessary if you're selling *Phantom of the Opera*. A one-man show means a one-man team. Don't use someone else if you can go yourself. Make your own phone calls. Deliver your own press kit. That was the success of my early career: I would take the opening-night tickets to each critic in Johannesburg in person on the day of the opening of the show. I did it because I didn't know who to ask to do it for me, but it was the best move of my developing career and I loved doing it. It gave me a feeling of working towards the success of the product. Maybe that's why today I enjoy marketing the apple more than eating it!

In my experience, radio is the most important means of spreading the word. Everyone has a radio on somewhere, be it in the car, the kitchen, the workplace or on a Walkman. Personal interviews can attract a lot of interest, and you can get so much detail of the show across with humour and excitement. There are also so many variations of radio programmes in which the information can easily be slipped in.

Audience investment doesn't have to start only once you've decided on a show and a title. A carefully planned campaign to keep the public informed and interested will make the eventual announcement of a new show a climax and not a discovery. So find ways of weaving a presence into unexpected areas, such as supermarket magazines, gay interest groups, and even political think tanks. Ladies' clubs are a wonderful way to pass on the news. Library meetings can focus on the writing of the piece, while corporate cabarets will help finance the production.

Don't ask for money from anyone if you can help it. Sponsorship will mean you are beholden to your financial lifeline. Subsidy brings with it the danger of self-censorship. If you want total freedom in this democracy, don't take the money. If you do, be prepared to suffer the consequences and bow down to the conditions. And once the money depends on the conditions, you've cut out your tongue. Arts Council support is lethal. If you have to be grateful to government for the help they give you, don't bite the hand that feeds you. It will be removed.

Arts festivals are now a national circuit of possibilities, and young performers have the chance to travel around and sharpen their satire. Performing on the fringes of festivals is essential for the development of your non-commercial alphabet. It's cheap, it's unstructured, it's a bit of a meat market, and if you attract attention with originality and passion, you make enough money for the petrol back home. And everyone at a festival will go to the theatre! At the festival, though, you have a trapped audience, which can lead to an artificial reaction. Often the success of a festival can flop when it moves to the mundane atmosphere of a commercial run in a city. Festivals are now the supermarket of the arts. It's exciting meeting colleagues and similar-minded eccentrics who also travel in battered transport with an entire show stacked on the back seat. One's courage is strengthened by meeting so many fellow-lepers.

If you can try out your show somewhere, do so. Even performing in your lounge to four people breaks the ice. The ice has to be broken some time: don't leave that horrible experience to an opening night! Rather present your show free as a work-in-progress, so that there is a chance to listen to audience feedback and rework the material for the next attempt. You want to challenge professional critics, so do it with a professional weapon. There's only one chance in professional theatre. If you blow that first exposure, the mud sticks to your silk gown for the rest of the run.

At Evita se Perron we have established a work-in-progress slot Sunday afternoons at 3.30. Anyone who wants to try out some material is welcome. It's free for them and for the audience. Those who are still there from the earlier Evita show are invited to bring their coffee, cat and kids into the small venue and see what's happening.

I've tried many sketches in this way, sometimes reading them from the script. Often, to my surprise, what I thought was not going to make sense hit a chord of delight and the audience loved it. Often the writing is still too academic and the sketch flops.

'Oh no, sis, that was horrible,' I say, and stop halfway. They laugh and agree.

A man puts up his hand.

'You explain too much in the beginning,' he says. 'If you started the story in the middle maybe?'

I start the story in the middle. It's better.

'Shouldn't it be in Afrikaans?' a woman shouts.

I do it, carefully translating into Afrikaans. It works even better and is funnier. They applaud. Now I have a hook on which to hang this future sketch.

Where else could I do something like this? It's the most rewarding part of the creation of a new piece.

It is here, during these sessions, that our township kids see how one puts things together. When they are shown documentaries about the Spice Girls and Madonna, it is the amount of work that happens off-stage that I accentuate, the need to understand discipline and preparation. And that everything has to start somewhere.

'No man, that's kak,' Sue-Ellen would say, watching another work-in-progress.

'Ja, but remember, next time it's less kak.'

Hopefully now, after seven thousand one-man performances, I'm the only one who sees what is still kak!

Previews are essential to the success of your new show. All theatres encourage them, so that a new production can get the feel of the space, the geography of backstage, the attitude of the staff and, of course, the audience. The first performance is always the worst. Never expose yourself on a first performance. Or even a second. Sell them to a charity, or have a R20-a-seat giveaway. Then open to the press and public on the third show. Don't rely on the usual first-night theatre mailing list. There is nothing more deadening than the same old crowd sitting there, sourly hating it, being jealous, being cynical, comparing and bitching. And being bored, because how many new tricks can you have up your sleeve for people who see every opening night of yours?

I give tickets to real people for the opening performance: the hairdresser and the dry cleaner, the waitress and the traffic cop. Recently I invited 200 vendors of the *Big Issue* magazine to an opening at the Baxter Theatre. They sat in the first few rows, much to the consternation of some smarty-arty-farty guests. It was a riot of enjoyment. They talked loudly along with me, and it felt like a soccer match. The adrenaline in the audience matched mine on stage. Magic.

The theatre programme used to be an important part of a night out. People bought them because they were informative and fun. Now no one seems to care, and for good reason: programmes are dull and just an excuse to sell advertising. Unless it's *Phantom of the Opera*, and then the programme costs nearly as much as the ticket itself! I have always regarded my programme as my First Act. In the 1980s it was essential to help people relax. The tensions outside were telling. Even today I know the men are usually only there because their wives bought the tickets. Today everyone is stressed by seven in the evening. Then to have to drive to a theatre, park and find your seat adds to the irritation. A good laugh at a witty programme is good therapy. It also gives them something to take away and reread at home.

Three programmes come to mind, all designed and produced for me by the remarkable Beni Stilborg, by profession a commercial artist, who understood so much of the shorthand of selling an image. And he has a rare, off-the-wall sense of humour. The programme for *Adapt or Dye* was based on familiar political figures and the rhubarb of parliamentary double-speak. *Farce About Uys* was a book of cut-out dolls, all representing the Bezuidenhout characters in the play. And the programme for *Rearranging the Deckchairs on the SA Bothatanic* was a sick bag!

Posters used to be essential. Now they get lost among the reams of paper flapping on street poles and in shop windows. If you can produce a poster that is smaller than usual, so much the better. There is no space in windows for the traditional A3 size. Handbills are useful, depending on where they are distributed, but it's a full-time job checking and refilling stocks.

There is a ridiculous lack of cooperation between our theatres. One management will not advertise a rival production. Instead of every foyer proudly supporting live theatre in those few venues still left, every stage becomes its own island. There is also a lack of national advertising. The arts pages in Cape Town seldom inform one about what is taking place in Johannesburg or Durban. And so our live theatre becomes suburban and small, unambitious and doomed to early silence. Unless it's *Phantom of the Opera*.

Press advertising is now so expensive and unreliable, it's crippling for a small management. Every newspaper should, as a public service, present the basic information on every theatre production for free: where it is, when it's showing, what it is, where to book. The media's lack of interest in live theatre, coupled with their resident critic's destruction of anything new and original, has resulted in the state of our local performance arts. The public are now otherwise engaged.

Which doesn't mean to say you can't get them away from their video games, their latest DVDs, their twenty-four-hour sport and their beers. *Phantom of the Opera* also had to start somewhere!

As a well-trained, old-fashioned stage manager, I am often amazed how badly trained today's technicians are. But it doesn't become an issue because at least I can do their jobs myself. There are always essentials in my dressing room. A stapler in case a hem comes loose. Needle and thread in case a trouser seam splits and your bum hangs out. A spare pair of reading glasses without which it is impossible to read the paper for new material, or read the material for that performance! A black koki pen can always fill in a blank white spot. Velcro is the penicillin of backstage and can cure a multitude of problems. A roll of clear medical tape can stick down the cord of a lapel mike. Black masking tape is good for instant repairs to set, props and stage – and to shoes! Strepsil for that threatening sore throat. A pair of scissors to cut the hair that's standing up like a porcupine's quill. A radio for the latest news and Classic FM. Pen and paper in case you're writing a book and get inspiration!

You travel with a show in a car or a plane. Neither of them needs more than one suitcase. No staircases, waterfalls or chandeliers. Unless it's *Phantom of the Opera*, which means you'll have your own plane! When you tour internationally, the less you have to transport, the happier your host-promoters will be. And don't forget Customs. Once, while going through Green at Heathrow Airport, I was stopped by a sour official who waved me aside.

He pointed at my suitcase.

With beating heart and guilty face I opened it. On top lay Evita Bezuiden-hout's high-heeled shoes, a handbag, a wig, the pink step-in and a blouse.

He looked at it all slowly, leant forward and scribbled a chalk mark on the side. Then he curtly indicated that I could go.

As I closed the case, relieved, he muttered without a smile, 'Sir? The handbag and the shoes don't match.'

Above all, remember you're on stage. You are there in flesh and blood. It's live. And it changes all the time. It's a reaction to an action. Plays are different from revues, more complex but often calmer, as there is always more time for character development. Cabaret is its own cocoon. And revue is shooting back with loaded guns. So kill them with kindness. Tickle them to death so that they come back and beg for more. Then give them something completely different!

18

THE *SOS* *SAGA*

There are two ways to introduce this chapter: The most interesting and eccentric project I attempted with Evita and her sister Bambi Kellermann was to put them on stage as actresses each in a play. Or: The most ridiculous and terrifying project I attempted with Evita and her sister Bambi Kellermann was to put me as them on stage each in a play!

In 2003, Bernard Jay, the CEO of the Johannesburg Civic Theatre, suggested that Evita act in a play that had just finished a successful run with a brilliant Gauteng actress in the lead. Called *The Woman Who Ate Her Husband*, it had attracted a good audience and justified a rerun, but the star had other commitments. Bernard suggested the most famous white woman in South Africa as a replacement. This was not the first time I'd toyed with the idea of having Evita act in a film or play, but coming from the director of a major theatre, the proposal was now a real possibility.

'You can't afford her, darling,' I joked.

'Try me!' he challenged.

I did, outrageously demanding a ridiculous fee, knowing he would laugh and withdraw his interest.

He laughed and didn't withdraw anything.

'It can be done,' he said. 'Nothing is impossible.'

That magic incantation took me back to my schooldays when Miss Nel looked into my frightened eyes and said: 'Pieter. Nothing is impossible.' Not even putting a non-existent actress in a play?

'Send me the script,' I added, taken off guard by the rush of adrenaline.

The play arrived and I read it. It was a racy modern black comedy with language to match. I rang Bernard.

'I love the play, but Evita ... but my client can't say those words.'

There was a pause.

'Your client?' murmured Bernard. 'I see ...'

Words like 'fuck' and 'cunt' are alien to the mouth of the Mother of the Boerevolk.

'But,' I added hastily, 'let's not throw the idea away. Let's find the right play.'

We hugged and kissed over the phone and that was that.

Cut to later that year. A packed Air France flight to Cuba. I'm in economy class with my ankles around my ears in the Joan Collins position, squashed between large and smelly people with their ankles behind each others' ears! Nothing to do but think.

Selle ou Storie!

A further reason why I hadn't even considered the play that Bernard had suggested was that it was someone else's work, and, no matter how we might love the novelty, no playwright should be subjected to having a man in drag play the female lead in his play! But I was the author of *Selle ou Storie*, it had a great leading part for an Afrikaans woman, it had a history of controversy behind it, and it would never be done again anyway. No one in their right mind would attempt the part after Christine Basson had given such a luminous performance in the seventies and eighties. Except Evita Bezuidenhout, who wouldn't have wanted to see it anyway and probably insisted that it be banned!

The Air France sandwich was hard and horrible, so I dropped it on the floor and did more thinking.

Same Old Story? I had the English translation from the days when the Afrikaans text was banned and we could only run the production on a text in English. Remember *Same Old Story*? Evita could act in both versions, which would make it accessible to those who didn't understand Afrikaans.

The can was now open and the worms saw the light and rose to the occasion.

This is what happened.

Bernard was excited by the proposal and listened with disbelief and delight on his face.

Evita Bezuidenhout would play the character of Ester Viljoen, the middle-aged Afrikaans stage actress living in her flat in Hillbrow in 1976 with her younger lover Rufus. While she goes out to an important dinner for potential work, he invites his former boyfriend Gregory over 'for old times' sake'. Ester has found out and comes back unexpectedly. When Gregory's current English girlfriend Sandra joins the quartet, it becomes a battleground of failed relationships, bitter ageing and arrogant power plays.

I was having second thoughts about Tannie performing in *Same Old Story*, though.

'But you said Evita would play in the English play as well?' Bernard said.

'No,' I replied. 'She's a terrible actress. She can play herself as Ester, but certainly not anything convincing in English. Besides, the English version cannot be set in South Africa.'

For purposes of subverting censorship it didn't matter, but reading the translation again, I realised that without Afrikaans there was no justification for the play to remain in a South African context. Ester Viljoen wouldn't speak English; it needed the Afrikaans. Unless ...

I went back to the original *Same Old Story*, which I'd written in London in 1970, where the character was called Yvonne Godard. It became frighteningly obvious. There was more work to be done here than just dieting! The *Same Old Story* we needed for now had to be completely rewritten, and set in London around the life of a faded English star. And not in 1976, but in 2004! And Yvonne Godard would be played by Evita's sister Bambi Kellermann! Who had a German accent, so Yvonne had to be German!

Bernard now ordered us strong drinks. We pushed the polite wine aside. We took off our jackets and brought out fresh pieces of paper.

The can of worms became the centre of our focus.

I didn't want the project to be just an excuse to wear women's clothing! The playwright in me wanted both plays to stand securely on their own feet. Not as vehicles for a middle-aged queen to indulge his drag fantasies, but as a dramatic unity that could be performed by any 'real' actress should that fateful bus squash the middle-aged queen to death. The producer in me always kept the option of 'next choice for part', especially when it came to plays that featured not just me, but other artists. This was going to be a job, not just a passion. Salaries had to be paid. Actors had mortgages and families to support. This was no longer the one-man show produced by the one-man band.

Lynne Maree was the obvious director. We had worked together so often during the thirty years of our friendship since the Space days. Her intense intelligence and delightful fuck-it solutions to the most ghastly problems made her unique. She was an actress who directed, not a director who acted, which made her the performers' closest confidante and friend. She had also performed the part of Sandra in the original saga, so she knew the play intimately. She would cast the other three roles: Rufus, Gregory and Sandra. The actors would play in both productions, the Afrikaans one set in 1976 and the English one in 2004.

So now we had two same old stories, one taking place in Johannesburg at the height of apartheid, and the other happening in Kensington, London, in the present. Both featuring middle-aged women fighting for their dignity and appeal, against the background of youthful sexuality and intrigues. Setting the plays in a political context was essential. It's bad writing as well as time-consuming to have to explain anything in a play that can be assumed: while the original action took place around 1973/4, I decided to set it on a fateful day in South African history, 16 June 1976, the day Soweto schoolkids rose up and burnt their schools, starting the domino effect that would result in the presidency of Nelson Mandela in 1994. It also gave the play a chilling political reality. The radio bulletins dotted throughout the action would mirror the events outside in the streets of black South Africa. But our Afrikaans characters are irritated and switch over to bland music. Which is what so many of us did at the time. *Same Old Story*, set in the terror-tense London of 2004, reflected a similar horror outside: car bombs in Riyadh, suicide bombers in Tel Aviv, terrorist attacks in Bali. And the people in the play switch over to something less upsetting and real.

1976 and 2004. It was, after all, the same old story. (Of course, after the events of 7 July 2005, the parallels would be even closer.)

Nico de Klerk designed a kitsch 1970s Hillbrow set for *Selle*, which could be adapted for *Same* as a retro-70s apartment in Blair's Britain, just by adding colour, flair and fashion. Two bright young designers, François Vedemme and Gideon from Durban, offered to dress both stars. An impressive cast of young professionals was found, who understood that they would be acting with two established female divas who did not exist, and they seemed ready for the experience.

My real excitement was the marketing of the productions.

Bernard Jay is a born showman, and the success of his Civic Theatre proves that. He saw the great possibilities of having our own Joan Crawford and Bette Davis together in the same theatre! Separate dressing rooms, different designs, and careful planning so that the two sisters never met face to face. This could all be explored through daily snippets in gossip columns in a media that was hungry for fun and, on the whole, keen on the crazy game.

My personal choice of PR was obvious. Brigid van Oerle and I had worked together for some years and understood the essence of the hard sell and what it entailed. There was no need to confirm every idea or decision. We both started our days at sunrise and quick calls solved long problems. But our short-hand relationship didn't help here. The Civic was a corporate concern and many people needed to be plugged into the daily decisions and processes. Too often I had to answer the question from Bernard, 'What's happening?' with 'I don't know.' This was fine when it was just two of us, but the lack of mundane detail led to a wedge between us as producers. So, as carefully as I could, I tried to divert my workhorse PR off the production for the sake of peaceful continuity. Bridget took it very well and stayed at my side unofficially, coming to my help on many occasions, when the PR company that took over the brief proved itself to be beyond useless. All this meant that the great marketing madness we had structured so carefully collapsed like a soggy soufflé.

Bernard and I hadn't realised how hard it would be to sell the season. I never seem to learn. How often in the past have I presented two productions simultaneously at a festival. No matter what I called the season, the public have a one-track mind. They come for one thing. They come for Evita! They want to laugh at short sketches. They don't understand that there are two, or maybe even three choices. This was our trip-up as well.

The Afrikaans play opened brilliantly, with a dazzling opening-night audience of friends, colleagues and former politicians, all coming to pay tribute to the play and to Mrs Bezuidenhout. Christine Basson was there, with Blaise Koch and Lynne Maree, remnants of the saga's history during the dark days of apartheid. The Minister of Foreign Affairs of that time, Pik Botha, was also present.

At the party afterwards, he made an impassioned speech, a glass in one hand and his other arm snugly around the now-thicker waist of his still beautiful and famous former Ambassador. Lynne said that watching them together was poignant, like an old Liz Taylor and her Richard meeting for the last time.

Pik Botha sang the praises of the play. He referred to the horrors of apartheid and came very close to an apology. But this was not the time and place for real things. It was a play. It was the theatre. Real was outside, where the same old story never goes away.

The few professional theatre reviewers left in Johannesburg gave the play glowing notices. But the audiences' responses were mixed.

The Afrikaans public didn't come, even though the advertising was extremely generous and expensive. Bernard Jay excelled himself for the sake of his two stars. Never in my career have I been so lavishly and colourfully publicised in the advertisements. But it didn't seem to make much difference in the old laager.

Afrikaners are not the most enthusiastic theatre-goers, but that's never a reason for blame. The Civic Theatre was not on their cultural roadmap, as they saw central Johannesburg as a dangerous black city. They didn't like my type of theatre. Or perhaps they didn't want to see their favourite Tannie Evita Bezuidenhout in a play. Some of those who did come were heard to wail somewhere in the first ten minutes of Act I: 'Maar sy's nie snaaks nie!'

Same Old Story was a different story.

Bambi Kellermann sunk her teeth into the character of Yvonne Godard and ran around the stage like a circus beast on heat! Her German accent and Eurotrash demeanour suited the part like a torturer's glove and she tore the fourth wall apart with her red nails and assaulted the audience's expectations.

They loved her! The reviews were excellent, and the one or two critics who had seen both plays could make interesting comparisons between the two stories. Audiences for Bambi's show grew daily. Evita could scarcely sell three seats a day!

We played each version for two weeks, and on Saturday nights you could see both plays: one at six and the other at nine. It became a very popular experience, and while the technicians and our remarkable stage manager swopped apartments from 1976 to 2004, the audience supped and sipped in the foyer restaurant, before coming back for Take 2 of the saga.

My Johannesburg season had started with fourteen performances as Ouma Ossewania in *Ouma Ossewania Praat Vuil*. This seventy-five-minute bloed-snot-en-trane monologue as Evita's mother looks back on her 102-year life – all in shockingly rude Afrikaans – was a clever marketing ploy. Now we had the mother and her two daughters in the same theatre! A unique season of three Poggenpoels! The ploy stayed clever on paper, as our PR company couldn't understand Afrikaans and didn't even bother to see the play!

The SOS Saga ran for a solid twelve weeks from August to October, an excellent time for theatre in this vibrant City of Gold. Our residence at the Civic was enjoyable and calm. Bernard treated us all like stars and gave us great inspiration, in spite of the dicey box-office proof. He also made certain that my performances as the three Poggenpoels wouldn't reactivate my three hernias.

As fate would have it, two weeks before my first performance as Ouma Ossewania, I'd had triple hernia surgery in Cape Town. Hospitals are never my cup of tea, and the prospect of being out of action for some time was terrifying. My frenzied research had reassured me that I'd be up and about within days. It allowed me to joke before going under. Peering at the doctor and nurses from under my drowsy eyelids, I think I said: 'Remember, this is a triple hernia on Pieter-Dirk Uys. Not a hysterectomy on Evita Bezuidenhout.' Their laughter was the last thing I heard. Well, if I died on the table, it was a good quote to be remembered by. Good career move.

A week after the operation, I was back on the Perron stage with an Evita show, testing my cogs and wheels before leaving for the Johannesburg season. I was wobbly, but all the bits seemed fine. Looking back now, it was daft and stupid, and if I'd had a manager I would've been pushed off the SOS project and left to recover like any other pensioner! I was still in agony and not protecting my pain. Very few people realise it, but acting is like running around a stage with a bag of cement above your head. Rehearsals can be akin to running a marathon through a minefield blindfolded!

I could have spoken to Bernard and suggested an alternative season of my award-winning one-man show *The End Is Naai*, having just completed a sold-out season in Cape Town. I could have put the SOS Saga off till a healthier time, but I couldn't think of putting the actors out of work. Or Lynne. Or to be shown to be a mere fifty-nine-year-old human being who is not Superman. Or Superwoman.

So Pieter-Dirk Uys would arrive at the Civic at 08.30 every morning, disappear into the dressing room and emerge as Evita Bezuidenhout. Why the need to dress up in the morning? For rehearsal, stupid! That was the key to the drama's success. It couldn't be a drag show. That's easy and would have been horrible. And for the sake of the three actors, I owed them a logical explanation for the absurdity of what we were doing.

The first rehearsal was a final read-through of the Afrikaans version.

The cast gave me a beautifully kitsch teacup for Mrs Bezuidenhout.

'Thank you, I said, but she's not here yet. She'll be here tomorrow. You won't see me again in rehearsal, because it's not me you have to play opposite. It's her.'

There was a pause and we looked at each other. I could see some expressions of amazed amusement.

'Evita is playing Ester. Evita is a woman. You must rehearse with the actress to find the acting.'

It was the right thing to do. The first ten minutes, with Evita sitting there like Elizabeth Taylor, were slightly stilted, and the embarrassed efforts to make her feel at home sounded like acting. But then Lynne suddenly took over and thanked Mrs Bezuidenhout for being there.

'Dankie Mevrou,' she said in her best Afrikaans. 'We are honoured to be in a play with you and hope to learn from your experience.'

Evita smiled.

'Dankie, Lynne skat. As you all know, I am not an actress. I will learn from you. But then, as a politician and a diplomat, I'm probably the best actress in the country!'

That broke the uys, as they say. Evita sipped Earl Grey tea from her beautiful kitsch cup, while the others drank from their polystyrene mugs.

Lynne was the first person I'd had to convince.

'You have to realise that you have two bad actresses here,' I explained. 'The one is a superstar in her own right and won't want to be told what to do. The other is an old stripper who could explore sex without smudging her lipstick. So you can't teach her how to suck eggs! You also have two old plays here that have been renovated to blow new air into this new century. Reinvention is the keyword here.'

Lynne gave a sigh and muttered her mantra.

'Wake me up when it's over!'

But it's not over until the fat lady sings. Mercifully, Evita doesn't do that, and even though my weight is now more rather than less, she always seems to stun the audience with her glamour, her style and her trim figure. In my new show *Icons & Aikonas*, I end my Evita sketch by taking off her wig and exposing myself, something I never do when the lady herself is around.

'Nice to be able to make fun of her,' I say. 'Mrs Bezuidenhout's in Cuba, so while she's gone I can drag up as her behind her back. It's not always as successful as it's been. I'm fatter than she is. Her legs are better. And she's much more of a racist than I am.'

A small pause magnifies a rustle of discomfort among an audience of non-racists.

'Although, with our democracy passing its tenth anniversary, I now realise that racism is like riding a bicycle. It's always there!'

Because she's ten years older than me, Mrs Bezuidenhout turns seventy on 28 September 2005. Inspired by the magnificent Sophia Loren, who will be seventy-one, I'm excited about seeing my oldest clown move into glamorous, contented maturity. The Unicity Council of Moorreesburg-Malmesbury, under whose jurisdiction Darling falls, has decided to rename a street in town after its most famous resident. By the end of September 2005, what was formerly Lower Church Street going into the Moorreesburg Pad, which passes through the coloured township, will be known as Evita Bezuidenhout Boulevard!

As she has always been led by politics, it is difficult to plan for her future. She is committed to the future of a democratic South Africa and her three grandchildren, Winnie-Jeanne, Nelson-Ignatius and La Toya Ossewania. Her son-in-law, Leroy Makoeloeli, has been sent to the South African embassy in Havana, taking his wife Billie-Jeanne and the children with him. That will give Gogo Evita the excuse to travel to Cuba to look after the kids.

It will also free me to get on with new work. While performing Evita is always a challenge, as I have to reinvent her with each performance, I look forward to finding dangerous new ways to attract irritated attention. We have been given this second chance to make our dreams come true; we will not get a third one. There is much subversive work to be done with the weapons of humour!

Recently I was at a dinner party hosted by Nelson Mandela and Oprah Winfrey to attract attention and funds for the AIDS issue that Madiba has so brilliantly taken on. I was asked to bring Evita to entertain the guests, who included pop stars, politicians and divas.

It was an early gig. Madiba doesn't like late nights, and Oprah can't afford them. She must have her hair done, and that takes fourteen hours. So by 8.30 my job was over and Evita was packed up in the box in the boot of my car. I could wear my little boy's clothes again for a change, which is nice, eat some excellent food and do the one thing I'd not been able to do all evening: go to the toilet. Because while I'm doing Mrs Evita Bezuidenhout, where do I go?

I found the toilet, which was a portable tent, a ten-star Zozo hut deluxe. Standing at the urinal, I looked beside me and saw a very famous black face in politics.

First I thought: 'Should I peep?'

But I didn't peep. Then I heard him laugh and I realised that *he* had peeped.

'Hey, Pieter-Dirk Uys,' he said, 'hell man, we love that Evita of yours. She's so beautiful and funny. You're so good in those high heels and with the wig and all. But then you gays are good with drag.'

I thought: 'Maybe now I should peep?'

But I didn't peep.

'Yes, you should stick to the drag and stop criticising the government.' He started laughing uproariously. 'We don't want to hear your opinions about President Thabo Mbeki and our Minister of Health. No man, Pieter, you should really shut the fuck up!' Gales of mirth from him as he shook it and zipped it up. 'Stick to the drag. Keep playing the queen. Okay, my brother.'

And he left and I hadn't even peeped. But, worse than that, I hadn't even made a peep! What the hell was wrong with me?

I should have said: 'Excuse me, Comrade, but this is now a democracy. I have freedom of speech, freedom of expression. I'm a citizen. I have the right to ask questions …'

I didn't say any of those things! Why didn't I say those things? Was it because he was black? Was it because I'm white? Or was it because he could have been right?

Here we are, having celebrated ten years of a young and fragile democracy that has exceeded all expectations. We must celebrate what has worked – and, believe me, so much has worked! We must give credit where it is due. We must be optimistic and hopeful and look forward with passion. And I must remember: I'm a middle-aged white drag queen and I must shut the fuck up. And entertain.

I look forward to the next time I can entertain my liberators. Because once it's over and Madiba has gone to bed and Oprah's gone to the hairdresser, I will look for the portable toilet. Because I need to find that politician again.

And this time I'm going to say: 'Remember, Comrade, what you told me last time? That I must stop giving bad news and slagging off the government? That I must stick to drag? Well, that's what I've been doing. I do Evita all over the world and never say a word about our politics!'

He might smile and say: 'Well now you know, Pieter. It is unpatriotic to criticise the ANC government.'

This time I will add: 'No, Comrade, you're wrong. A patriot is someone who protects his country from its government!'

And then I'll peep!

19

DEATH AND OTHER IMPORTANT BITS

'Do you know what democracy is?' I ask the children sitting on the floor of their school hall.

They nod and many call out various answers.

'No apartheid! Freedom of speech! Vote! Mandela!'

I nod.

'Yes, but there is one thing no one tells us about. Being in a democracy, as we are now, means that each one of you is the most important person in South Africa.'

There is a pause, a gasp, a freeze-frame of surprise.

'No one is more important than you are.' I look at a young twelve-year-old going on forty. 'What is your name?'

'Sipho.'

'Well, Sipho, you are as important as Madiba!'

'No!' He blushes.

'Yes. You are as important as President Mbeki.'

'Okay!' He laughs.

'You are as important as anyone and everyone you look up to.'

A girl puts up her hand and waves it wildly, keenly, importantly.

'Yes?'

She stands.

'My name is Norma. Am I important also?'

'Norma, you are the most important person in the world!'

A sea of hands shoot up. It takes time, but soon everyone feels important. It's fun and ends happily, but you can see the lights go on in small eyes. No one has ever told them that. No one has ever said to these young people: You are important.

'If you die, the world will be a poorer place. You must live. You must fight to live. You must be educated to live. You must not be too scared to live!'

Where the hell did this come from?

No one ever said that to me. I've also never bothered to read the motivational books that fill the shelves with their mumbo-jumbo claptrap.

Sometimes the terminal optimist in me tends to applaud any focus on hope, but the memory of my mother's death slaps me down.

Helga Bassel thought she was going mad. She had a thyroid problem, and the treatments in 1969 were not easy or clear. The pills she'd been given would take her way down before they helped her up. No one told her. And when she was way, way down, with no help to believe that she would have faith in hope again, she drove her car to Chapman's Peak and jumped off the cliff.

'I don't want to be a burden. Forget me. I love you Hannes, Gerhardt, Pieter, Tessa.'

That was on 26 May 1969. Every year, that date is branded on our memories. Every year it still feels like yesterday.

When children lose their parents, it must be the worst moment of their lives, even if they are over fifty. But then they become adults, because there is no one left to protect them. The edge of the cliff is under their feet. They can jump if they wish. They will jump if they're terrified. They always leave someone behind.

That experience of death, so close and so terrible, blew a fuse in my life. Since then I cannot be shocked by death. I can be sad and sorry, but it is part of a journey now. My mother tore the wrapping off the secret and showed me the true gift. Whatever her motivation, and we will never really understand it, it was a terribly brave, horribly frightening action. But it was not as terrible and frightening as the feared madness she was leaving behind. I respect that and admire her courage.

Ma's death changed our lives completely. The empty frame in the centre of my vision will always be blank. That's where she used to be. She is gone. I am here. Live with it and celebrate what was good and important. And if memory fails, mythologise and create a better picture.

Not everything I write here is exact. A lot has to be squashed into a paragraph while it took a year to live. We don't have years in stories; we have sentences and words. But the truth is here and it is not always very pretty. I have no shame about my life, except for those many, many, many times when I was too scared to venture out into the darkness and see the bright stars. The regret of what I didn't do overpowers the regret of things done badly.

Take a chance and make a stand.

*   *   *

Then my father died, and my life changed gear once more.

But this was a very different farewell. Pa was in his eighties, and he had been sick for some years. A constant problem with heart failure brought on by septicaemia. He had to have a pacemaker replaced with a stronger machine, and during the process the infection set in that would eventually kill him. He was slowing down. He was cold. Frightened. Tessa was due back for Christmas, and Pa was so excited, sitting in his green chair, covering his chilled legs with a mohair blanket and fascinated by the small white Maltese terrier I'd given him for his birthday. He was the life and soul of his party, telling wonderful stories and making jokes at which he laughed the loudest.

Sannie was back in attendance, rubbing his neck gently. After years of exile, she had taken up residence in Sonskyn again, as his nurse, his helper, his healer, memory and friend. Tessa was coming home and, Pa had said and we all agreed, we would have a wonderful Christmas together in Sonskyn as always. Then he ended up back in hospital. His circulation was failing.

I drove him to Groote Schuur Hospital, helping him into the car, making sure the wind didn't steal the small hat off his head, the hat he always wore, no matter what the weather. The small hat I now also wear, and when I see my reflection somewhere, I realise I look just like Pa and it makes me very pleased.

As we reversed out of the driveway into Homestead Way, he looked up at the thatched roof of the home he had made for us since 1948.

He said very softly, 'This is my end.'

I patted him gently on his cold hand.

'We love you, darling,' was all I could say, making it all sound so Noël Coward while it felt like the end of the world. This tiny bundle of a person scarcely making a dent in the seat where Hannes Uys had once sat, robust and full of life and himself.

Then Pa started crying.

No! Parents don't cry! Fathers don't die! Mothers don't jump off mountains! Jesus, when did I become head prefect of this family?

At the hospital he perked up, surrounded by the familiar faces of the nursing staff, who loved him and welcomed him back with open arms. He made it clear it was only for the one night. He wanted to be strong for Tessie, who was coming from London the next day.

Sannie and I went home and waited at the phone. It rang early the next morning. We rushed up to Groote Schuur, Sannie still wearing her house slippers.

Pa was dying. I don't think he even saw us when we arrived. I kissed his cold forehead. Sannie held his hand. There was a terrible sound coming from his throat. This was one time I didn't look away.

Pa held my hand as he died. He squeezed it so hard I nearly cried out. And then he was gone, going through the door from the room in which we remained, to the room beyond where the others were waiting for him.

The nurses and doctors were moved to tears. They loved Pa. I comforted them as best I could. Hannes Uys was a great star. I was just his stage manager now, packing up his book, his glasses, his teeth, his spare pyjamas. And his little hat he always wore no matter what the weather.

We drove home to Sonskyn in Pinelands. Sannie and me. The remnants of the troupe that had once inhabited that small part of Homestead Way.

I walked into the empty house. The small dog stared up at me with busy eyes.

Pa was dead. Tessa was still in the air on her way home.

What do I do?

I went to Pa's writing desk in the sitting room. There were two drawers. I opened the top drawer, hearing his voice: 'If something terrible happens, grab the top drawer and run to the neighbours.'

The drawer held all the important papers. Insurances. Wills and certificates. Our Eisteddfod diplomas. Our mother's suicide letter from 1969, which was the last terrible thing that had happened.

But now something terrible had happened again.

I stood in the middle of the room, holding the drawer in my hands. On top of all the envelopes, tied with pink ribbon, was a letter addressed to me.

'Pieter my son ...' The handwriting was scrawled and uneven.

I sat on the carpet and opened the letter.

'Pieter. When you read this, I am dead. Now do the following ...'

And he had listed neatly from 1 to 34 all the things that had to be done to tie up the loose ends of his life.

'Phone Mr Olivier at the funeral parlour. Here is the number ... He knows what to do. Phone Tannie Anna, she knows what to do ...'

He listed where the insurances were. The debts and bills to be paid. The birthdays to remember. Who gets the Maggie Laubser. Who gets the Hugo Naudé. Who gets the house.

Within an hour, the end of Hannes Uys's life had been sorted out. His death was over. Now we would celebrate his memory.

That was fifteen years ago, and it's also like the day before yesterday.

* * *

And then there was Sannie.

They eventually managed to contact me through the Perron. I had been touring the country, visiting schools with the AIDS programme. Although my cellphone was always taking messages like a good Japanese secretary, they didn't have the number. When I got back home, I listened to the many messages they'd left on the answering machine.

'BLEEP. Hello Pieter, this is Sannie's daughter. Listen, Pieter, Mammie's fallen and she's broken her hip. Please phone. Thank you, Pieter.'

'BLEEP. Hello Pieter, this is Sannie Abader's daughter again. I don't know if you remember me, but Sannie is now in hospital. She must have a hip operation, so phone me, please Pieter. Thank you, Pieter.'

'BLEEP. Hello Pieter. I hope this is the right number. I'm Sannie's daughter, Sannie who was your nanny when you were small, and she's in hospital and the operation is over and she wants to see you. She keeps saying: Where's my Pieter. Thank you, Pieter.'

'BLEEP. Pieter, Sannie's dead. Oh Pieter, Sannie's dead. Oh Pieter, she's gone. Goodbye Pieter.'

By now the message from the Perron was clear.

'Your old nanny is dead.'

Sannie was never my nanny! She was my other mother. She was my friend and my teacher. She showed me how to play dominoes. She gave me the tune of the language of the Cape Flats. She was the most constant energy in my life from seven to sixteen. And she treated apartheid with the utter contempt it deserved.

She'd come back into our lives when I was forty-six. When Pa was so ill after a heart operation and there was no one to look after him, once Tess and I had careened off on our careers. Sannie came back and looked after Pa, and, when he died, she closed his eyes.

And now she was dead too.

I phoned the family.

'Sorry I wasn't in Darling when you phoned. What can I do?'

'Come to the funeral, Pieter. Seven thirty tomorrow morning. Bonteheuwel.'

In the rain, everything on the Cape Flats seems to glisten and shimmer. It's either plastic or tin or corrugated iron. The sky was low and dirty brown. It was early and the traffic was hell. Half of Cape Town was getting out of the city and half of the Flats was trying to get in. Buses and trucks and taxis and cars and bicycles and pedestrians and umbrellas.

The township of Bonteheuwel is violent and ignored and poor. The people are magnificent and proud and smart, and they will not give up the hope that tomorrow will be a better day. Sannie had moved into her son's house there after Pa died. Her son was also ill. Her grandchildren needed her. We built her a flat in the backyard, but through bad management it was never properly completed. It leaked and was cold and damp. There were constant repairs.

Sannie never complained.

'Ag, darling, my grandchildren need me.'

I wanted to scream: 'So do I. My mommy and daddy are dead and I am over fifty and I need you!'

'BLEEP. Pieter? Pieter my darling? This is Sannie? Where are you? Pieter can you hear me?'

Because she spoke so loudly, we always teased her that she didn't need a phone. She would scream messages into my machine. I would phone back and arrange to fetch her to spend a weekend in Darling, usually when Tessa was playing a concert at the Perron.

On one occasion Auntie Sannie was given a lift by two friends in their state-of-the-art fast car.

Sannie was most upset.

'Nay man, sies, those boys drive like the devil, nee asseblief!'

She arrived in a twinset suit with pearls, clutching the little dog we called Kittie, a white Maltese who had been Pa's present on his last birthday and was Sannie's best friend until he was killed by a huge stray Rottweiler in Bonteheuwel during a morning walk.

'Sannie,' I explained loudly, noticing that her hearing aid was missing, 'this is my house, this is the bathroom, here is your bedroom ...'

'Where's the TV?' she asked impatiently.

I showed her. She spent the whole three days in Darling watching television. Dog in arms. Like in Bonteheuwel.

And now she was dead and I hadn't been there when she wanted me.

Her coffin was open. Her small face was lined gently with balls of cotton-wool. The hint of moustache was still on her top lip, always part of her and never a reason for ridicule or even question. She had been brought up Christian and married a Muslim. So the funeral was a wonderful combination of both.

There were long, sad, slow songs in Afrikaans. There were more songs. And more songs. I held the piece of paper in my hands, reading the religious words that I did not know, fascinated by the woman priest who was leading the service. Her love for the dead woman was clear. The power of Sannie's matriarchal hold on the family was obvious. This was something I had never been part of. Sannie's hold over me was that of care and love. She was my guardian angel. Here she was Marlon Brando's Godfather.

During the singing I noticed how many family members and friends would wander up to the open coffin and softly feel Sannie's forehead. To check if she had a temperature? I still don't know why, but I think they just wanted to touch the person they loved before she was put away forever. This was the first funeral I could face with calm and understanding. My parents were buried and cremated and scattered, and I remembered little. But Sannie's funeral was clear and precise, and I wanted to focus on every moment. I didn't look away from anything.

To begin with, I was the only white person there. But I felt Evita Bezuidenhout was there too. They all looked at me with that glazed stare of fans. It didn't allow me to be one of them. The other son. The one that got away. The one with the grand car. The one with the picture in the paper. The one who wasn't there when she needed him.

The small coffin was carried to the white hearse.

'She did pay into a fund for her funeral, Pieter, but we feel she deserves better.'

'Yes,' I said, 'I'll pay for that. Get her the best.'

The cost of the best for Sannie was less than a meal for four queens at Rozenhof restaurant in Kloof Street. And yet it was good for the friends and the family. In the dingy wet street without structured sidewalks or drainage stood a shiny white hearse. It was full of flowers. There was going to be food at the church too. Halaal snacks. Fizzy cooldrinks.

In the church, Muslims and Christians and me, the Jew, sat together and waited for the service to start. By now there were a few more white people. Middle-aged men and women who were also Sannie's children, from the time she left us in the sixties to look after other young families. We nodded to each other like relatives.

'Pieter? Hello, Pieter, I'm Sannie's niece. Will you give the speech?'

It was one of the greatest compliments of my life. To be asked to be part of this family of which I'd always felt a part.

The spooky echo of fame followed me to the microphone. Did they see Evita or just a cartoon of the little boy they remembered as Pietertjie Uys from Pinelands, now a grown man who owed so much of his sense of humour to the small person sleeping in the white box?

'Sannie broke down the barriers of apartheid for me,' I began. 'She started as a coloured woman in the kitchen and ripped down every barrier between us. For Tessa and me, she was the most important friend in our lives as children. And now as big people. I'm honoured that you have asked me to speak here. I thank you for allowing me to be part of her family. And to say with you:

Here was a great mother and a great grandmother and a great friend. And a wonderful South African. And no one could tell a joke like Sannie!'

And we all laughed, because we remembered her unchecked cheeky cackle of delight.

I have kept a small ball of cottonwool that touched her cheek. They covered her with the lid and screwed it down and Sannie was gone. But she will never be gone. She will always be with me, in the forefront of my army of heroes, loving me from a distance, helping me from within, caring for me and wanting me. I look forward to seeing her again.

* * *

Ten years after Miss Nel asked me to write a poem, I had one published in an anthology for high schools. I now meet parents who remember reading it as schoolkids.

This is for Miss Nel.

> When I was young
> time never flew
> and summer was green and winter was airy
> the mornings felt fresh
> and pocket money a fortune
> cats made me sneeze
> it was a big deal to tease
> ag it was like the other day mos
> When I was starting
>
> Then smoking was a sin
> and girls boring and polluted with scent
> and comics a swoppable commodity at the old Savoy
> skiet-met-'n-kettie a squirrel for a rand a tail
> cars were stored in a scruffy inventory
> like, ek sê, that's ten Chevs for me
> and two Fords and jislaaik ou maat
> that's nogal one more Ford than like you got
> Ek sê
>
> Bioscope-flicks-films-movies: The Devil
> on a Saturday morning and vreet jou dik aan sweets
> scream for hero in white hat
> boo for everything in black, horse daarby
> and the only blood happened on your nose

when your sweets were rukked in the toilet
and you stood up for bubble gum and Smarties
like any self-respecting young boytjie would
forget the weak knees and o gaats hier kom hy
Eina ek sê!

The Hardy Boys and Enid Blyton and Debbie Reynolds
'Put Your Sweet Lips a Little Closer to the Phone'
and homework?
No come right now ek sê
I'll do it tomorrow
and don't tell me about That, Pa
I know about That!

That?
Chat behind the bikeshed at school
but sis that's not what was in that book
Stan brought to class when teacher was sick
Who needs girls, ek sê
Ugh!

When I was young and believe me we were
parents were immortal and perfect
and mothers never cried and if they did
it was truly the end of the world
Pa's just gave hassles if you didn't water the garden properly
and never was sick and always moeg
and oumas were hels old and religious
always giving socks and handkerchiefs for birthdays
ag no man ek sê

When I was young
all older people were uncles and aunts even if they weren't
and younger sisters a drag and not even pretty
even if you knocked off her glasses and ran
restaurants on Sunday after church were special
and the most expensive thing on the menu was the only choice
when I was young

And now we're the uncles and aunties
and little cousins have babies
and mothers are dead

sisters are stunning and friends'
smoking makes me sick
and there are no more grannies
time always flies
Jislaaik ek sê
where can I find comics to swop at the Savoy
Swop for Enid Blyton and Elvis
and the most expensive item on the menu
like when I was young.

20

BETWEEN DARLING
AND THE DEEP BLUE SEA

Children make me happy. No, that's a dangerous generalisation, because too many children need so much help, so much care, so much consideration, that artificial happiness gets in the way of one's focus. The tragedy of the lives of unwanted and unloved children is the daily obituary to the once-treasured knowledge that we cared for each other.

I can only revel in the experiences I have with my community of Darling here on the West Coast of the Cape. Since I moved here in 1995, my involvement with the community has been my priority. There are 5000 people in Darling, and 75 per cent of them do not have access to funds, luxuries or secure futures. But in spite of it all they can laugh – and that is catching.

The kids come to Evita se Perron to the Elsie Balt Art School and the Perron Piano School. Although not all of them want to take part in 'arty things', we have a core of young people who can paint and perform with the confidence of professionals. Sue-Ellen is one of them.

It was Christmas, and we decided to take twelve of our little Perronistas to Cape Town, to go to the movies. I asked Sue-Ellen to help me organise the event.

She chose the film.

'*Harry Potter.*'

I didn't argue.

'And ice-creams?'

Yes, and Tannie Evita would buy them each something from Mr Price, the clothing store with lovely things for little people. Our transport was the theatre panel van, with cushions on the floor to accommodate the dozen kids and the two adults. We would leave at noon to be there for the two o'clock movie.

Some of the kids arrived an hour early. The little girls were dressed to the nines, with ribbons in their hair and small handbags. Sue-Ellen wore tiny lace gloves like a fairy princess. I saw her cellphone tucked into her belt.

'I'll switch it off in the movies, I promise, Pieter,' she confided.

I didn't know it, but most of them had never been as far as the perimeter of their small town, let alone into the Big City. This I discovered when the van panted its way up the steep road that runs across the meadows beyond the town and up a hill. From there, one can see Table Mountain in the distance. The smallest boy sat between me and a parent. As we travelled up the hill, his tension was palpable: his fists were tightly clenched and he looked very frightened. Another urgent toilet stop, I wondered.

As we reached the top of the hill, he gave a funny little squeak.

'Jon-Erik?' I asked. 'What's the matter?' (His name, too, was inspired by a soap opera.) He opened his eyes and stared at the vista ahead. Then, with a small smile, he looked up at me.

'There's more ...!' he whispered.

He'd thought the world ended at the top of that hill! He'd never been that far, and no one had told him that the world went on further than the eye could see. It was the first of many magical moments in this exhausting and exhilarating day of discovery.

I asked the oldest boy to count every head in the troupe regularly, so we wouldn't lose anyone at the mall. He did.

'Theodore? How many are we?'

'Twelve,' he said, not counting us oldies.

We went to the ice-cream parlour and sat down.

Now they were quiet and inhibited by the crowds and the colours and lights around them. Little Jon-Erik hung onto my T-shirt and wouldn't let go. They all ordered what I ordered. Yes, they were all eating their first ice-cream. They were shocked how cold it was.

Then to the clothing store. I told them that Tannie Evita would allow each of them to choose something nice. The little girls had now regained confidence and knew exactly what to go for.

'Can we choose an ensemble?' Sue-Ellen asked, indicating the T-shirts, skirts, shoes and bracelets.

Jon-Erik pointed at the first thing he saw, a shirt that was meant for a teenager twice his age. He'd never been into a place like this before and it frightened him. Theodore, meanwhile, had discovered some small pocket games in the shop next door, and to my relief Jon-Erik showed huge excitement in owning one. Soon he did.

We made our way to the cinema.

By now everyone was talking at the same time and discussing their purchases. They carried their colourful plastic bags like trophies.

'How many are we, Theodore?' I asked.

He counted.

'Fourteen.'

We stopped.

'But Theodore, the last time you counted we were twelve,' I suggested, a clammy feeling of fear reminding me that I was responsible for the lives of other people's kids.

We all counted. Theodore was right: fourteen. We'd picked up two little urchins from the car park, who were now also holding their Mr Price packets with T-shirts from Tannie Evita! And so they came along to see *Harry Potter*.

Before the movie, it was time for toilet and popcorn.

All fourteen were each presented with a bucket of warm kernels and a cooldrink. We adults were more excited about the popcorn than anyone dared admit. I noticed all the kids huddle together and count things out in their hands. They'd clubbed together to buy me a cooldrink as well!

The cinema dazzled the children.

Two little girls clutched their handbags and looked around the glittering foyer with wide eyes.

'It's like church!' the one said to Sue-Ellen, who sighed like someone well travelled and knowing it all.

Harry Potter is a long film, and so our row was constantly disrupted into standing by a constant flow of kids visiting the toilet. Except Jon-Erik, who sat on the floor and stared at the film through the space between the seats in front of him.

'Are you okay?' I asked. He nodded and squeezed my ankle nervously.

The day ended with Big Macs for everyone.

And trust McDonald's to have a playground as part of the eating area!

'Swing and slide first; hamburger last,' I suggested.

But that didn't happen. There was a lot of chucking-up behind plastic chairs, and we ended up at the tap in the parking area, cleaning up and wiping down remnants of the feast. We said goodbye to our two local urchins, who wanted to know when we'd be back.

On the way home I drove on the coast road. Everyone sat very quiet and stared through the open windows at the great waves crashing on the white beach.

Jon-Erik's little fingers dug into my arm.

'Why is it so cross?' he whispered.

I was too shocked to explain. I'd just realised that they had never seen the sea before, even though they lived twenty minutes from the ocean.

'What's that?' He pointed at the dark monster visible above the swell.

'That's Robben Island.'

*　　*　　*

As children we would visit Robben Island for our Sunday school picnics, playing on the beach, having a braai and eating watermelon. There was no knowledge of what took place behind the wattle trees that hid the jail.

My play *Panorama* took up from there. Set in the bull's eye of political symbols, the play premiered in 1987 at the Grahamstown Festival. The action takes place in the small house of the two local primary-school teachers, Karin and Rosa. They spend their evenings watching the panorama of Table Mountain through their picture window. It helps them ignore the reality of the terrible prison beyond their fence.

It is a play about terror. Fear of the black political prisoners behind the walls. Fear of what they stood for and what was hidden by censorship and laws. Fear of forgotten dreams and lost chances. Fear of loneliness and spinsterhood. And fear of change.

Rosa is sexy and brash, while Karin is dumpy and timid. Grobbelaar, the policeman who visits, is young and blond, unlike the beer-swilling, arse-scratching thug-cops so familiar at the time. Sibi, the black woman who is forced to spend the night with the teachers while visiting her sick father in prison, is sophisticated and witty, not fitting the easy picture of the black woman who made more sense in the kitchen than on a sofa, sipping a martini. And because she's a banned person, only allowed to be in the room with one person at a time, Karin waits off-stage during the dinner, constantly moaning that someone must leave so she can also come and eat!

In 1987 Nelson Mandela was no longer on Robben Island, but the others were. There was a State of Emergency throughout South Africa, and the darkness of PW Botha's iron fist suffocated all aspects of life. During the Grahamstown Festival season of *Panorama*, there were riots in the township across the valley from the theatre in which we played. People were arrested and locked up. It was illegal even to think. We did more than think. We entertained with the unmentionable.

Rosa is alone with Sibi Makhale. Karin has gone to bed, terrified of being in the room with them both, illegally. Rosa is tense and regards everything Sibi says as an attack on her.

'Don't drag politics in, please!' she snaps.

Sibi shrugs.

'Everything is political: eating, houses, schools, God, love, sex, hate. Even the sun shines down to make your skin dark, while it bleaches our land white.'

'You're here because of politics.'

'Only after you people forced it on me.'

The wind has started to howl round the house. Through the window the darkness of the night obliterates the lights of the city across the bay.

Sibi thinks about what Rosa had asked her.

'Yes, I also had dreams. Not to be a jogger like you. I don't even run from the riot police. No, I wanted to be a nurse, like my mother was before she was forced to give it up.'

Rosa is impressed. 'You became a nurse?'

Sibi laughs. 'I planned and then fought with my mother, who wanted me to get a decent job and not work for whites ...' She notices Rosa's expression of surprise. 'Oh yes, I once worked for whites to earn money to make my dream come true.'

'Couldn't you get a bursary?'

'Come on, teacher, we're talking about the years when it wasn't fashionable to sponsor a black face. Not with a father in jail and a mother in exile.'

Rosa has never had a conversation like this with a black person.

'You could've gone to the press.'

'The overseas press had just discovered the Ayatollah ... So I spent my dream carrying letters from his lawyer to her lawyer, keeping their marriage alive with little messages, dodging police and informers. I inherited the burden of revenge. I got involved. So here I am.'

Rosa sees the bigger picture and smiles.

'Did you throw bombs?'

'That would be so simple, wouldn't it?' Sibi sighs. 'No, I talked. I made speeches. I visited friends.'

'Russia?'

'Russia? What the hell is this white obsession with fucking Russia? Why must everything anti-apartheid come from Russia? Look, I've never been north of Joburg!'

It turns out that Sibi is pregnant. The father is a married white man. Suddenly all the preconceptions crumble and collapse. They are just three South African women trying to come to terms with the three threatened worlds they each inhabit. By meeting, their lives have been changed forever and so have ours.

The evening passes, troubled by a stormy black south-easter and clashing emotions. Sibi retires to Karin's room for the night. Karin and Rosa lie on the couch in their living room, looking out of the window at the panorama.

'Rosa?'

'What is it?'

'Do you think it will be okay tomorrow?'

'Ja.'

'Promise?'

'Ja, unless the wind blows again.'

'Oh God, I hope not.'

'Let's see what happens, okay?'

'Okay.'

The silence is only broken by the howling wind. The women stare out into the darkness.

*　　*　　*

On the other side of the bay, across from the Island, our Christmas treat was drawing to a close, sixteen years after *Panorama*. The children around me hadn't even been born in 1987. Some of them didn't know what Robben Island represented.

It was time to go home.

The drive back to Darling was a joyous celebration of conquering the world. They sang their school songs and told jokes and laughed constantly. We stopped in the coloured township and they all got out. Their parents would fetch them, they promised. It became clear that some of them didn't have that luxury.

Little Jon-Erik was the last to leave the vehicle. I handed him his plastic carrier bag with the pocket game, bits of popcorn, a serviette from the ice-cream parlour, a toilet roll from the cinema loo and an empty Big Mac container – his souvenirs.

'You okay?' I asked.

He looked up at me, his four-year-old face breaking into a great grin.

'Ja,' he said, nodding, 'I'm so happy.'

He handed me a grey feather.

'Where did you find this?' I asked.

He looked up into the dark sky and shrugged.

*　　*　　*

My journey in theatre, which started at the Little in Orange Street, was to find its climax in Darling. Working with Wim Visser and Inge Bos, Dutch impresarios who had bought a house in the town and were now part of the community, we created the Voorkamerfees. With eighteen homes in our community as our canvas, this yearly festival takes place in the front rooms of the people of Darling. Suddenly the small box house of Sally Pieterse, with its three windows and two doors, becomes the Sydney Opera House.

Jan Bruin's pondok is New York's La Mama. Phil and Siena's living room is the London Palladium, and Bella and her three children present the Vienna Staatsoper. Rediscovering the essence of entertainment, it is a concept that doesn't need the overloaded structures of the usual theatre festivals. It happens because the people open their doors and their hearts.

This was uncharted territory, especially the thirteen township venues where white people never venture, let alone to be entertained. Audiences would buy a ticket to three homes. On the first stop they would discover a singer from Indonesia presenting twenty-five minutes of song in the potter's workshop up Long Street, then on to an intense actor doing his monologue in the home of Mr Botha the schoolteacher downtown, and finally a magic show in the RDP home of Sally Pieterse.

RDP homes were built through the Reconstruction and Development Programme, which the ANC launched in 1994. One million houses in five years, they said. We teased: one house in a million years? They eventually built many, not very sturdy or secure, but at least a roof of sorts over heads once protected only by corrugated iron or cardboard.

Sally had cleared her small space of the bed, the cupboard, the table and the three chairs. Even her TV was outside under the bush, covered with a piece of black plastic. In its place stood fifteen chairs. That was the extent of her theatre. Fifteen guests who sat in Sally's home and watched the magician from Leeds do his tricks. Surrounded by the small children of the community, Harold Jones, aka Mad Max, brought forth rabbits and steam engines, made sounds like birds and bombers, sang songs like Jagger and Bon Jovi. The kids mimicked him and copied him, and by the third performance took over the show, to his delight.

The Voorkamerfees was what theatre has always promised. Letting the people entertain each other. Letting their homes be their castles. And inspiring those who always thought they had nothing, to know that the world was in their front rooms.

After the three days were over, I visited Sally at her home. All her things were back in their original places. The only hint of the past miracle was Mad Max's signature on the wall above her TV set.

'I'll be back, baby!' it promised in funny, florid, red curly letters.

'So, how was it all, Sally?' I asked over rooibos tea and small cakes.

'No man, it was great. Hell, I couldn't believe so many people here?'

I looked around and couldn't believe it either.

'How many performances in all?' I asked.

'Twelve, Pieter, I swear! A hundred and eighty people in my house! Laughing! Clapping! Taking photos of me!'

She looked around the room and shook her head.

'I can't wait for next year.'

'Is Mad Max coming back?' I asked, indicating his message.

She laughed.

'Shame, our kids do his show now. Poor Max must think of something else. But I've had an idea.'

'You'll do the show?'

I could see Sally put on the whole *Phantom of the Opera*.

'Me? Come on, man, I'm just a cleaning lady. No, Pieter, I think I want to turn my place into a B&B. You know? At night, for the people to sleep over.'

I looked at the little overcrowded square.

'How?'

'Easy. You put a wire down the middle. Hang some blankets. On this side me and the kids sleep. On that side: the B&B.'

I had to laugh.

'Bed and breakfast? Here?'

'Ja.' She looked at me with narrowed eyes and a slight smile. 'Don't you think it can happen?'

I shrugged.

'How?'

'Sis man, Pieter-Dirk Uys. And you always tell us: Nothing is impossible?'

The Box Under the Bed

Here it is. A chronological list of my plays, revues, films, videos and books. I've added the casts and the director, as well as where the piece was originally performed. Funny feeling to look at a list like this. The person responsible for all this must be stark-staring bonkers!

FACE⨍ IN THE WALL *play*
1969   London Film School: Pieter Uys, Ian Lowe, Vari Sylvester – dir: PDU
1973   Space: Chris Prophet, Val de Klerk, Peter Piccolo, Sue Boekstein – dir: PDU
1980   Market: Terry Norton, Roberta Durrant, Jonathan Rands,
       Murray Angus-Leppan – dir: PDU

POPCORN *play*
1973   Space: Bill Flynn, Peter Piccolo, Val de Klerk, Paddy Canavan – dir: PDU

PITY ABOUT PEOPLE *play*
1974   Space: Blaise Koch, Val Donald, Michele Maxwell – dir: PDU
1974   The Company JHB: Ziona Garfield, David Eppel, Kathy Kahn – dir: PDU

⨍ELLE OU ⨍TORIE *play*
1974   Space: Christine Basson, Lynne Maree, Marthinus Basson, Johann van
       Heerden – dir: PDU
1975   The Company JHB: Christine Basson, Val de Klerk, Danny Keogh, PDU
       – dir: PDU
2004   Civic JHB: Evita Bezuidenhout (PDU), Greg Melvill-Smith, James van
       Helsdingen, Michelle Bradshaw – dir: Lynne Maree

JU⨍T HILDA! *revue*
1974   Space: PDU

⨍NOWHITE & THE ⨍PECIAL BRANCH *revue*
1974   Space: Lynne Maree, Bill Curry, Vincent Ebrahim, Jonathan Sherwood,
       Andrea Fine, Neels Bezuidenhout, Diane Vlotman, Marthinus Basson
       – dir: PDU
1976   Labia Theatre CT: Mary Dreyer, Dawie Malan, Trix Pienaar, Chris
       Galloway, PDU, Martin Clohessy – dir: PDU MD: Peter Brauer
       double-billed with BLACK BEAUTY & THE BO⨍⨍ *revue*

251

GOD'*S* FORGOTTEN *play*

1975   Space: Christine Basson, Lynne Maree, Jacqui Delhaye, Esther van Ryswyk, Blaise Koch – dir: PDU

1976   Market: Christine Basson, Lynne Maree, Michele Maxwell, Wilma Stockenström, Blaise Koch – dir: PDU

1979   La Mama NYC: Maggie Soboil, Lisette Lecat, Madeleine le Roux, Christina Avis-Krauss, Joel Rooks – dir: Mavis Taylor

KARNAVAL *play*

1975   Space: Trix Pienaar, Cornelia Stander, Vincent Ebrahim, Christine Basson, Grethe Fox, Margot Luyt, PDU – dir: PDU

1981   Market: Magda Beukes, Dale Cutts, Kevin Smith, Lynette Luyt, Joey de Koker, Margi Lewis – dir: Dawie Malan

*S*TRIKE UP THE BANNED *revue*

1975   Space: Trix Pienaar, PDU, Vincent Ebrahim, Jacqui Delhaye, Maria Jensen – dir: PDU

1976   Grahamstown Festival and tour: Lynne Maree, Blaise Koch, Wilma Stockenström, Michele Maxwell, PDU – dir: PDU

1978   Market: PDU, Rika Sennett – dir: PDU

*S*KOTE! *play*

1976   Hoërskool Jan van Riebeeck students, Limpie Basson – dir: Esther van Ryswyk

THE RI*S*E AND FALL OF THE FIR*S*T EMPRE*SS* BONAPARTE *play*

1977   UCT students, Margot de Villiers, Robin Lake, John Caviggia – dir: PDU

1983   PACT: Jacqui Singer, Ron Smerczak, Michael McCabe – dir: William Egan

PARADI*S*E I*S* CLO*S*ING DOWN *play*

1977   Grahamstown Festival and tour: Val de Klerk, Melanie-Anne Asher, Christine Basson, William Meyer – dir: PDU

1977   Market: Cal de Klerk, Melanie-Ann Sher, Magda Beukes, William Meyer – dir: PDU

1978   Edinburgh Festival and London: Naomi Buch, Barbara Kinghorn, Helen Bourne, Frank Williams – dir: Roberta Durrant

1980   Granada TV: Estelle Kohler, Naomi Buch, Shelley Borkum – dir: Howard Baker

DIE VAN AARDE*S* VAN GROOTOOR *play*

1977   Baxter: Antoinette Kellermann, Mary Dreyer, Chris Galloway, Bill Curry, Lida Botha, Marthinus Basson – dir: Dawie Malan

1978   Market: Magda Beukes, Eon de Vos, Rina Nienaber, Antoinette Kellermann, Allan Dysel, Nomsa Nene – dir: Dawie Malan

INFO ſCANDALſ *revue*
1979   Pretoria: Richard Haines, Sybil Coetzee, PDU – dir: PDU
1979   Baxter/Market: Chris Galloway, Lida Botha, Bill Curry, Zaza Vorster
       – dir: Dawie Malan

UYſCREAMſ FROM THE WIMPY ARCHIPELAGO *revue*
1980   Market: PDU, Tessa Uys, Martin Clohessy – dir: PDU

UYſCREAMſ WITH HOT CHOCOLATE ſAUCE *revue*
1980   Market/Baxter: PDU, Tessa Uys, Thoko Ntshinga – dir: PDU

ADAPT OR DYE *revue*
1981   South Africa: PDU
1985   Tricycle Theatre / 1986 Boulevard Theatre Soho / 1988 Purcell Room
       London / 1988 Edinburgh Festival Traverse Theatre / 1988 Hackney
       Empire and Donmar Warehouse London
1987   Toronto, Canada
1988   Holland

HELL Iſ FOR WHITEſ ONLY *play (aka* BEYOND ALL REAſON*) play*
1982   Market: Amanda Strydom, Bill Curry, Denise Newman, Margi Lewis, John
       Whiteley, Marius de Vos – dir: PDU

APPAſſIONATA *play*
1982   Pretoria/Market/Baxter: Tessa Uys, Chris Galloway – dir: Mario Schiess

FARCE ABOUT UYſ *play*
1983   Market/tour/Baxter: PDU, Chris Galloway, Thoko Ntshinga – dir: Dawie
       Malan

TOTAL ONſLAUGHT 1984 *revue*
1984   Pretoria/Market/Baxter/tour: PDU – dir: Dawie Malan

ſKATING ON THIN UYſ *film*
1985   Brigadiers/BME: PDU, Thoko Ntshinga, Chris Galloway – dir: Bromley
       Cawood

BEYOND THE RUBICON *revue*
1986   Market/tour/Nico Malan: PDU – dir: PDU

AN UYſ UP MY ſLEEVE *TV special*
1986   SABC: PDU – dir: Roy Sargeant

ACROſſ THE RUBICON *TV special*
1986   PBTV/USA: PDU – dir: Lionel Friedberg

NO ONE'S DIED LAUGHING *book*
1986   Penguin

PANORAMA *play*
1987   Grahamstown Festival: Lynne Maree, Susan Coetzer-Opperman, Thoko
Ntshinga, Richard van der Westhuizen – dir: PDU
1988   Pretoria/JHB: Lyn Hooker, Susan Coetzer-Opperman, Thoko Ntshinga,
Robin Smith – dir: PDU
1988   Cape Town: Bo Petersen, Marion Holm, Lulu Gallo, Peter Krummeck
– dir: Ralph Lawson
1988   London King's Head Theatre: Jemma Redgrave, Natasha Williams, Di Kent,
Ken Sharrock – dir: Penny Cherns

PW BOTHA: IN HIS OWN WORDS *book*
1987   Penguin

REARRANGING THE DECKCHAIRS ON THE SA BOTHATANIC *revue*
1987   Market/Baxter/tour: PDU, Chris Galloway – dir: Ralph Lawson

SKATING ON THIN UYS *revue (title for* ADAPT OR DYE*)*
1987   Sydney Footbridge Theatre Australia: PDU

CRY FREEMANDELA – THE MOVIE *revue*
1987   Market/Nico Malan 1988: PDU, Chris Galloway, Sello Maake ka Ncube
(later Arthur Molepo) – dir: PDU

JUST LIKE HOME *play*
1989   Baxter/Market/UK: Shaleen Surtie-Richards, Robert Finlayson, Royston
Stoffels, Paul Savage – dir: PDU

EVITA'S INDABA *TV series*
1989   M-Net: PDU, Lizz Meiring – dir: Bill Faure

BITE THE BALLOT *TV special*
1989   Channel 4 UK: PDU – dir: Penny Cherns

EVITA'S LAST DECADE *TV special*
1989   M-Net: PDU, Lizz Meiring – dir: Bill Faure

SCORCHED EARTH *play*
1989   Market: Margaret Inglis, Fiona Ramsay, Val Donald Bell, David Butler,
Pierre Knoesen, Gaynor Young, Arthur Molepo – dir: PDU

A KISS ON YOUR KOEKSISTER *revue*
1990   Market/Baxter/UK/Holland: PDU – dir: Janice Honeyman

A PART HATE A PART LOVE *book*
1990   Random Century
1994   Hond (2nd edition)

AN AUDIENCE WITH EVITA BEZUIDENHOUT *revue*
1990   Market/Baxter/tour/UK/Holland: PDU, Lizz Meiring – dir: PDU

ſÜD-AFRIKA IN FARBE *revue*
1991   Germany: PDU

EEN LEVEN APART *book*
1991   Jan Metz

MEſſAGE TO MAJOR *TV special*
1991   BBC: PDU, Lizz Meiring – dir: Francis Gerard

ſTAND UP ſOUTH AFRICA! *revue*
1992   Israel: PDU

DIE VLEIROOſ *play*
1992   Nico Malan/tour: Lynne Maree, Chris van Niekerk, Theresa Cloete,
       Joey de Koker – dir: PDU
1995   Civic JHB: Trix Pienaar, André Stolz, June van Merch, Anna-Mart van der
       Merwe – dir: Lynne Maree

JEZUſ IN JOHANNEſBURG *book*
1992   Amber (Amsterdam)

PARADIſE Iſ CLOſING DOWN (REVIſITED) *play*
1992   Grahamstown Festival/Wits JHB: PDU, Chris Galloway, Stephen Raymond,
       Randall de Jager – dir: Lynne Maree

AN EVENING WITH PIETER-DIRK UYſ *revue*
1992   Baxter: PDU

THE POGGENPOEL ſIſTERſ *revue*
1993   CT/tour/JHB: PDU, Godfrey Johnson

AN AUDIENCE WITH AN AFRICAN QUEEN *revue*
1993   UK: PDU, Lizz Meiring

NEGERKÜſſE *revue*
1993   Germany/Austria/Switzerland: PDU

ONE MAN ONE VOLT *revue*
1994   SA/USA/Holland: PDU

EVITA*S* FUNIGALORE TV *series*
1994   M-Net: dir: Pieter Cilliers

BAMBI *SINGS* THE FAK *SONGS* *cabaret*
1995   CT/JHB/tour: PDU, Godfrey Johnson

YOU ANC NOTHING YET *revue*
1995   Baxter/tour/UK/Holland/USA: PDU

TRUTH OMI*SS*ION*S* *revue*
1996   Baxter/tour/UK/Holland: PDU

TANNIE EVITA PRAAT KAKTU*S* *monologue*
1996   Perron/tour: PDU

LIVE FROM BOERA*SS*IC PARK *revue*
1997   Baxter/tour/UK/Holland: PDU

THE E*SS*ENTIAL EVITA *book*
1997   David Philip

OUMA O*SS*EWANIA PRAAT VUIL *monologue*
1997   Perron/tour: PDU

NO *S*PACE ON LONG *S*TREET *play*
1997   Baxter: PDU – dir: Lynne Maree

GOING DOWN GORGEOU*S* *play*
1998   Perron/tour: PDU
2000   SATV series – dir: Robert Davis

NOËL & MARLENE *play*
1998   Perron/tour: PDU, Godfrey Johnson

BAMBI'*S* XMA*S* KEREL*S* *revue*
1998   Perron: PDU, Godfrey Johnson

TANNIE EVITA'*S* CRY*S*TAL BALL*S* *monologue*
1998   Perron: PDU

DEKAFFIRNATED *revue*
1999   Market/Baxter/tour/UK/Holland: PDU

THE MAR*S*HRO*S*E *play* 1999

CONCENTRATION CAMP *cabaret*
2000   Perron: PDU (Bambi Kellermann), Godfrey Johnson
2000   Grahamstown Festival
2000   On Broadway, CT

FOR FACT'S SAKE *revue*
2000   Perron/tour: PDU

SYMBOLS OF SEX AND STATE *revue*
2000   CT: PDU, Warona Seane – dir: PDU
2000   JHB: PDU, Nomsa Nene – dir: PDU

TANNIE EVITA'S COOKSISTERS *monologue*
2000   Perron: PDU

EVITA: LIVE AND DANGEROUS *TV talk show*
2000   e.tv: PDU – dir: Roger Smith

TREKKING TO TEEMA *novel*
2000   www.teema.iol.co.za
2001   ComPress

FOREIGN AIDS *revue*
2001   SA/tour/UK/USA/Holland/Australia: PDU

ELECTIONS & ERECTIONS *book*
2002   Zebra Press

HAVING SEX WITH PIETER-DIRK UYS *video*
2002   Lodestar: PDU – dir: Roger Smith

SURVIVAL AIDS *video*
2003   Lodestar: PDU – dir: Roger Smith

AUDITIONING ANGELS *play*
2003   Pieter Toerien Productions/JHB and CT: Clive Scott, Jo da Silva, Thoko
           Ntshinga, Paul du Toit, Nandi Nyembe – dir: Blaise Koch

THE END IS NAAI *revue (aka* ELECTIONS & ERECTIONS *outside SA)*
2004   Perron/tour/UK/Australia: PDU

IT'S JUST A SMALL PRICK *video*
2004   Lodestar: PDU – dir: Roger Smith

ƒAME OLD ƒTORY *play*
2004 Civic JHB: Bambi Kellermann (PDU)/Greg Melvill-Smith/James van
      Helsdingen/Michelle Bradshaw – dir: Lynne Maree

ICONƒ & AIKONAƒ *revue*
2005 Perron: PDU

BETWEEN THE DEVIL AND THE DEEP *book*
2005 Zebra Press

MANY OF THE PLAY TEXTƒ ARE NOW FREELY AVAILABLE AT:
www.pdu.co.za
www.pieterdirkuys.co.za
www.pieterdirkuys.com

If You Want to Help

If you want to be part of extraordinary self-help groups that are doing so much to improve lives and dreams, here are some details:

WOLA NANI
www.wolanani.co.za
Wola Nani is committed to providing a caring and developmental service that enables people living with HIV to respond positively to their status. Through counselling, care, training, increased awareness and community support, people with HIV are empowered to take control of their lives with confidence, dignity and hope.
E-mail: wolanani@wolanani.co.za

Visit the Wola Nani shop:
Third floor
76 Long Street
Cape Town
South Africa

NAZARETH HOUSE CHILDREN'S HOME
www.nazhouse.org
E-mail: nazhouse@netactive.co.za
PO Box 12116
Mill Street
8010

THE DARLING TRUST
www.evita.co.za
To make the impossible the extraordinary.
The Darling Trust is a charitable trust set up to act as a vehicle for the transformation of our community and to be a transparent and accountable channel for funding for the community.

Registration No.: IT 2598/2003
Banking details: Standard Bank/Darling (05-01-11)
The Darling Trust a/c no.: 08 – 326 – 482 – 5

Do you have any comments, suggestions or feedback about this book or any other Zebra Press titles? Contact us at **talkback@zebrapress.co.za**